Black–White
Income Differentials

Empirical Studies and
Policy Implications

Institute for Research on Poverty
Monograph Series

Vernon L. Allen, Editor, *Psychological Factors in Poverty*

Frederick Williams, Editor, *Language and Poverty: Perspectives on a Theme*

Murray Edelman, *Politics as Symbolic Action: Mass Arousal and Quiescence*

Joel F. Handler and Ellen Jane Hollingsworth, *"The Deserving Poor": A Study of Welfare Administration*

Robert J. Lampman, *Ends and Means of Reducing Income Poverty*

Larry L. Orr, Robinson G. Hollister, and Myron J. Lefcowitz, Editors, with the assistance of Karen Hester, *Income Maintenance: Interdisciplinary Approaches to Research*

Charles E. Metcalf, *An Econometric Model of the Income Distribution*

Glen G. Cain and Harold W. Watts, Editors, *Income Maintenance and Labor Supply: Econometric Studies*

Joel F. Handler, *The Coercive Social Worker: British Lessons for American Social Services*

Larry L. Orr, *Income, Employment, and Urban Residential Location*

Stanley H. Masters, *Black–White Income Differentials: Empirical Studies and Policy Implications*

In Preparation
Irene Lurie, Editor, *Integrating Income Maintenance Programs*

Black–White Income Differentials

Empirical Studies and Policy Implications

Stanley H. Masters
University of Wisconsin–Madison

ACADEMIC PRESS   New York   San Francisco   London

A Subsidiary of Harcourt Brace Jovanovich, Publishers

This book is one of a series sponsored by the Institute for
Research on Poverty of the University of Wisconsin pursuant to
the provisions of the Economic Opportunity Act of 1964.

Academic Press, Inc.
111 Fifth Avenue, New York, New York 10003

United Kingdom Edition published by
Academic Press, Inc. (London) Ltd.
24/28 Oval Road, London NW1

Library of Congress Cataloging in Publication Data

Masters, Stanley H   (date)
        Black-White income differentials : empirical studies
and policy implications.

        (Institute for Research on Poverty monograph series)
        Includes bibliographical references and indexes.
        1.   Income distribution—United States.   I.   Title.   II.   Series:
Wisconsin.   University—Madison.   Institute for Research
on Poverty, Monograph series.
HC110.I5M33 1975   331.6'3'96073   74-17984
ISBN 0-12-479050-X

Printed in the United States of America

Dedication

To three generations of the Masters family

Malcolm H. and Claire M.
Julie J.
Sarah and Joe

The Institute for Research on Poverty is a national center for research established at the University of Wisconsin in 1966 by a grant from the Office of Economic Opportunity. Its primary objective is to foster basic, multidisciplinary research into the nature and causes of poverty and means to combat it.

In addition to increasing the basic knowledge from which policies aimed at the elimination of poverty can be shaped, the Institute strives to carry analysis beyond the formulation and testing of fundamental generalizations to the development and assessment of relevant policy alternatives.

The Institute endeavors to bring together scholars of the highest caliber whose primary research efforts are focused on the problem of poverty, the distribution of income, and the analysis and evaluation of social policy, offering staff members wide opportunity for interchange of ideas, maximum freedom for research into basic questions about poverty and social policy, and dissemination of their findings.

Contents

List of Tables   **xiii**

Foreword   **xv**

Preface   **xvii**

1 Economic Theories of Discrimination   1

    I. Economic Theories of Discrimination   2
        A.   Becker's Theory   *2*
        B.   Criticism of Becker by Kreuger, Welch, and Arrow   *6*
        C.   Thurow's Theory   *10*
        D.   The Radical Analysis and Other Group Conflict Theories   *14*
    II. An Empirical Test of the Radical Analysis versus the Becker Model   19
    III. Policy Implications of the Theories   21

2 A Review of Empirical Studies of Discrimination against Blacks   25

    I. Discrimination in Employment   25
    II. Segregation and Discrimination in Housing   31
    III. Discrimination in Education   36
    IV. Changes over Time in the Black–White Income Ratio   43
    V. A Preview of the Remaining Chapters   47

                            ix

3   The Effect of Migration on Black Incomes   49

I. The Data and the Measures of Migration Status   51
II. Results for Black Lifetime Migration   53
III. Explaining the Results for Lifetime Migration   56
IV. Results for Recent Migration   62
V. Conclusion   66

Appendix 3A: Independent Variables Used in the Regressions   68

**4   The Effect of Housing Segregation
      on Black–White Income Differentials   69**

I. Empirical Results Concerning the Effect of Housing
   Segregation on Black–White Earnings Ratios   74
II. Conclusion and Qualifications   88

Appendix 4A: Results for Relative Employment Ratios   91
Appendix 4B: Means and Standard Deviations for the Variables 95

**5   Estimating the Relative Importance of Labor-Market
      Discrimination versus Differences in Productivity
      between Blacks and Whites   97**

I. The Conceptual Framework   104
II. Empirical Results from the 1960 Census   106
III. Empirical Results from 1967 Survey of Economic
     Opportunity   111
IV. Results Using Predicted Test-Score Performance
    Instead of Years of School to Measure Educational Attainment 116
V. Conclusion   122

Appendix 5A: Variables Used Plus National Regression Results   123

I.   National Regressions   123
II. Subregion Regressions   125
III. National Regression Results Using 1/1000 and
     Comparable SEO Samples (Regression Coefficients and
     t-values)   125
IV. National Regression Results for Full-Time SEO Sample
     (Regression Coefficients and *t*-values)   127

**Appendix 5B: Demonstration That the Results in
Section IV Are Likely to Underestimate Labor-Market Distribution 128**

6 Alternative Policy Perspectives   131

I. The Conservative View   131
II. The Liberal View   133
III. The Radical View   137
IV. Empirical Evidence on the Three Views   140
V. Conclusion   149

7 Policy Recommendations   151

I. Combating Discrimination in Employment   151
   A. *Substantive Issues in Eliminating Employment Discrimination*   *153*
   B. *Affirmative-Action Requirements*   *157*
   C. *The Advantages and Disadvantages of Affirmative-Action*
      Requirements   *161*
   D. *Alternatives to the Present Emphasis on Affirmative Action*   *164*
II. Combating Discrimination in Education   168
   A. *Reducing Racial Segregation*   *169*
   B. *Educational Vouchers*   *171*
   C. *Community Control of Schools*   *174*
III. Concluding Comments   181

Author Index   185

List of Tables

2.1 *Differences in Teacher Effectiveness for Black and White Students*   40

2.2 *Changes in Relative Occupation Status of Black and White Males over Time*   46

3.1 *Economic Status of Black Lifetime Migrants and Nonmigrants*   52

3.2 *Percentage Distribution of Migrants and Nonmigrants, by Age and by Years of School*   54

3.3 *Net Effect of Black Lifetime Migration on Economic Status*   55

3.4 *Percentage Distribution of Blacks, by Years of School, 1960*   57

3.5 *Net Effect of Lifetime Migration for Blacks, by Years of School*   58

3.6 *Net Effect of Black Lifetime Migration on Economic Status Relative to Those Left Behind in the South*   59

3.7 *Net Effect of Lifetime Migration on Economic Status for Black Males and Females*   61

3.8 *Percentage Distribution of Occupation of Blacks, Lifetime Migrants and Nonmigrants*   62

3.9 *Economic Status of Recent Migrants and Nonmigrants*   64

3.10 *Net Effect of Recent Migration*   65

3.11 *Net Effect of Recent Migration by Sex for All SMSAs*   66

4.1   Results from Simple Regressions   79
4.2   Regression Results for Potential Control Variables
      (Dependent Variables and Sample)   82
4.3   Results from Multiple Regressions, Nonagricultural
      Sample   87
4.A1 Results for Relative Employment Rates   93
5.1   Michelson's Results for Racial Earnings Gap   98
5.2   Revised Version of Michelson's Results   98
5.3   Duncan's Estimates for the Components of the Racial
      Income Gap   100
5.4   Duncan's Results with Component for Mental Ability   101
5.5   Gwartney's Income Indices   103
5.6   Decomposing the Racial Earnings Gap: Results from
      1/1000 Sample, 1960 Census   108
5.7   Decomposing the Racial Earnings Gap: With and
      without Standardization for Weeks Worked, Results
      from 1/1000 Sample   109
5.8   Decomposing the Racial Earnings Gap: The Effect of
      Differences in Years of School, Results from 1/1000
      Sample   110
5.9   Decomposing the Racial Earnings Gap: Results from
      Survey of Economic Opportunity, 1967   112
5.10 Decomposing the Racial Earnings Gap: Comparative
      Results from 1/1000 and SEO Samples, All Results as a
      Percentage of $\bar{E}_W$ 113
5.11 Decomposing the Racial Earnings Gap: Results from
      Persons in the Labor Force All Year, SEO   114
5.12 Decomposing the Racial Earnings Gap: Results for
      Effect of Differences in Years of School, 1/1000
      and SEO   115
5.13 Decomposing the Racial Earnings Gap: Results Using
      Predicted AFQT Scores Compared with Results Using
      Years of School, SEO   119
6.1   Changes in the Nonwhite–White Male Income Ratio,
      1960–1971   144
6.2   Median Black–White Male Income Ratios, 1959–1969, by
      Age and Years of School   145
6.3   Changes in the Black–White Income Ratio, by Location   146
6.4   The Residuals for Equation (2), Where the Dependent
      Variable (Y) Is the Black–White Income Ratio   148

Foreword

The problem of poverty in the United States concerns income gaps and relative deprivation. For a variety of complex and interacting reasons, some families and individuals find themselves at the bottom end of the distribution of income and wealth—with resources that are insufficient to provide for their needs. Among the primary reasons for the phenomenon of economic poverty are the initial endowments of ability and motivation; human investments in education, training, migration, and the inheritance of wealth; and the structure and performance of (primarily labor) markets. A central task of research on poverty is to disentangle these causes and to evaluate the contribution of each to the problem of income gaps and relative deprivation. It is through such efforts that basic research can enlighten the choices of policymakers seeking effective instruments for closing income gaps or reducing poverty. Professor Masters's book on black–white income differences is in this research tradition.

Past theoretical and empirical contributions have suggested that labor-market discrimination may not be a significant cause of black poverty and the income differentials between blacks and whites. It has been suggested, for example, that the migration of southern blacks to large northern cities is the major cause of the observed income differentials in these areas, or that segregation in housing has thrown up impediments to black workers seeking attractive employment opportunities. It has been suggested that productivity differentials (measured by schooling duration or performance) account for the income gap rather than discrimination in the labor market. After reviewing the literature on labor-market discrimination, Professor Masters undertakes empirical tests of the primary hypotheses that suggest the relative unimportance of discriminatory behavior in labor markets.

His statistical results indicate that neither the south–north migration hypothesis nor the housing segregation hypothesis is a sustainable explanation for the black–white income gap. In testing the validity of the productivity hypothesis, he concludes that the contribution of productivity differentials to racial income differentials depends crucially on the assumptions that one makes about the reliability of the schooling variables as measures of productivity. At best, the result is ambiguous. Masters concludes that even under the most extreme assumptions, much of the black–white income gap must be attributed to racial discrimination in labor markets. Although this result is not inconsistent with the beliefs of many citizens, it is significant in that it verifies in an empirical, scientific way the power of economic discrimination in employment as a cause of income differentials and, hence, of poverty.

The final sections of the book draw policy conclusions that are based upon the statistical analysis. Masters's proposals are aimed, first, at securing reductions in labor-market discrimination and, second, at improving educational opportunities available to racial minorities. These policy proposals are in the liberal tradition: As Professor Masters states, "While conservative and radical prescriptions are also considered ... the experience since the Civil Rights Act of 1964 is consistent with predictions by liberals concerning the effectiveness of such legislation."

This study began in 1970, when Professor Masters joined the staff of the Institute for Research on Poverty as a Visiting Professor. The work has been an important part of the Institute's Seminar on Segregation, Discrimination, and Poverty. It is a welcome addition to the literature on the economics of discrimination and a valuable contribution to the Institute's Monograph Series.

Robert H. Haveman
Director, Institute for Research on Poverty

Preface

Racial discrimination has received much attention in recent years from both the general public and the economics profession. One purpose of this work is to attempt to summarize some of the literature that has developed on the economics of discrimination. As the literature review indicates, however, there are many hypotheses in this area that have not been tested very thoroughly. Thus, a considerable portion of the book is devoted to empirical testing of various hypotheses. Such tests are designed not only to improve our understanding of discrimination, but also in the hope that they will be of assistance to policymakers who are attempting to reduce such discrimination. Consequently, the book concludes with a discussion of various policy measures that appear deserving of serious consideration. Although this policy discussion must depend on the author's value judgments and on his subjective assessments regarding political feasibility, I believe the book's empirical analysis also can make a significant contribution by helping to focus attention on some of the more important policy areas, like labor-market discrimination.

The policy discussion emphasizes the difficulty of achieving color-blind standards and the need for such policies as affirmative action and black community control of schools. A related issue is whether whites like myself should play an active role in the economic analysis of racial discrimination and in making policy recommendations in this area, or whether the field should be left primarily to blacks and other minority groups. In my view, whites should remain active in this area, in part because I believe discrimination is an issue that diminishes the discriminator as well as his victim. Consequently, whites as well as blacks have a stake in seeking both to understand and to combat discrimination.

The study focuses on racial income differentials for males, primarily because the racial discrimination issue is very complex even without attempting to separate interactions between racial and sexual discrimination (or between racial discrimination and sexual roles). Fortunately, sexual as well as racial discrimination has been receiving considerable attention in the past few years. In my view, interrelations between these two kinds of discrimination should represent a fruitful area for future research.

Although many people have made valuable contributions to this book, I would like especially to acknowledge the research assistance of Burt Barnow and Edward Lin; suggestions from referees Orley Ashenfelter, Lester Thurow, and Phyllis Wallace; and the overall advice and encouragement of Irv Garfinkel and Robert Haveman.

1

Economic Theories of Discrimination

Racial discrimination can occur in many areas, including employment, education, and housing. From the point of view of economics, the net result of such discrimination is to lower the relative real incomes of blacks and other minority groups. This introductory essay discusses the economic theories of discrimination that have been developed in recent years. Chapter 2 reviews evidence on the magnitude of different kinds of discrimination and serves as an introduction to three statistical investigations. Each empirical essay presents evidence concerning an hypothesis which, if true, would imply that discrimination in employment is relatively unimportant as an explanation for black–white urban income differentials. These hypotheses are: (1) southern migrants are a major reason for the low average income of blacks living in northern cities;[1] (2) housing segregation causes significant employment problems for urban black males;[2] and (3) differences in productivity (especially differences in educational attainment) are more important than labor-

---

[1] For example, see Edward C. Banfield, *The Unheavenly City* (Boston, Massachusetts: Little, Brown, 1968), p. 68.

[2] The classic statement of this position occurs in John F. Kain and Joseph J. Persky, "Alternatives to the Gilded Ghetto," *The Public Interest* (Winter 1969).

1

market discrimination in explaining why black males have lower earnings than whites.[3]

The first two of these hypotheses are shown to be false while the validity of the third depends upon what assumptions one is willing to make about the reliability of years of school or test-score performance as measures of productivity. Even under the most extreme assumptions, however, it appears that much of the racial differential in earnings (or income) should be attributed to labor-market discrimination. Therefore, in the policy analysis of the concluding essays, we concentrate first on proposals to reduce labor-market discrimination and second, on strategies to improve the educational opportunities available to blacks.

While conservative and radical policy perspectives are also considered, we concentrate on policies in the liberal tradition—in part because our analysis in Chapter 6 indicates that, thus far, the experience since the Civil Rights Act of 1964 is consistent with predictions by liberals concerning the effectiveness of such legislation.

I. Economic Theories of Discrimination

In this section, we discuss the major economic theories of discrimination. Then we examine the rather limited attempts that have been made to test the empirical validity of these theories, and finally, we consider the policy implications of each theory.

A. Becker's Theory

The first major attempt to relate discrimination to economic theory was made by Gary S. Becker in *The Economics of Discrimination*.[4] Becker begins by criticizing definitions that equate discrimination with behavior toward an individual which "is not motivated by an 'objective'

---

[3] James Gwartney reaches this conclusion while studying racial income differentials for urban males. See James Gwartney, "Discrimination and Income Differentials," *American Economic Review* 60 (June 1970). Also see Lester C. Thurow, *Poverty and Discrimination* (Washington, D.C.: The Brookings Institution, 1969) for a similar conclusion with regard to the total population.

[4] Gary S. Becker, *The Economics of Discrimination* (Chicago, Illinois: University of Chicago Press, 1957). A second edition was published in 1971, but we shall use the page references in the original (unless otherwise specified). Note that there are few changes in the substance of the second edition.

consideration of fact." Rather than get involved in what is (and what is not) an objective consideration of fact, Becker proposes a different definition.

> If an individual has a "taste for discrimination" he must act *as if* he were willing to pay something, either directly or in the form of a reduced income, to be associated with some persons instead of others. When actual discrimination occurs, he must, in fact, either pay or forfeit income for this purpose.[5]

While this definition applies to an individual discriminator, market discrimination is defined as the difference between the actual ratio of black to white wages (or incomes) and the ratio that would exist if no individuals had a taste for discrimination. For example, if there were no differences in productivity between blacks and whites, then any difference between black and white wages would represent discrimination in employment.

Becker then makes a sharp distinction between market discrimination and market segregation, with the latter being defined in terms of the amount of physical contact between blacks and whites. For example, if some firms refuse to hire blacks, this refusal will automatically produce some racial segregation. However, if blacks can obtain equally good jobs elsewhere, then the fact that they are excluded by some firms would not lead to market discrimination since there would still be no income differential (aside from any differences in productivity).

In applying these concepts to the real world, Becker looks at total discrimination and then separately at discrimination by employers, employees, consumers, and the government. We will begin by looking at discrimination by employers. If black and white labor are perfect substitutes in production,[6] if perfect competition prevails in both the product and labor markets, and if there is no discrimination aside from that by employers, then the extent of discrimination depends on (*1*) the distribution of employers' tastes for discrimination, (*2*) the relative supply of black and white labor, and (*3*) the ability of the less discriminatory firms to expand their output without severe increases in unit cost.

---

[5] Ibid., p. 6.

[6] In other words, we are assuming that blacks and whites have identical abilities and tastes, that there is no discrimination in education, and no discrimination by employers or consumers.

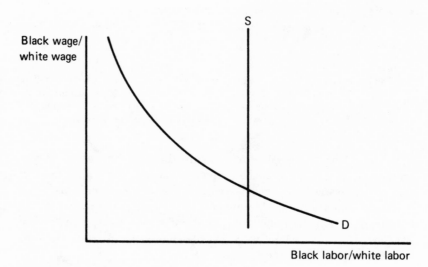

FIGURE 1.1   *Supply and demand for labor by race at different relative wage rates.*

Since black and white labor are assumed to be perfect substitutes, firms will hire either all white workers or all black (that is, complete segregation) depending on whether or not the employer's taste for discrimination is adequately compensated by the market differential between black and white wages. This situation can be analyzed in terms of a supply and demand diagram as shown in Figure 1.1. The lower the ratio of black to white wage rates, the more firms will prefer to hire blacks. Employers' tastes for discrimination determine the shape of the demand curve, D, while the relative labor supplies are assumed to be inelastic with respect to relative wage changes. For a given demand curve, the relative wages of blacks will be lower the larger their relative supply.

Of course, if there is discrimination, firms who hire blacks will obtain a competitive advantage, and, depending on their production functions, such firms may be able to significantly expand their share of the market. If they can, then the demand curve, D, will shift upward to the right and the ratio of black to white wages will increase. Therefore, given an identical distribution of employers' tastes for discrimination and similar relative supplies of black and white workers, the racial wage differential should be lower in competitive industries than in monopolistic ones where there are fewer competitive pressures.

Next we turn to discrimination by employees rather than employers. In this case, we assume that white employees will require a higher wage if they are to work alongside black employees but that employers have no tastes for discrimination. If black and white workers are perfect substitutes in production, then Becker predicts complete segregation of work forces, since it is more costly for a firm to hire black and white workers simultaneously than to hire those of just one race when there is employee discrimination. Although there should be complete segregation, there should not be any market discrimination since each firm would hire whichever race would work for the lower wage, thereby leading to equal wages by race under equilibrium conditions.

If white and black labor are not perfect substitutes, they may work together at some firms doing different jobs. In this case a racial wage differential will exist (independently of differences in productivity) since employers must pay white employees more in order for them to work with blacks. Therefore, even if tastes for discrimination against blacks are greatest among whites who are close substitutes for blacks in production (as is usually assumed), the tastes of whites who provide complementary labor may still have a greater effect on market discrimination.[7]

Next, Becker shows that tastes for discrimination by consumers can be analyzed in much the same fashion as such tastes by employers or employees. With respect to housing, he argues that if, ceteris paribus, whites prefer to live near other whites and blacks prefer to live near other blacks, then this is an explanation for housing segregation but not for housing discrimination. Given the existence of housing segregation, Becker suggests that, at least in northern cities, housing discrimination may result primarily from market adjustment lags in the face of large-scale black immigration.

Although Becker is primarily concerned with discrimination in the marketplace, he does briefly discuss governmental discrimination. Becker shows that under a democracy, if racial discrimination is the only issue, then the government should be expected to act in accordance with the median taste for discrimination among the electorate. On the other hand, if there are a number of related issues (as there almost always are) then black voters may be able to have a disproportionate influence on

[7] See Becker, *Economics of Discrimination*, pp. 52–53.

governmental racial policies. The argument here is that, if blacks feel more strongly about a racial issue and if whites feel more strongly (and are divided) on some other issue, then blacks can trade their support on the second issue in return for enough white support to gain a majority for the black view on the racial question. Writing in 1957, Becker argued that this analysis explains why blacks appeared to have much more political influence in the North than in the South since (*1*) blacks were more likely to be disenfranchised in the South[8] and (*2*) racial prejudice among whites may have been less intense in the North.

Up to this point, we have discussed Becker's analysis of discrimination on the part of employers, employees, consumers, and the government. In addition to looking separately at discrimination by each group, Becker puts considerable emphasis on his analysis of discrimination by the entire white community. Here, he uses a simple one-commodity international trade model with whites exporting capital to blacks and importing black labor. In this model, discrimination acts as a barrier to trade, analogous to a transportation cost (or possibly a tariff).

According to the principle of comparative advantage, both blacks and whites could benefit from free trade. Thus Becker demonstrates that discrimination by whites reduces the net income of both blacks *and* whites. On the other hand, the factors of production that are scarce in each society—namely white labor and black capital—stand to gain as a result of such discrimination.

B. *Criticism of Becker by Kreuger, Welch, and Arrow*

Although Becker's work represents a very valuable, pioneering effort to study discrimination with the tools of economics, his analysis has been subjected to a number of serious criticisms. First, Kreuger has criticized the usefulness of Becker's international trade analysis.[9] As she emphasizes, Becker's conclusions apply only to the effect of discrimination on *net* income, defined as money income minus the psychic costs of whites who have to deal with blacks. If we assume that, in the absence of a white taste for discrimination, whites do have economic dealings with blacks, then it should not be surprising that whites are worse off if they find these dealings to be distasteful rather than simply a matter

[8] Note that Becker does not attempt to explain why or how blacks are disenfranchised.

[9] Anne O. Kreuger, "The Economics of Discrimination," *Journal of Political Economy* 71 (October 1963): 481–486.

of indifference. As Kreuger indicates, the more interesting question (and the question Becker should have been asking given his definition of discrimination) is what happens to white *money* incomes when whites discriminate against blacks. Using the international trade model, she argues that whites may be able to gain money income even if blacks retaliate.[10]

Since blacks are a relatively small minority in the United States and have much less capital (both physical and human) per capita than whites, both Becker and Kreuger agree that blacks are likely to suffer significant economic losses if they refuse to trade with whites. On the other hand, a strategy of black separation could still be quite rational since black separatists might be willing to pay these economic costs in order to attain greater dignity and self-respect for the black community.[11]

Welch and Arrow have criticized Becker for not giving enough attention to the following question: Why is it that competitive forces do not act to eliminate discrimination in the long run?[12] Certainly economic theory suggests that, if some employers (e.g., blacks) have no taste for discrimination against blacks, then in a long-run competitive equilibrium there should be no discrimination by employers since such discrimination implies below average (and thus negative) profit.[13] Since both Welch and Arrow believe that the economy is reasonably competi-

---

[10] As the Wohlstetters point out, however, in "Third Worlds Abroad and at Home," *The Public Interest* (Winter 1969): 89–90, "in other literature on discrimination, it is widely assumed that the loss imposed on nonwhite laborers is a net gain to the white employers—that is, that the loss to nonwhites equals the gain to whites." Therefore, when we compare Becker's analysis (even as modified by Kreuger) with this view, it appears that "the argument for reducing discrimination has greater appeal to the self-interest of whites (in Becker's model) than if the relationship between whites and nonwhites were truly that of a zero-sum game [Ibid.]."

[11] Note that the Wohlstetters quote Quevara and others to show that militant exponents of self-sufficiency in the less-developed countries have often modified their position once they became aware of the extent of these economic costs. On the other hand, separation may increase black political power, since blacks are actually a minority element in a white society rather than a separate society. Thus separatism could conceivably lead to economic gains for blacks if whites have been enforcing discrimination through a governmental mechanism. (See the discussion of Thurow's analysis in Section C.)

[12] Finis Welch, "Labor Market Discrimination in the Rural South," *Journal of Political Economy* 75 (June 1967); and Kenneth J. Arrow, "Models of Job Discrimination," in *Racial Discrimination in Economic Life*, ed. Anthony H. Pascal (Lexington, Massachusetts: Heath, 1972).

[13] This analysis assumes that firms will go out of business rather than assume losses indefinitely. On the other hand, the firm's owner may be willing to keep the firm going by accepting a low rate of compensation for his capital or labor.

tive but that discrimination has existed for a long time, they are faced with an apparent paradox.

Welch deals with this problem by assuming that black and white workers have different skills and are, thus, complements in production.

> This complementarity implies that the joint product of two laborers with unequal education is greater than the sum of their individual products. But, if the laborers are of different races, their joint product is assumed to be less than if they are of the same race.[14]

Thus, we can have discrimination as long as (*1*) the first factor is stronger than the second and (*2*) there is a significant difference in skills between blacks and whites (e.g., as a result of unequal educational attainment).

Arrow presents several other hypotheses to explain why discrimination can continue for a long time, even in a competitive economy. First, as Becker indicates, if black and white workers are perfect substitutes in production and whites have tastes for discrimination, then the employer can minimize his costs by hiring all white or all black workers. This means that, if racial wage differentials change, the employer should either do nothing or else replace his entire work force with workers of the other race. However, if the employer has made an investment in his present work force, he will lose some of the returns on that investment if he hires a new work force. Thus, when blacks move into a white economy, the influence of past investments by firms may keep them from replacing whites with blacks even if the black wage rates would be lower. While Arrow is correct in arguing that past investments will retard the movement to a new equilibrium, he is not convincing when he suggests that the equilibrium will never be achieved. If the economy is as competitive as Arrow believes, then, since there is considerable growth in the economy, there should be enough new firms entering to allow the economy to reach its long-run equilibrium position with regard to racial wage differentials.

Arrow's second argument is also more convincing as an explanation for why a new equilibrium might be reached slowly rather than not at all. According to this argument, employers discriminate against blacks because they believe them to be inferior workers. In other words, skin

[14] Welch, "Labor Market Discrimination," pp. 227–228.

color is used as a cheap source of limited information.[15] Such information is potentially useful whenever it is costly for the employer to hire the worker and then simply see how he does on the job, a situation that occurs whenever the firm must make an initial investment in its workers. Arrow summarizes this theory:

> We have two primary elements in this model: The employer's investment of personnel capital will be wasted if the employee turns out not to (be qualified); and the employer cannot know beforehand whether or not the employee is qualified. But the employer does know the race of the individual, however, and he holds some subjective beliefs about the respective probabilities that white and black workers are qualified. It is of course immediately obvious that if the subjective probability in the mind of an employer that a white worker is qualified, is higher than that a black worker is qualified, there will have to be a wage difference if the employer is to hire any blacks at all.
>
> The effects of this model are similar to those based on tastes, but the causes are different. We would still want to know why the subjective probabilities are different. The simplest explanation is prejudice, in the literal sense of that term; that is, a judgment about abilities made in advance of the evidence and not altered by it. Of course, the persistence of prejudice really should not be left unexplained. One possible explanation is to be found in theories of psychological equilibrium, such as Festinger's theory of cognitive dissonance. If an individual acts in a discriminatory fashion, he would, according to this theory, tend to have beliefs that justify his actions. Indeed, precisely the fact that discriminatory behavior is in conflict with an important segment of our ethical beliefs will, according to this theory, intensify the willingness to entertain cognitive beliefs that will supply a socially acceptable justification for this conduct.[16]

While this argument almost certainly has some validity, it does not explain why, in the long run, the less prejudiced employers do not drive their more prejudiced rivals out of business. Arrow has a third model, however, that may be relevant in this regard. In this model, there are no innate differences between blacks and whites, but whites have initially developed better work habits or some other aspect of superior productivity which is not immediately obvious. Then, employers would be justified in preferring whites to blacks when each has the same readily observable characteristics. If, as a result, employers do favor whites and give them a better opportunity to prove themselves in the better jobs, then whites will receive a higher return than blacks for investing in the

[15] This point is also stressed by Peter B. Doeringer and Michael J. Piore in Chapter 7 of *Internal Labor Markets and Manpower Analysis* (Lexington, Massachusetts: Heath, 1971).

[16] Reprinted by permission of the publisher, from *Racial Discrimination in Economic Life*, edited by Anthony H. Pascal (Lexington, Massachusetts: Lexington Books, D. C. Heath and Company, 1971), p. 97. Copyright 1971 by The Rand Corporation.

development of such work habits. Therefore, the economy may never reach the nondiscriminatory equilibrium where blacks and whites would have an equal incentive to invest in these work habits or other similar skills.[17]

C. Thurow's Theory

So far, we have considered criticisms of Becker's analysis that have been made by economists who are prepared to accept his basic approach. Next we consider some important criticisms aimed at Becker's general assumptions.

Thurow and Bergmann argue that Becker gives too little attention to how tastes for discrimination vary according to the kind of job involved. For example, Thurow writes:

> Discrimination is not simply demanding a premium to associate with Negroes, as described by Becker. The discriminator may want to work with, buy from, or hire Negroes, but he insists on specifying the relationships under which the two parties will meet and how the Negro will respond. Perhaps it is more accurate to say that whites maximize a utility function with social distance rather than physical distance as one of its arguments. A desire for social distance can lead to a very different set of actions. The discriminator may prefer to hire Negro maids, Negro garbage collectors, or to work with Negroes if he can be in a position of authority.[18]

Or, in Bergmann's view:

> The most important feature of an economy in which discrimination is practiced is the simple fact that some jobs are open to Negroes and some are not. The jobs open to Negroes are not a random selection, even allowing for Negroes' relatively lower education. They tend to be predominantly low in status and to be concentrated very heavily in a few occupations.[19]

Bergmann goes on to emphasize that restricting blacks (or other groups) to certain occupations increases the relative supply and decreases the relative wage for those occupations.

While Bergmann's criticism of Becker leads to this "crowding" hypothesis, Thurow challenges the individualistic approach of Becker's

---

[17] This argument has been more extensively developed in recent work by Stiglitz, who also discusses other reasons why wage discrimination could be consistent with a competitive equilibrium. See Joseph E. Stiglitz, "Approaches to the Economics of Discrimination," *American Economic Review* 63 (May 1973): 287–295, and the references cited therein.

[18] Thurow, *Poverty and Discrimination*, p. 117.

[19] Barbara R. Bergmann, "The Effect on White Income of Discrimination in Employment," *Journal of Political Economy* 79 (March–April 1971): 295.

model. According to Thurow, it is more useful to view discrimination in the context of whites acting collectively, as a rational monopolist (or cartel), in their dealings with blacks. Therefore, in contrast with Becker's conclusions, Thurow believes that whites—as a group—can frequently improve their economic and social position by discriminating against blacks. Although he does not put the argument in these terms, Thurow would probably be receptive to economists treating racial barriers as a "public good" when viewed from the standpoint of the white community. For example, all whites with a taste for discrimination stand to lose (utility if not income) if blacks, rather than whites, get top jobs or move into good neighborhoods.[20] In short, the theory of inter-dependent utility functions in welfare economics appears to provide some of the microeconomic foundation for Thurow's approach, in contrast to Becker's reliance on the theory of the firm and of the household.

In evaluating Thurow's contribution to the economic analysis of discrimination, the main issue is the plausibility of his assumption that the white community acts qua community to exploit the black community. As he notes, some whites can often gain an individual advantage by violating a general policy of discrimination. In response to this problem, Thurow cites two main mechanisms by which the white community can enforce its discriminatory policy: (*1*) law or other governmental activities and (*2*) mutual reinforcement achieved by various forms of discrimination.

First, we look at the governmental mechanism. Examples of discrimination by the government range from the provision of inferior schooling opportunities and discrimination in governmental hiring and promotion policies, all the way to imposing legal penalities on private parties who educate blacks or hire them for skilled positions. While such action can sometimes be extremely effective (as carried out in the antebellum South or contemporary South Africa, for two extreme examples), it appears to be less relevant in the contemporary United States. Even when a clear majority of our electorate wants to discriminate, there are judicial constraints—based largely on the Fourteenth Amendment. Moreover, in the last few years the legislative and executive branches of the federal government (and many state and local governments as well) have been willing to go on record as officially opposed to a wide variety of forms of

[20] When people have utility functions with this property, racism exists according to the definition of Alexis. For a further discussion of this issue, see Marcus Alexis, "A Theory of Labor Market Discrimination with Interdependent Utilities," *American Economic Review* 63 (May 1973): 296–302.

discrimination. Although passing laws and issuing judicial decrees against discrimination does not necessarily mean they will be widely obeyed or vigorously enforced, such actions do suggest that in our society government is less likely to be a major vehicle for enforcing a *prodiscrimination* policy now[21] than it was prior to 1964 or 1954.[22] However, "the government" is far from monolithic and many components (both federal and local) still discriminate against blacks, either directly or indirectly. For example, subsidies to wealthy white farmers are much more prevalent than those to poor black agricultural workers.[23] Or, to take a quite different kind of example, public education may often reinforce white tastes for discrimination. We will return to the issue of the government as an enforcement mechanism later.

Second, we consider Thurow's "mutual-reinforcement" mechanism for enforcing a community-wide discrimination policy. Thurow argues that, because of discrimination in education, there are few blacks that are qualified for the best jobs. Therefore, employers are under little effective pressure to hire blacks for such jobs. Consequently, blacks also have less income, which also makes it easier to exclude blacks from the best housing neighborhoods. Finally, as a result of low incomes and housing discrimination, blacks are not in a position to either (*1*) send their children to white schools or (*2*) generate enough political and/or economic power to establish high-quality schools in black neighborhoods.[24]

To analyze this argument, we begin by looking at the links between poor education and restricted job opportunities. While it is obviously true that the *total job opportunities* for blacks are restricted if blacks receive a low-quality education, Becker's analysis suggests that labor-market discrimination will be less in this case since the few well-qualified blacks can probably all be hired by a few whites with relatively low tastes for discrimination.[25] A similar argument also applies to the link between

[21] For evidence that fair employment laws do have some effect on reducing discrimination, see William M. Landes, "The Economics of Fair Employment Laws," *The Journal of Political Economy* 76 (July–August 1968).

[22] For an interesting further discussion of the role of government as a mechanism to maintain discrimination (with special reference to recent changes in the importance of this mechanism in the United States) see Richard B. Freeman, "Decline of Labor Market Discrimination and Economic Analysis," *American Economic Review* 63 (May 1973): 280–286.

[23] See Senator Ernest F. Hollings, *The Case Against Hunger* (New York: Cowles Book Co., 1970), especially Chapter 7.

[24] Throughout this discussion, we will assume that an individual's political influence is positively related to his command over economic resources.

[25] In fact, there may be no discrimination (or reverse discrimination) if there are some firms that do not discriminate (or discriminate in favor of blacks).

job opportunities and housing. However, this criticism does not apply to the link between low income and housing discrimination and poor schools, since the quality of schooling is determined politically rather than in the market place. Therefore, as long as the courts do not prohibit discrimination in education based on de facto segregation, the effect of low income and housing discrimination on black educational opportunities is likely to be the most important link in Thurow's chain of interaction effects.[26]

To test whether the "mutual-reinforcement" mechanism can maintain an equilibrium position where competition and discrimination coexist, let us assume that the initial level of market discrimination is determined collectively by the white community and is quite high. Competitive pressures should lead to reduced discrimination in employment and housing, and then interaction effects should work to *reduce* discrimination in education since diminished discrimination in employment and housing should increase the economic and political power of blacks, thereby enabling them to obtain better education for their children.

While the mutual-reinforcement mechanism probably cannot maintain a discriminatory equilibrium, it is important as a means of slowing competitive pressures to eliminate discrimination. As such it appears closely related to the view that discrimination is becoming more institutional than overt (e.g., the handicaps blacks face in the labor market are now due less to overt discrimination and more to factors like inferior education or reduced aspirations which result from past discrimination).

We have suggested that the "mutual-reinforcement" mechanism can only slow down movement toward a Becker-model equilibrium and that, in the contemporary United States, the importance of the governmental mechanism is difficult to evaluate. Next we consider whether other mechanisms exist which would support Thurow's model.

For example, consider discrimination in housing.[27] Note that white vigilante actions (e.g., burning crosses on a black's front yard) or

---

[26] Note that the California Supreme Court has ruled that it is illegal to finance schools through a local property tax unless measures are taken to insure that children are not discriminated against by coming from communities with low levels of per capita wealth or income. See *Serrano* v. *Priest*, 487 P. 2d 1241, 91 Cal., Rptr. 601 (1971). However, the United States Supreme Court has refused to make an analagous ruling.

[27] Discrimination in employment will be discussed later. Since education is normally provided by the government, the earlier discussion of the government as an enforcement mechanism can be applied to this form of discrimination.

ostracism may be quite simple and effective methods for enforcing a white policy of discrimination. Also, housing developers, real estate agents, and banks may be subject to reprisals from white customers, other white businessmen, or the white political structure if they act to encourage integration. In this regard, consider the following quotation:

> A Philadelphia builder recently told an interviewer that he would very much like to sell suburban houses to Negroes, but that it was impossible because it would ruin him economically. "If I sold just one suburban home to a Negro, the local building inspectors would have me moving pipes three-eighths of an inch every afternoon in every one of the places I was building; and moving a pipe three-eighths of an inch is mighty expensive if you have to do it in concrete."[28]

Although a national fair housing law now exists and attitudes have perhaps changed since this story was related in 1958, the *fear* of economic (and social) reprisals may still be important in discouraging housing integration. If so, then such fears provide support for Thurow's view that communities discriminate as communities (at least in part) rather than simply as a set of individuals.[29]

D. The Radical Analysis and Other Group Conflict Theories

While Thurow's theory appears useful in explaining housing discrimination, it appears somewhat less helpful when we deal with employment.

---

[28] John F. Kain, ed., *Race and Poverty: The Economics of Discrimination* (Englewood Cliffs, New Jersey: Prentice-Hall, 1969), p. 25.

[29] In this context consider Becker's view that housing discrimination in the northern cities is a temporary phenomenon resulting from the combination of housing segregation and the large increase in the black population of such cities as a result of migration from the South. While expansion of the black population has undoubtedly aggravated the problem of housing discrimination, it is not at all clear that discrimination would cease if there there were no black population growth. Let us assume that a black incurs extra costs when he moves into a white neighborhood. These costs, which do not occur if he moves into a black neighborhood or if a white moves into a white neighborhood, could result from a wide variety of factors, including fear of violence or social ostracism, less assistance from realtors, or higher mortgage costs. If these costs do exist, then the black would not move into the white neighborhood unless the market price of housing were enough cheaper to compensate for these "racial" costs. Therefore, in equilibrium, racial differences in the market price of housing can exist as long as they are no larger than the "racial" costs that would be incurred by the marginal black who is discouraged from moving into a white neighborhood. As a result, we should not expect housing discrimination in the northern cities to disappear even if their black populations should stop growing— although a decrease in the black migration to these cities probably would alleviate the housing shortage for blacks and thus reduce the magnitude of discrimination.

The main difficulty is that Thurow's model neglects class issues—such as those between employers and employees (white as well as black). On the other hand, radical "Marxist" economists, such as Baran and Sweezy, emphasize the importance of class conflict in economics. With regard to race, one of the radicals' main themes has been that

> employers benefit from divisions in the labor force which enable them to play one group off against another, thus weakening all. Historically, for example, no small amount of Negro migration was in direct response to the recruiting of strikebreakers.[30]

In addition to weakening the strength of unions, such divisions are also seen as helpful to employers as a means of reducing the political power of labor (e.g., less effective pressure for programs to reduce unemployment and to provide workers with generous benefits under employment–security-type programs). Since political power for the employer (or capitalist) class is a collective good where each employer benefits from the efforts of his colleagues, standard economic theory suggests that relatively little of this political activity will occur unless employers can organize as a group and impose some kind of tax on their members. Otherwise, each employer is assumed to act solely in terms of his narrow self-interest. On the other hand, the radicals expect capitalist political activity to be highly important, even in the absence of any explicit organization by the capitalists, since the radicals assume (*1*) that individuals (especially capitalists?) are motivated by class as well as individual self-interest and (*2*) that the economy is not competitive enough to force firms to act strictly on the basis of individual profit maximization.[31] Racial political strategies by capitalists have been employed frequently in the United States, at least since the capitalists' successful effort to defeat the southern populist movement in the 1890s.[32]

---

[30] Paul A. Baran and Paul M. Sweezy, *Monopoly Capital* (New York: Monthly Review Press, 1966), pp. 263–264. While Baran and Sweezy also stress a number of other points, this one has probably received the widest acceptance. For example, see Morris Silver, "Employee Tastes for Discrimination, Wages and Profits," *Review of Social Economy* 26 (September 1968). Also reprinted in *Economics: Mainstream Readings and Radical Critiques*, ed. David Mermelstein (New York: Random House, 1970).

[31] In addition to the importance of noncompetitive market structures such as oligopoly, the radicals also emphasize the importance of dynamic factors that limit the relevance of the long-run price competition model. Such dynamic factors include changes in technology and in consumer tastes, both of which are at least partially under the control of firms.

[32] For example, see C. Vann Woodward, *Tom Watson: Agrarian Rebel* (New York: Macmillan, 1938).

The policies of the early Nixon administration have been analyzed in these terms by Rustin[33] who suggests that the Philadelphia Plan was designed to increase antagonisms between the labor movement and the black community.

In addition, the radicals argue that white workers obtain psychological, if not economic, benefits from racism.[34] For example, Reich maintains that

> capitalist society . . . encourages the formation of racism. Whatever the origins of racism, it is likely to take root firmly in a society which breeds an individualistic and competitive ethos, status fears among marginal groups, and the need for visible scapegoats on which to blame the alienating quality of life in America.[35]

In a similar vein, Baran and Sweezy suggest that

> the gratification which whites derive from their socio-economic superiority to Negroes has its counterpart in alarm, anger, and even panic at the prospect of Negroes attaining equality. Status being a relative matter, whites inevitably interpret upward movement by Negroes as downward movement for themselves.[36]

Recently Gordon has developed a radical view of the labor market which draws heavily on the literature of the dual labor-market hypothesis.[37] Gordon argues that by the end of the nineteenth century workers in the United States were being drawn together in large work places. As a result, capitalists faced the danger that the workers would more effectively perceive their common interests and demand both better working conditions and a larger share of the total product.

At the same time, as production processes were becoming more complex and interdependent, firm-specific skills were becoming increas-

---

[33] See Bayard Rustin, "The Blacks and the Unions," *Harper's* 242 (May 1971).

[34] The radicals also emphasize that union members can sometimes gain by excluding blacks. For a good treatment of this issue see Becker, *Economics of Discrimination*, 2d ed., 1971, pp. 63–74. This material was originally written by Becker as "Union Restrictions on Entry," in *The Public Stake in Union Power*, ed. P. Bradley (Charlottesville, Virginia: University Press of Virginia, 1959).

[35] See Michael Reich, "The Economics of Racism," in *Problems in Political Economy: An Urban Perspective*, ed. David M. Gordon (Lexington, Massachusetts: Heath, 1971), p. 110. A slightly revised version also appears in *The Capitalist System*, ed. Richard C. Edwards, Michael Reich, and Thomas E. Weiskopt (Englewood Cliffs, New Jersey: Prentice-Hall, 1972).

[36] Baran and Sweezy, *Monopoly Capital*, p. 266.

[37] David M. Gordon, *Theories of Poverty and Underemployment* (Lexington, Massachusetts: Heath, 1972).

ingly important. Consequently, firms were becoming more dependent on maintaining a stable work force, thus making it more difficult for them to combat worker organization by such means as importing strike breakers.

Gordon describes the response of employers to this problem:

> It becomes increasingly useful for employers to try to organize job structures and to define the nature of job clusters in such a way that those jobs requiring employee stability are clearly separated from those which do not. The devices necessary to insure stability often become expensive—through whatever special work adjustments and monetary incentives may prove necessary—and it becomes increasingly efficient for employers to confine those extra expenses to the narrowest range of jobs they can.[38]

But Gordon also suggests that such procedures could be used to reduce the threat of workers organizing effectively against the employers, since employers would try to minimize the extent to which those in less desirable jobs could identify with those in the better jobs.

> If they could, they would try to segregate white-collar workers from blue-collar workers, create or permit the development of a class identity among more advantaged white-collar workers to distinguish them from blue-collar workers, and to impose some sharp barriers between the different kinds of jobs, like educational requirements. To the extent that employers could accomplish this stratification, it became more likely that blue-collar workers would accept their poorer working conditions (relative to those of white-collar workers) because they did not have the necessary credentials and education to move on to jobs with better opportunities.
>
> [In addition], employers were likely to seek to sharply segregate those blue-collar or secondary workers who could potentially identify with white-collar workers—and who might therefore develop class consciousness—from those blue-collar or secondary workers who were not likely to develop class consciousness, in order, obviously, to limit the potential costs of concessions to workers who make determined demands. Employers would seek to do this in two ways. First, they would seek to stratify jobs in order objectively to separate job clusters from each other and consequently to establish "fire trails," as it were, to limit the potential spread of costly concessions. Second, they were likely to try to fill the worst jobs with those who were least likely to identify with advantaged workers. Gradually, as the composition of the American labor force changes, it becomes relatively easy for employers to reserve the most "secondary" jobs for teens, women, and minority group workers with quite confident expectations that they would not identify with more advantaged workers.[39]

[38] Reprinted by permission of the publishers, from *Theories of Poverty and Underemployment* by David M. Gordon (Lexington, Massachusetts: Lexington Books, D. C. Heath and Company, 1972), p. 71.

[39] Ibid., pp. 73–74.

While this view seems plausible, it is also possible to explain the segmentation of labor markets by starting with the assumption that certain groups of workers were able to gain power through unionization—including the economic or political power to effectively prohibit the firm from substituting nonunion for union labor. Thus the importance of firm-specific training could be viewed as a natural response of firms to the reduced turnover that should occur as unions improve wage and working conditions and help develop industrial relations systems that put more emphasis on seniority.

Even if we accept this latter view rather than the radical analysis, the emphasis on group conflict remains important. The main distinction is that the analysis is likely to become more complex. Instead of either (1) the capitalist's being generally successful in a strategy of divide and conquer or (2) the worker's uniting to gain the upper hand (and establish socialism?), a more general bargaining situation exists with a wide variety of results possible and with the particular outcome dependent largely on the bargaining power and skill of the various parties. Such bargaining can occur in many different contexts (e.g., between civil rights groups and firms or unions, between firms and unions, or within unions), but the most important ones are likely to occur in the political arena. For example, Thurow's view of discrimination being enforced by the government can be viewed as a polar case of this bargaining model, where the white community has all the political power and the black community has none. On the other hand, it appears more realistic in most situations to assume that blacks have some political influence, although not as much as whites.

As this book goes to press, a more extensive version of the bargaining model has been developed by Ray Marshall, who summarizes his views in the following passage:

> This model distinguishes between overt and institutional discrimination, calls for an analysis of the motives of various actors impinging on the employment decision, emphasizes the need to examine the power relations between these actors, and stresses the need to examine the broader social and economic context within which the actors establish formal, informal, and institutionalized rules governing racial employment relations.[40]

[40] Ray Marshall, "The Economics of Racial Discrimination: A Survey," *The Journal of Economic Literature* 12 (September 1974): 869–870. The discussion in the text is based partly on an earlier version of Marshall's work which he presented in a lecture at the University of Notre Dame in the spring of 1973.

II. An Empirical Test of the Radical Analysis versus the Becker Model

An empirical attempt to distinguish between alternative policy perspectives, including liberal as well as radical and conservative (à la Becker) views, will be presented in Chapter 6. Although the present literature attempting to test alternative theories is surprisingly limited,[41] a recent study by Reich is sufficiently important to warrant our careful consideration.[42] Reich seeks to determine empirically whether the radical view or Becker's trade model is a better description of the economics of racism in the United States. As we indicated earlier, Becker's trade model implies that white employers (or capitalists) lose from discrimination since discrimination acts as a barrier to trade and reduces the ability of white employers to export capital. By similar reasoning, the trade model implies that white workers gain from discrimination since the trade barrier reduces the importation of black labor. On the other hand, the radical analysis suggests that white capitalists gain from discrimination and that white workers lose since discrimination reduces the relative economic and political power of the working class. Assuming that white capitalists normally have higher incomes than white workers, Reich argues that under Becker's view more discrimination (or racism) should reduce income inequality among whites, while more racism would lead to greater inequality if the radical analysis is correct.

To test these predictions, Reich uses 1960 Census data for forty-eight large Standard Metropolitan Statistical Areas (SMSAs). As his measure of racism, he uses the ratio of black median family income to white median family income. For the inequality of the white income distribu-

---

[41] Several economists have found that discrimination is highest in industries where profits or concentration ratios are highest. While this result is consistent with Becker's theory, it is also consistent with the radical analysis. Also see the discussion in footnote 44.

For empirical results on this issue see Becker, *Economics of Discrimination*, Chapter 3, and the criticism of his results by Raymond S. Franklin, "A Framework for the Analysis of Interurban Negro–White Economic Differentials," *Industrial and Labor Relations Review* (April 1968). Also see Robert P. Strauss, "Discrimination against Negroes in the Labor Market: The Impact of Monopoly Power on Negro Male Employment Patterns," Institute for Research on Poverty Discussion Paper 72-70, University of Wisconsin–Madison; and William S. Comanor, "Racial Discrimination in American Industry," Technical Report No. 5, Graduate School of Business, Stanford University, Palo Alto, California.

[42] See Reich, "Economics of Racism."

tion, he concentrates on two measures: (*1*) the percentage share of all white income that is received by the top one percent of white families, and (*2*) the Gini coefficient of white incomes. Control variables are included for the following characteristics of the SMSAs: (*1*) industrial and occupational structure, (*2*) region, (*3*) average income, and (*4*) proportion black. On the basis of these regressions, Reich concludes:

> Racism as we have measured it was a significantly disequalizing force on the white income distribution, even when other factors were held constant. A 1 percent increase in the ratio of black to white median incomes (that is, a 1 percent decrease in racism) was associated with a 0.2 percent decrease in white inequality, as measured by the Gini coefficient. The corresponding effect on the top 1 percent share of white income was two and a half times as large, indicating that most of the inequality among whites generated by racism was associated with increased income for the richest 1 percent of white families.[43]

While these results do not support Becker and are consistent with the radical view,[44] they are also open to other interpretations. For example, let us assume that unionization reduces income inequality among whites and increases the black–white income ratio.[45] Then differences in the importance of the union movement across SMSAs could be responsible for Reich's results. As Reich indicates, however, differences in racism may be a primary determinant of union power. Therefore, on the basis of cross-section evidence across SMSAs, it does not appear possible to distinguish between the radical view and the view that unions (or some

[43] Ibid., p. 318.

[44] Other results that appear to conflict with the Becker model have been presented by Robert J. Flanagan in "Racial Wage Discrimination and Employment Segregation," *Journal of Human Resources* 8 (Fall 1973). For a positive test of Becker's theory of employee discrimination relative to two versions of the crowding hypothesis, see Barry R. Chiswick, "Racial Discrimination in the Labor Market: A Test of Alternative Theories," *Journal of Political Economy* 81 (November–December 1973).

[45] Both Ashenfelter and Reich find a positive relation between black–white income ratios and the extent of unionization. Ashenfelter interprets this finding to mean that unionization improves the relative position of blacks while Reich views it as meaning that racism affects the extent of unionization.

other factor) are responsible for Reich's empirical results. However, other approaches do provide some support for the radical interpretation.[46]

To return to the validity of the alternative theories of discrimination, we find the radical theory to be at least as plausible as Becker's or Thurow's in explaining labor-market discrimination. Certainly, its emphasis on group conflict appears useful, although a generalized bargaining model like Marshall's appears more realistic than assuming the ultimate power of the capitalist class. Thurow's analysis can be viewed as another special case of such a model, with just two groups—white and black—and with whites dominant. As indicated earlier, this theory appears especially useful for explaining discrimination in housing. While the group conflict view of discrimination appears fruitful, we do expect that Becker's analysis of discrimination by individual employers and employees will be useful in many situations. Moreover, his political analysis can be regarded as an interesting illustration of the group conflict bargaining view.

III. Policy Implications of the Theories

To conclude this chapter on the various economic theories of discrimination, let us look at their policy implications. We begin with the radical position. According to this view, the capitalist system must be replaced with some radical socialist alternative (perhaps similar to Castro's Cuba). While the radicals generally concede that it will not be easy to overthrow the present system, they hope that a black revolution will lead eventually to this solution.

While radicals are divided over what, if any, tactics are most applicable in furthering the development of a revolutionary consciousness in the

---

[46] For evidence that racial factors are more important than class factors, see Otis Dudley Duncan, "Inheritance of Poverty or Inheritance of Race?" in *On Understanding Poverty*, ed. Daniel P. Moynihan (New York: Basic Books, 1969).

There is also considerable historical evidence, especially for the late nineteenth century South, to support Reich's view that the white upper class can benefit economically by dividing the political power of the laboring class through an emphasis on racial issues. Such policies included actions to control the votes of dependent blacks in order to defeat populist candidates and then to disenfranchise blacks. After disenfranchisement, racial issues became primary and the populist movement went into eclipse. For example, see the analysis in C. Vann Woodward, *The Strange Career of Jim Crow* (New York: Oxford Univ. Press, 1966), especially Chapter 3. For an analysis of Nixon administration policies that support Reich's position, see Rustin, "The Blacks and the Unions."

United States, this author finds Sherman's view the most appealing. According to his perspective, "patient, nonviolent, socialist education seems the only useful radical tactic in America—though this educational process will include strikes, sit-ins, marches, and other practical activities."[47]

Consider the policy implications that follow from the theories of Becker and Thurow. Although Becker does not explicitly consider policy issues, some policy implications do appear to be implicit in his analysis and have been explicitly developed by Friedman.[48] If his theory is correct, then it makes sense to fight discrimination primarily by changing people's tastes for discrimination and secondarily by making the economy more competitive. Since tastes are exogenous to the theory, however, it provides no guidance for anyone who might wish to change society's tastes for discrimination. And, since most economists favor making the economy more competitive for other reasons, it seems unlikely that an additional economic argument for competition is likely to have much effect in the political arena.

Thurow's theory stresses the role of collective action in discrimination. Therefore, to increase the economic opportunities available to blacks, it would be necessary to disrupt the governmental or other mechanisms that enforce this collective discrimination. As Thurow puts it: "Many of the effects of discrimination rest on monopoly or monopsony powers of whites. Governments and Negroes can attempt to break down these powers in government, labor, and business institutions."[49] However, Thurow does not explain why governments should be expected to combat discrimination if: (1) whites are a majority of the electorate, and (2) the white community gains from discrimination. Thus, it would appear, once again, to be necessary to change society's tastes in order to achieve any significant reduction in discrimination.

We have already discussed the radical view of tastes for discrimination. Next recall how Arrow, a more traditional economist, has dealt with this issue. In his view, it is reasonable to assume that the average white is reluctant to discriminate consciously against blacks but that he

[47] Howard Sherman, *Radical Political Economy: Capitalism and Socialism from a Marxist Humanist Perspective* (New York: Basic Books, 1972), p. 198. Alternative policy perspectives, including the rather different radical views of Sherman and Baran and Sweezy will be discussed in more detail in Chapter 6.

[48] See Milton Friedman, *Capitalism and Freedom* (Chicago, Illinois: University of Chicago Press, 1962), Chapters 1 and 7.

[49] Thurow, *Poverty and Discrimination*, p. 130.

is quite prepared to rationalize the extent of discrimination by various means (e.g., "Blacks are just lazy").[50] Thus Arrow, like Sherman, appears to suggest that more information and education may be important in changing attitudes.

We will return to the issue of changing tastes for discrimination in Chapter 6. Based on the aforementioned analysis, however, we can preview the basic theme of this book. The next four chapters suggest rather strongly that discrimination (especially labor-market discrimination) does exist and that the low incomes of blacks should not be attributed mainly to other factors. Proposals for combating discrimination are then discussed in Chapters 6 and 7. If whites can be made more aware of discrimination and its consequences, then hopefully greater political support can be generated for efforts to reduce discrimination.

The approach outlined in the preceding paragraph is based on the assumption that careful empirical analysis may have an effect on racial attitudes. Such analysis will also aid in determining where discrimination is most important (e.g., education, housing, or employment) and thus may be of some assistance for policymakers who are seeking to combat current discrimination and who must decide where to concentrate their scarce resources.[51] In the next chapter we begin our empirical analysis by summarizing some empirical results on the magnitude of racial discrimination.

[50] See the quote from Arrow on p. 9.

[51] Of course, a good benefit–cost analysis of alternative policies would be much more helpful. Knowing relative magnitudes will only give a little information on potential benefits of policies in different areas. However, a policymaker may still find such information quite useful, especially when combined with other information, such as his assessment of political benefits and costs of different policies.

2

A Review of Empirical Studies
of Discrimination against Blacks

In this chapter, we review empirical studies of discrimination in employment, housing, and education and also look at changes in the black–white income ratio over time. This review will serve to introduce the empirical investigations of Chapters 3 through 5. In addition, many of the conclusions from this literature review will be utilized in the following chapters.

I. Discrimination in Employment

We begin by examining how economists attempt to measure labor-market discrimination. The usual approach is to estimate the effect of race on earnings, after standardizing for other factors such as years of school, performance on achievement tests, age, sex, and other variables. Hansen, Weisbrod, and Scanlon (HWS) have done such an analysis for 2400 men, aged 17–25, who were rejected for military service because of failure to pass the Armed Forces Qualification Test (AFQT).[1] After standardizing for AFQT score, years of schooling, training outside of

[1] W. Lee Hansen, Burton A. Weisbrod, and William J. Scanlon, "Schooling and Earnings of Low Achievers," *American Economic Review* 60 (June 1970).

school, age, region, and a couple of family status variables, they find that being nonwhite leads to an expected decrease in annual earnings of $362 (about 20 percent), statistically significant at the 99 percent level. If we assume that the variables other than race represent reasonably good controls for differences in productivity, then the net effect of race on earnings provides us with a reasonably good measure of employment discrimination for the HWS sample.

Griliches and Mason (GM) have analyzed a sample of 1454 men, aged 21–34, who had previously served in the armed forces (and thus passed the AFQT).[2] After standardizing for schooling, AFQT score, experience in armed forces and current occupation, age, location, marital status, and father's position, they also find that nonwhites earn about 20 percent less than whites. Note that GM get very similar results to those of HWS despite using a different sample.[3] However, both studies are using quite similar independent variables. Also note both studies are for relatively young males. As Thurow demonstrates, holding schooling constant, earnings increase with experience—especially for the first few years in the labor force *and especially for whites*.[4] Therefore, the HWS

[2] Z. Griliches and W. Mason, "Education, Income, and Ability," *Journal of Political Economy* 80 (May–June 1972), Supplement.

[3] Griliches and Mason obtain a lower estimate (7 percent) for the effect of race when they replace the variable for actual AFQT score with a predicted AFQT variable, with the prediction based on race, schooling before military service, father's schooling, and father's occupation. Since these latter three variables are then excluded from the regression explaining income differences, this approach assumes that these factors affect earnings only by way of their effect on ability. However, this assumption seems less plausible than the assumption that AFQT scores are reasonably good measures of ability. For example, father's background may affect at least the initial job openings available to the son. More important, schooling probably has a significant effect on earnings independent of its effect on ability measures like the AFQT. For an interesting discussion of the issues, see Herbert Gintis, "Education, Technology, and the Characteristics of Worker Productivity," *American Economic Review* 61 (May 1971). Thus we place more reliance on GM's original estimates of the effect of race on earnings, where actual rather than predicted AFQT variables are used. Note that their first approach is very similar to that of HWS.

Other studies [e.g., H. M. Miller, *Income Distribution in the United States* (Washington, D.C.: United States Government Printing Office, 1966), p. 140] have shown that prior to the late sixties the ratio of black to white male earnings falls as years of school increase, holding age constant. At first glance, such results might appear inconsistent with the fact that similar estimates for labor-market discrimination have been derived for this period for those above and below the minimal standards set by the armed forces. However, there are a number of possible explanations including the fact that test-score differentials by race may be more important (relative to schooling differentials) at higher schooling levels.

[4] Lester C. Thurow, *Poverty and Discrimination* (Washington, D.C.: The Brookings Institution, 1969), p. 80.

and GM results might not apply to older workers. If Thurow's results on racial differentials by experience occur because those with more schooling and better test scores (mainly whites) get more on-the-job training, which depresses their wages initially but increases them later on, then our estimates of labor-market discrimination based on the HWS and GM studies may be too low, since these studies cannot control very adequately for such differences in training. If blacks are subject to greater discrimination in higher paying jobs and thus have much more difficulty than whites in earning promotions, then we also should obtain larger estimates of labor-market discrimination for older workers.

In attempting to measure labor-market discrimination, a major difficulty is standardizing for all factors that may be correlated with race and which may lead to lower incomes for blacks even if there were no discrimination in the labor market. The next two chapters will evaluate the effect of two such factors. Chapter 3 examines the hypothesis that urban blacks have been severely disadvantaged as a result of their recent migration from the rural South. Then Chapter 4 evaluates whether urban blacks are being seriously handicapped by the existence of large-scale housing segregation together with the rapid growth of suburban jobs. Neither of these hypotheses receives any appreciable empirical support. Thus the results of HWS and GM do not have to be modified because they do not standardize for such factors.

All efforts to separate the effects of labor-market discrimination from the effects of racial differences in productivity run into the problem of measuring productivity differences. While the HWS and GM studies appear to be the best, broad-based studies currently available, they still cannot accurately measure the actual skills needed on various jobs. In fact, most employers probably are not very well informed in this regard.[5] To try to get around this information problem, two studies have been made of organized baseball, where good productivity data are available as a result of the wealth of statistics on batting averages, home runs, times at bat, innings pitched, and games won.[6] Both studies agree that black players in the big leagues generally outperform their white counterparts, thus indicating discriminatory entry into this quite

---

[5] For example, see Ivar Berg, *Education and Jobs: The Great Training Robbery* (New York: Praeger, 1970).

[6] Anthony H. Pascal and Leonard A. Rapping, "Racial Discrimination in Organized Baseball," in *Racial Discrimination in Economic Life*, ed. Anthony H. Pascal (Lexington, Massachusetts: Heath, 1972); and Gerald W. Scully, "Discrimination: The Case of Organized Baseball," in *Government and the Sports Business*, ed. Roger G. Noll (Washington, D.C.: The Brookings Institution, 1974).

lucrative occupation. Although the studies use the same data, they disagree as to whether there is discrimination against those blacks who do make it into the big leagues. While the original study by Pascal and Rapping found no such discrimination, Scully's less aggregative approach does indicate significant discrimination even after blacks make it into the major leagues.

As indicated in Chapter 1, the role of racial entry barriers in the better occupations is central to Bergmann's view of racial discrimination in employment.[7] As part of a study of the effect of discrimination on white incomes, she has documented barriers to entry among occupations that have traditionally had low educational requirements (those where a majority of male employees have less than twelve years of school). Bergmann summarizes her results on racial imbalance by occupation as follows:

> For each of these occupations, an "expected" number of nonwhite (male) employees was computed by assuming that nonwhites would share in employment in each occupation to the degree that they shared in the educational achievement shown by all persons in the occupation. On this basis, of the twenty-nine occupations, eighteen had significant deficits of nonwhites and eight had surpluses. Of the eighteen deficit occupations, fifteen had deficits of nonwhites of more than 50 percent. The surpluses of nonwhites were heavily concentrated. Two occupations, service workers and nonfarm laborers, accounted for 82 percent of the surplus.[8]

These results, together with the fact that nonwhites are concentrated in the lowest paid occupations,[9] indicate important racial barriers to entry.[10] Such barriers not only reduce the chances of blacks obtaining jobs in high-paying occupations, but are also likely to lower the wages in those occupations where blacks are welcome, since the supply of labor in these occupations will be artificially high—a view often referred to as the "crowding" hypothesis.[11]

[7] See Barbara R. Bergmann, "The Effect on White Income of Discrimination in Employment," *Journal of Political Economy* 79 (March–April 1971): 295.

[8] Ibid., p. 297.

[9] More than 98 percent of the surplus is accounted for by three occupations, each of which is among the four lowest paying (mean earnings) of the twenty-nine occupations in Bergmann's sample.

[10] Although Bergmann cannot standardize for differences in educational quality, such differences probably only account for a relatively small portion of the racial imbalance, since little educational attainment is needed in these occupations.

[11] For some evidence supporting Becker's model as opposed to this crowding hypothesis, see Barry R. Chiswick, "Racial Discrimination in the Labor Market: A Test of Alternative Hypotheses," *Journal of Political Economy* 81 (November–December 1973): 1330–1352.

Next let us seek to determine where labor-market discrimination is most severe and what economic groups or institutional mechanisms are most responsible for such discrimination. Bergmann's results suggest that blacks with more education may be subject to greater discrimination, either in the labor market or at school. In this regard, Becker and Hanoch both calculate that blacks generally receive a lower economic rate of return on additional education than do whites.[12] As Becker demonstrates, under apparently plausible assumptions, the lower rate of return implies greater discrimination in the labor market against the more highly educated blacks[13]—a result that appears to conflict with the implications of Becker's trade model of discrimination, since those with the most education have the most human capital. However, the conclusion that discrimination is greatest against blacks with the most education should not be accepted too readily. First, Becker and Hanoch both measure education solely in terms of years of schooling. When test scores are also included in the analysis, the HWS and GM studies indicate that there may be little difference in discrimination against blacks of different abilities.[14] Perhaps of greater importance, several recent studies indicate that the differential between black and white earnings gains for additional years of school has declined substantially since 1960.[15]

It is not easy to separate the effect of discrimination by employers and by nonunionized employees. However, it is possible to compare the effects of unions on the relative wages of blacks. Ashenfelter examines this issue using cross-section data for individuals, industries, and states.

[12] Gary S. Becker, *Human Capital* (New York: Columbia Univ. Press, 1964), pp. 94–100; and Giora Hanoch, "An Economic Analysis of Earnings and Schooling," *Journal of Human Resources* 2 (Summer 1967).

[13] Of course, there is also discrimination against unskilled blacks. For a particularly thorough case study documenting this point, see David P. Taylor, "Discrimination and Occupational Wage Differences in the Market for Unskilled Labor," *Industrial and Labor Relations Review* 21 (April 1968).

[14] More precisely, there appears to be little difference in discrimination against those of low as opposed to average ability. These studies do not enable us to conclude anything about differences against those of average versus high ability.

[15] See Leonard Weiss and Jeffrey Williamson, "Black Education, Earnings, and Interregional Migration: Some New Evidence," *American Economic Review* 62 (June 1972): 372–383; Richard B. Freeman, "Decline of Labor Market Discrimination and Economic Analysis," *American Economic Review* 63 (May 1973): 280–286; and Finis Welch, "Black–White Differences in Returns to Schooling," *American Economic Review* 63 (December 1973): 893–907. Using similar data, however, Bennett Harrison has found that blacks living in urban ghettos still obtain very small economic gains from more years of school. See Bennett Harrison, "Education and Underemployment in the Urban Ghetto," *American Economic Review* 62 (December 1972): 796–812.

After standardizing for differences in years of school and other variables, he concludes that

> a higher ratio of black to white wages is consistently found in labor markets organized by industrial unions than in unorganized labor markets. It is also consistently found that the ratio of black to white wages in labor markets organized by craft or "referral" unions differs little from that ratio in unorganized labor markets. At the same time, the proportion of black workers who are unionized differs little from the proportion of white workers who are unionized in the industrial union sector, but the former is about cne-half of the latter in the craft union sector. Under certain simplifying assumptions, these results taken together imply that in 1967 the ratio of black to white male wages might have been 4 percent higher in the industrial union sector and 5 percent lower in the craft union sector than they would have been in the absence of all unionism. The average of these two effects is positive, however, so that the ratio of black to white male wages may have been some 3.4 percent higher in 1967 than it would have been in the absence of unionism.[16]

Some of the differences between the craft and the industrial unions can be attributed to the fact that craft unions are more likely to exercise their influence over wage rates in part by control of the labor supply rather than relying exclusively on the strike threat, as is the case in most industrial unions. A strike is not likely to be effective if there are blacks working at competing plants or blacks who can serve as strikebreakers. Therefore, an industrial union excludes such workers from its jurisdiction (either directly or by treating them so badly that they leave the union) only at considerable economic cost. On the other hand, craft unions that control the supply of labor to their craft can exclude blacks at little cost.

As Ashenfelter emphasizes, his results do not imply that the average union does not discriminate against black workers. Instead these results suggest .that whatever discrimination exists in the average unionized labor market is likely to be less severe than in the average nonunion labor market. Also any union influence in narrowing wage differentials by skill level would tend to benefit blacks relative to whites.

In conclusion, it is easier to document the existence of labor-market discrimination than to determine which groups are most responsible for its existence. Although unions have received much unfavorable publicity for their racial policies and although some unions are undoubtedly highly discriminatory, it appears that, on the average, unions have had little effect on labor-market discrimination. In fact, they may have reduced it slightly.

[16] Orley Ashenfelter, "Racial Discrimination and Trade Unions," *Journal of Political Economy* 80 (May–June 1972): 462–463.

Up to this point, our attention has been focused on the relation between employment discrimination and racial differentials in annual earnings. These earnings differentials can occur either because of differentials in hourly earnings or because of differentials in the amount of employment. In analyzing unemployment rates by race, Gilman has found that standardizing for differences in education, age, occupation, industry, and region accounts for about half the racial differential in unemployment.[17] While he concedes that the residual may be at least partly the result of imperfect standardization for skill differentials, Gilman argues that wage rigidities are a more important factor. More specifically, his argument runs as follows:

> Under complete wage flexibility, the majority's preference for discrimination will result in higher wages for white than for nonwhite workers (e.g., the Becker model). However, if there are legal or quasi-legal pressures towards nonwhite–white wage equality, discrimination may take the form of reducing the employment opportunities of nonwhite relative to white workers. Thus, we would expect a greater effect of such factors as statutory and union minimum wages on the employment opportunities of nonwhite than of white workers; employment opportunities should fall more for nonwhite than for white workers.[18]

Then Gilman goes on to argue that the higher unemployment differentials in less skilled occupations, in the regions outside the South, and in more recent years are all consistent with this wage rigidity hypothesis because union power and minimum wage legislation are more important in each of these cases. These results also suggest that fair employment laws limiting pay differentials between blacks and whites may result in greater unemployment for blacks—unless employment provisions of the law are also enforced.[19] The issue of fair employment laws and other efforts to combat labor-market discrimination will be discussed in Chapter 7.

II. Segregation and Discrimination in Housing

In considering the effect of race on housing markets, we shall start by looking again at segregation since it is much easier to measure than

---

[17] Harry J. Gilman, "Economic Discrimination and Unemployment," *American Economic Review* 55 (December 1965).

[18] Ibid., p. 1091.

[19] Landes does find some increase in unemployment differentials between blacks and whites as a result of fair employment laws. See William M. Landes, "The Economics of Fair Employment Laws," *Journal of Political Economy* 76 (July–August 1968): 507–552.

discrimination. The classic study of nonwhite housing segregation is *Negroes in Cities* by Karl E. and Alma F. Taeuber.[20] Their basic measure is a segregation index that indicates the percentage of nonwhites that would have to move in order for each block of a city to have the same percentage of nonwhites.[21] Using 1960 Census data, they calculated values of this index for 207 cities (all those where block data were available and where there were at least 1000 housing units with a nonwhite head). The values ranged from 60.4 in San Jose to 98.1 in Fort Lauderdale, with a median of 87.8. Although these values are very high, the Taeubers believe that they would have been still higher if the index had been calculated only for blacks and majority (non-Spanish surname) whites. After reviewing "a variety of miscellaneous information on the residential segregation of minorities in comparison to that of Negroes," they conclude that "these data provide strong and consistent support for the conclusion that Negroes are by far the most residentially segregated large minority group in recent American history."[22]

For the nation as a whole there appears to be little change in segregation over time. The Taeubers found a slight average increase (two percentage points) between 1940 and 1950 and a slight decrease (one percentage point) between 1950 and 1960. These changes may result primarily from changes in the tightness of housing markets since fewer neighborhoods may be shifting from white to black when the housing market is tight (as in 1950) than when it is looser (as in 1940 and 1960).[23]

[20] Karl E. Taeuber and Alma F. Taeuber, *Negroes in Cities: Residential Segregation and Neighborhood Change* (Chicago, Illinois: Aldine, 1965).

[21] As the Taeubers note, a completely unsegregated residential distribution could be obtained by moving fewer people, if both whites and blacks move. See Taeuber and Taeuber, *Negroes in Cities*, p. 30, n. 1. As Reiner points out, a value of zero for the Taeuber index does not imply that blacks and whites are distributed randomly across the city. See Thomas A. Reiner, "Racial Segregation: A Comment," *Journal of Regional Science* 12, no. 1 (1972).

Ideally we would prefer results for entire metropolitan areas (SMSAs) rather than just for cities. Unfortunately, data on blocks are limited to cities and a handful of suburbs, but data for Census tracts (a larger unit) are available for all parts of many SMSAs. The Taeubers calculate segregation indices by tracts for twelve SMSAs and also for the corresponding central cities. They interpret their results as follows: "From the results from tracts . . . , we hypothesize that if block data were available for entire metropolitan areas, there would be a high correlation, both cross-sectionally and through time, between the series for cities and the series for metropolitan areas [Taeuber and Taeuber, *Negroes in Cities*, p. 62]."

[22] Taeuber and Taeuber, *Negroes in Cities*, p. 68.

[23] Using data for thirteen special Censuses since 1960, Farley and Taeuber find a slight increase in segregation levels. See Reynolds Farley and Karl E. Taeuber, "Population Trends and Residential Segregation since 1960," *Science* 159, no. 3818 (March 1968).

In the South, housing segregation used to be less pronounced than in the North, but it has been steadily increasing so that "by 1960, average levels of residential segregation were somewhat higher in Southern than in Northern cities."[24]

Given the large values of the segregation indices, let us consider to what extent this segregation is economic rather than racial. The Taeubers investigated this question by (1) picking a set of economic-status characteristics (e.g., tenure plus value or rent of occupied dwelling unit) and a set of cities, (2) calculating the expected percentage of nonwhites for each census tract in each city by applying the proportions nonwhite in each economic-status category for the city to the economic-status distributions for each tract, (3) calculating the variance of this "expected" percentage across tracts, and (4) comparing this variance with the variance of the actual percentages. Since the "expected" variance is based on the assumption that there is economic segregation but no additional racial segregation, the relative importance of economic segregation will be greater, the greater the ratio of the "expected" to the total variance.

Using data for fifteen cities in 1960 and the tenure–value–rent set of economic-status categories, the expected variance is always less than 20 percent of the actual and the median is less than 10 percent.[25] When occupation or housing quality is used to measure economic status, the expected variance is even smaller. Therefore, if the cities chosen are at all representative, it would appear that economic segregation accounts for very little of the racial segregation in housing.[26] Moreover, the

---

[24] Taeuber and Taeuber, *Negroes in Cities*, p. 4. In Kain, *Race and Poverty: The Economics of Discrimination*, p. 21, the author gives the following interesting discussion of housing segregation in the South. Although it applies to larger geographic units (the clustering of "black" blocks into ghettos), a similar analysis would probably apply to segregation within blocks. "In older Southern cities the central ghetto is often less dominant, and several smaller Negro residential areas often replace the 'massive' central ghetto found in Northern cities. This pattern is a vestige of an earlier period, when residential segregation was not needed to enforce social segregation and when accessibility to the Negro (servant) population was valued by the white population. . . . With increased pressure by civil rights groups for integration in schools, restaurants, and other aspects of urban life, Southern metropolitan areas appear to be moving rapidly toward emulating the 'classic' ghetto model of Northern cities."

[25] The classification by tenure–value–rent involves thirteen categories, thus, adding extra categories seems unlikely to have any significant effect on the results.

[26] In "The Economics of Housing Segregation" (Santa Monica: The Rand Corporation, Memorandum RM-5510-RC, 1967), Anthony H. Pascal concludes—on the basis of an empirical analysis using data for Chicago and Detroit—that economic

relative importance of economic segregation appears to be decreasing, especially in southern cities.[27]

In Chapter 4 we examine whether the extensive racial segregation of blacks has had any significant impact on the job opportunities of blacks. Contrary to the view of many economists, we find that it has little, if any, affect on their relative earnings.

While housing segregation may not handicap blacks in the labor market, it may facilitate discrimination against blacks in the housing market.[28] The major focus of this book is on black–white income differentials. In this context, discrimination in housing (and in the purchasing of other commodities) is important since such discrimination implies that the ratio of black-to-white money income overestimates the corresponding ratio of real incomes. Housing discrimination is much more difficult to measure than segregation since it is defined as the extra price blacks must pay for *comparable* housing. The key difficulty is in determining when two different housing units should be considered comparable. Although it is obviously impossible to standardize for all differences, several studies have made a significant effort to take into account a number of the most important factors.

[27] See the analysis in Taeuber and Taeuber, *Negroes in Cities*, Chapter 4.

[28] For example, see Becker's analysis of housing discrimination in northern cities where such discrimination is hypothesized to result from a combination of housing segregation and market-adjustment lags in the face of large-scale black immigration.

---

factors account for about 50 percent of housing segregation by race. There appear to be two main differences between his approach and that of the Taeubers: (*1*) Pascal's measure of the effect of economic factors is the *coefficient of determination* of a regression where the units of observation are housing neighborhoods, the dependent variable is percent black, and the economic variables (including housing price and type) are independent variables; and (*2*) Pascal includes an independent variable representing the accessability of housing sites to the work places of nonwhites. In both respects, his approach appears inferior to that of the Taeubers. See the critique of Pascal's work by Karl E. Taeuber in his article, "Patterns of Negro–White Residential Segregation," *Millbank Memorial Fund Quarterly* 47 (April 1970): 81. For another approach to this issue see Raymond G. Zelder, "Racial Segregation in the Urban Housing Market," *Journal of Regional Science* 12, no. 1 (1970).

For an interesting analysis, which shows how neighborhoods may become highly segregated by race if most whites do not want to live in neighborhoods where there are more than a small percentage of blacks, see Thomas C. Schelling, "A Process of Residential Segregation: Neighborhood Tipping," in *Racial Discrimination in Economic Life*, ed. Anthony H. Pascal (Lexington, Massachusetts: Heath, 1972). This analysis also explores the effect of other factors, such as black preferences for the neighborhood's racial composition and the role of speculation.

An early study by Luigi Laurenti investigates what happens to values of homes when blacks enter a white neighborhood.[29] Downs summarizes Laurenti's major conclusion as follows:

> When nonwhites enter a previously all-white neighborhood consisting primarily of single-family residences, and no other changes in neighborhood character occur, then prices of residential property in the area will probably not decline and may very well rise in comparison with prices in similar neighborhoods that have remained all-white.[30]

In the absence of housing discrimination, these increases and decreases should appear at random. However, if blacks must pay more for housing due to discrimination, then, ceteris paribus, prices should rise when blacks enter a new neighborhood. Otherwise a differential would be maintained between what blacks had to pay in the new area relative to those areas that were previously available. But under these conditions, there should be a large excess demand by blacks for housing in the new area, which should lead to price increases.

Empirically Laurenti found that of thirty-four comparisons made over a five-year period (1950–1955) between test and control neighborhoods in San Francisco, Oakland, and Philadelphia, the relative price of houses in the test neighborhood increased more than 5 percent in sixteen cases, decreased more than 5 percent in five cases, and changed less than 5 percent in thirteen cases.[31] These results appear consistent with the hypothesis that blacks have to pay more for comparable housing because of discrimination. Housing discrimination has also been documented recently in quite sophisticated case studies in St. Louis (Kain and Quigley) and New Haven (King and Mieszkowski).[32]

[29] Luigi Laurenti, *Property Values and Race: Studies in Seven Cities* (Berkeley, California: Univ. of California Press, 1960).

[30] Anthony Downs, "An Economic Analysis of *Property Values and Race*," *Land Economics* 56 (May 1960): 181.

[31] Since the demand by blacks is greatest for relatively inexpensive housing, houses are often converted into apartments when blacks move into a neighborhood. Such situations are not considered in Laurenti's study, although the higher density (combined with scare tactics on the part of "block-busting" realtors) would usually result in at least a temporary decline in the value of houses as whites move out.

[32] See John F. Kain and John M. Quigley, "Measuring the Value of Housing Quality," *Journal of the American Statistical Association* 60 (June 1970); and Peter Mieszkowski and A. Thomas King, "Racial Discrimination, Segregation, and the Price of Housing," *Journal of Political Economy* 81 (May–June 1973). The latter study also indicates special reasons why discrimination was not found in case studies of Chicago by Bailey and of Dallas by Lapham.

This conclusion is also consistent with Rapkin's results for rental housing in central cities, based on the 1/1000 sample of the 1960 Census.[33] After standardizing for monthly rent (<50, 50–79, >79), number of rooms (1–2, 3–5, greater than 5), SMSA size (less than 500,000 or not), and region, Rapkin found that for almost every cell blacks were much more likely than majority whites to live in substandard housing.[34] Moreover, taking account of other factors might lead to even larger differences by race. In Rapkin's words:

> Even within central cities, neighborhoods differ in the community facilities available to them and the undesirable uses which impinge upon the residential structures. Though low-rent housing occupied by whites may be in as unpleasant location as that available to Negroes, neighborhoods in which more expensive housing restricted to whites is located are generally superior to those in which equally expensive housing is available to Negroes.[35]

In fact, Kain and Quigley argue that the difficulty of obtaining certain kinds of housing is a more serious problem for blacks than the racial price differential that exists for those kinds of housing that are readily available.[36]

III. Discrimination in Education

In education as in housing, racial segregation is easier to measure than discrimination and has been the subject of more extensive empirical investigation. Therefore, we begin by examining data on the extent of school segregation. In 1965, the Coleman report indicated that about two-thirds of all black first graders were attending schools where at least

[33] Chester Rapkin, "Price Discrimination Against Negroes in the Rental Housing Market," in *Essays in Urban Land Economics* (Los Angeles, California: Real Estate Research Program, University of California, 1966). Also reprinted in *Race and Poverty: The Economics of Discrimination*, ed. John F. Kain (Englewood Cliffs, New Jersey: Prentice-Hall, 1969).

[34] Standardizing with finer breakdowns of these dimensions might lessen the comparative disadvantage of blacks to some extent, but probably would not change the major conclusion. For example, blacks in a given rental category often have more substandard housing than whites in the next lower rental category. For an interesting empirical analysis of some of the factors affecting inter-SMSA differences in the ratio of rents paid by blacks and whites, see R. A. Haugen and A. J. Hein, "A Market Separation Theory of Rent Differentials in Metropolitan Areas," *Quarterly Journal of Economics* 81 (November 1969).

[35] Rapkin, "Price Discrimination," in Kain, *Race and Poverty*, p. 121.

[36] See John F. Kain and John M. Quigley, "Housing Market Discrimination, Homeownership, and Savings Behavior," *American Economic Review* 62 (June 1972).

90 percent of the students were black.[37] For twelfth graders, about half the black students were attending such heavily black schools.

Using 1967 data for public elementary schools in sixty large cities, Farley and Taeuber measure segregation in terms of an index of dissimilarity very similar to that used by the Taeubers for housing segregation; a measure that represents "the percentage of Negroes (or non-Negroes) who would have to be shifted among schools to achieve complete integration," where complete integration means that each school in the system has the same racial composition as the system as a whole.[38] Using this measure, Farley and Taeuber find very high levels of segregation for elementary school pupils (an average value of 87 for southern cities and 74 for those in the North). For teachers there is somewhat less segregation, especially in the North (an average value of 82 in the South versus 58 in the North). However, there is a greater discrepancy in the North between the percentage of black teachers and the percentage of black pupils (16 versus 30 percent in the northern cities and 32 versus 36 percent in the southern cities). Under pressure from the courts, a number of these cities have instituted significant desegregation programs since 1967. In most cities, however, there is little dispute that school segregation remains high.

Although the Supreme Court has ruled that separate schools cannot be equal, there quite clearly is not a perfect correlation between the extent of segregation and the degree of discrimination. To an economist, the standard approach to discrimination is to see if white schools have more and better resources than black schools. Fortunately the Coleman report provides extensive data on average school characteristics for pupils of different races.[39] As summarized by Bowles and Levin, the report found

[37] James S. Coleman *et al.*, *Equality of Educational Opportunity* (Washington, D.C.: United States Department of Health, Education, and Welfare, 1966), pp. 5, 7.

[38] Reynolds Farley and Alma F. Taeuber, "Racial Segregation in the Public Schools," Institute for Research on Poverty Discussion Paper 121–72, University of Wisconsin, Madison. In contrast to the measures used in the Coleman report, this index of dissimilarity is unaffected by the percentage of all students who are black. If one is dealing with relatively autonomous units, such as SMSAs, then it appears very appropriate to use a measure with this property. When dealing with city school districts, however, this index of dissimilarity ignores the extent of segregation between a city and its suburbs. While the Coleman report approach does not really get at this issue very well either, it does provide a useful supplement to the results using the index of dissimilarity within cities.

[39] We are not aware of any national data on school-expenditure differentials by race. Moreover, if such data do exist, they might be quite misleading. For example, expenditures for police protection may be much greater in black than in white schools.

"relatively minor differences in the measured characteristics of schools (e.g., class size, age of school, and characteristics of teachers) attended by different racial and ethnic groups."[40]

For the Coleman report data to be useful for our purposes, however, we also need estimates of the relation of such characteristics to student achievement. While student achievement has many dimensions, including intellectual ability, physical and emotional health, creativity, and socialization, most studies have focused on test-score measures of intellectual attainment. With regard to the effect of school characteristics or test-score achievement, the Coleman report concluded (as summarized by Jencks), "Despite popular impressions to the contrary measured differences in schools' physical facilities, formal curriculums, and teacher characteristics had very little effect on either black or white students' performance on standardized tests."[41] While this conclusion has been the subject of considerable controversy, we need not enter into this controversy here.[42] Instead we shall merely illustrate the economists' methodology for determining discrimination in education and discuss some of its shortcomings.

We start with the following results of Hanushek:

> In general, Hanushek found two teacher characteristics that were consistently related to the verbal scores of sixth graders . . . years of teacher experience and teacher's verbal score . . . . For each additional point of teacher's verbal score, the Negro student showed an increment of .175 points and the white student an increment of .179 points in student verbal score. For each additional year of teacher experience, the test scores of Negro students were about .108 points

---

[40] Samuel Bowles and Henry M. Levin, "The Determinants of Scholastic Achievement—An Appraisal of Some Recent Evidence," *Journal of Human Resources* 3 (Winter 1968): 4.

Recently Jencks has done a more extensive analysis based on the Coleman report data and arrived at the following conclusions: (*1*) There was racial bias in the allocation of resources among northern urban elementary schools in 1965, but it was very slight relative to the variation caused by other factors; (*2*) there was also social class bias in the allocation of resources among northern urban elementary schools, but again it was slight relative to the variation caused by other factors.

However, it is not clear how he arrived at these conclusions or what the "other factors" are. See Christopher S. Jencks, "The Coleman Report and the Conventional Wisdom," in *On Equality of Educational Opportunity*, ed. Frederick Mosteller and Daniel P. Moynihan (New York: Random House, 1972), p. 70.

[41] Jencks, "Coleman Report," p. 69.

[42] For example, see Mosteller and Moynihan, *On Equality*, pp. 28–34. Also note the criticisms of the Coleman report data on resources allocation that are made by Hanushek and Kain in the Mosteller–Moynihan volume.

higher and the test scores of white students were about .060 points higher. (The mean student scores were 26.7 for Negroes and 35.7 for whites.)[43]

While it is not always clear which way the causation runs (e.g., teachers with more experience may be able to obtain classes with better students),[44] we shall assume for illustrative purposes that the causation does run from teachers' verbal ability and experience to students' test scores. We shall also make the somewhat questionable assumption that verbal test scores are a valid measure of student achievements.

The differences in teacher experience and verbal score, by the student's race, and the net effect on student achievement are presented in Table 2.1. The net effect of these differences in teachers' experience and verbal scores is to give an advantage to white students. While this analysis is very crude, it does illustrate how economists can attempt to measure discrimination in education.

Economists usually concentrate on discrimination that affects the allocation of resources to different schools, as we have done in the preceding analysis. When schools are completely segregated (administrators, teachers, and students being all of the same race), this level of analysis is probably quite appropriate. When schools are not completely segregated, however, then other aspects of discrimination may be very important. In schools that are run by whites but have mostly black pupils, there may be considerable discrimination in the sense that given financial resources will be spent less efficiently (at least in terms of local "community" goals) than in schools that are run by and for whites. Moreover, within desegregated schools (especially those that have desegregated only as a result of outside pressure), there may be considerable discrimination against black students. For example, tracking systems have often been instituted when schools desegregate, with most blacks assigned to bottom tracks.

The policy implications of the above analysis will be discussed in Chapter 7. Before concluding this discussion of racial discrimination in education, however, we should give some attention to the broader issue of racial differences in educational attainment. This issue is important as

---

[43] Quoted in Henry M. Levin, "A Cost-Effectiveness Analysis of Teacher Selection," *Journal of Human Resources* 5 (Winter 1970): 28–29. Note that Hanushek's results are for metropolitan schools.

[44] See Jencks, "Coleman Report," pp. 82–83. If causation runs from student performance to teacher's experience, but from teacher's verbal ability to student performance, then our analysis later underestimates the discrimination against black students.

TABLE 2.1

Differences in Teacher Effectiveness for Black and White Students

	Student verbal scores		Elementary school teachers	
	Mean	(Standard deviation)	Experience (in years)	Verbal score
Pupils				
White	35.7	(4.5)	12	23.4
Black	26.7	(4.2)	13	20.2
Difference	9.0	—	−1	3.2
Effect on pupil test scores				
Based on coefficients for black				
sample (.108 and .175)			−.108	.560
Based on coefficients for white				
sample (.060 and .179)			−.060	.573

SOURCE: Henry M. Levin, "A Cost-Effectiveness Analysis of Teacher Selection," *Journal of Human Resources* 5 (Winter 1970): 27; James S. Coleman *et al.*, *Equality of Educational Opportunity* (Washington, D.C.: United States Department of Health, Education, and Welfare, 1966), p. 131; and calculations by the author.

background for our analysis in Chapter 5 of the relative importance of labor-market discrimination versus differences in educational attainment (and other characteristics related to productivity) in accounting for differences in the black–white earnings ratio.

While racial differences in years of school completed for young people are now very small, there are still considerable differences in test-score performance by race. For example, the Coleman report found that black children average about one standard deviation below whites on a wide variety of different tests.[45] While we recognize that such tests may be culturally biased, they are still important as a measure of how well a youth is prepared for competition in the labor market.[46] The poorer

[45] Coleman *et al.*, *Equality of Educational Opportunity*, p. 20.

[46] Since we are interested in test scores because of their relation to a person's (potential) income, we need not be very concerned whether people with higher test scores really are more productive. For example, employers may overestimate the importance of additional education for their workers [e.g., see Ivar Berg, *Education*

test-score performance can be attributed to some combination of the following five factors: (*1*) present discrimination in the schools; (*2*) differences in family background, resulting in large part from past and present discrimination of various kinds; (*3*) effects of expected discrimination on children's aspirations and current educational performance; (*4*) cultural biases in the test; and (*5*) innate differences in ability between blacks and whites. We have already discussed the first factor and also the fourth to a very limited extent. Factors two through four will be given some attention in Chapter 5. The one issue that needs further discussion at this point is the possibility of innate (genetic) differences in ability by race.

Throughout this book, we shall assume that there are no innate differences in ability between blacks and whites. We must, however, take some note of Jensen's recent revival of the old argument that racial differences in education may occur primarily because of genetic factors rather than discrimination.[47] While Jensen is obviously correct in arguing that genetic differences *could* be a major factor, he is on much shakier ground when he asserts that "the preponderance of the evidence is, in my opinion, less consistent with a strictly environmental hypothesis than with a genetic hypothesis."[48] This latter statement has been widely criticized, perhaps most persuasively by Kagan, who argues that "the essential error in Jensen's argument is the conclusion that if a trait is under genetic control, difference between two populations on that trait must be due to genetic factors."[49] Kagan then goes on to cite empirical evidence to suggest that environmental factors could easily account for racial differences in educational performance.

[47] Arthur R. Jensen, "How Much Can We Boost IQ and Scholastic Achievement," in *Environment, Heredity, and Intelligence* (Cambridge, Massachusetts: Harvard Educational Review, 1969).

[48] Ibid., p. 82.

[49] Jerome S. Kagan, "Inadequate Evidence and Illogical Conclusions," in *Environment, Heredity, and Intelligence* (Cambridge, Massachusetts: Harvard Educational Review, 1969).

---

and Jobs: The Great Training Robbery (New York: Praeger, 1970)], or education may be more important for its effects on the personality traits of students than for students' cognitive development [e.g., see Herbert Gintis, "Education, Technology, and the Characteristics of Worker Productivity," *American Economic Review* 61 (May 1971)]. For evidence that test scores are related to income see the HWS and GM studies referred to in Section I. Also note that years of school appear to have an important effect on income independent of their effect on test scores (see HWS, GM, and other studies summarized in the Appendix to Gintis, ibid.).

Thus even if genetic factors do explain much of the individual variation in IQs, they may not explain average differences between the races. As Daniels indicates, however, it is by no means certain that genetic factors do explain a major portion of individual differences in intellectual ability.[50]

As indicated earlier, we shall assume that genetic differences by race have no appreciable effect on racial differences in education (or other aspects of productivity). While this view appears consistent with the limited empirical evidence available, the rationale for making this assumption is not entirely scientific. As Wohlstetter and Coleman argue, "The mischief to be done by rejecting a true hypothesis that there are no substantial genetic factors disabling nonwhites from contributing on a par with whites is so large compared with the consequences of accepting that hypothesis if it is false, that the null hypothesis seems the appropriate one on moral and political grounds as well as scientific ones."[51]

In addition, we shall assume that there are no racial differences in preferences for money income vis-à-vis either leisure or nonmonetary rewards for work, except insofar as such differences may be caused by discrimination. Although this assumption is fairly strong since it ignores all differences with regard to the experiences of blacks in Africa and whites in Europe, we suspect that most families of both races have been in this country for enough generations to be rather thoroughly Americanized.

As a result of the above assumptions plus an assumption of no racial differentials in luck, we can attribute the entire difference between black and white incomes to various forms of discrimination. While these assumptions may not be entirely true, we suspect that they are at least a reasonably good first-approximation to reality. Of course, changes in the black–white income ratio will still not give us an accurate reflection of changes in current discrimination since such ratios also are influenced by other factors, such as changes in past discrimination (e.g., differences in education) and migration to areas of higher average wages and prices. In the next section, we discuss what conclusions can be made on the basis of a time-series analysis.

---

[50] Norman Daniels, "The Smart White Man's Burden," *Harper's* (October 1973): 24–40.

[51] Albert Wohlstetter and Sinclair Coleman, "Race Differences in Income," in *Racial Discrimination in Economic Life*, ed. Anthony H. Pascal (Lexington, Massachusetts: Heath, 1972), p. 47.

IV. Changes over Time in the Black–White Income Ratio

In looking at time-series analyses of the ratio of black to white incomes, the two most interesting questions concern *(1)* the underlying trend and *(2)* the effects of changes in the overall unemployment rate or other measures of labor-market tightness. The importance of the trend is obvious, since we want to know whether blacks have been improving their relative position, ceteris paribus. With regard to the importance of tight labor markets, perhaps the best known discussion is that of Tobin, who argues that in slack labor markets *(1)* employers are more likely to use race as a screening device for good jobs and *(2)* unions and other craft groups are likely to be more discriminatory as they seek to preserve control over scarce jobs.[52] Consequently, he argues that blacks suffer more than whites from increases in total unemployment, long-term unemployment, and involuntary part-time unemployment, while slack labor markets also hurt their relative position because of changes in relative wage rates,[53] decreases in labor force participation among black males,[54] and decreases in the migration from agriculture to better paying jobs.

Turning to empirical results, we shall start with a relatively simple,

---

[52] James Tobin, "Improving the Economic Status of the Negro," *Daedalus* 94 (Fall 1965). Batchelder also called attention to this issue and showed that the relative income of black men fell during the 1950s—a period when labor markets became slacker. See Alan B. Batchelder, "Decline in the Relative Income of Negro Men," *The Quarterly Journal of Economics* 78 (November 1964). Also note the related comment by Rashi Fein in *The Quarterly Journal of Economics* 80 (May 1966).

[53] Note that the wage differential between skilled and unskilled workers normally is reduced when labor markets are tight. See Richard Perlman, *Labor Theory* (New York: Wiley, 1969), Chapter 4. Therefore, since blacks are disproportionately represented in the less skilled jobs, their relative wage levels should be expected to improve when labor markets are tight. Note that unskilled workers of all sorts (and not just blacks) suffer disproportionately from slack labor markets. See Edward Kalachek and James Knowles, "Higher Unemployment Rates 1957–1960: Structural Transformation or Inadequate Demand," Subcommittee on Economic Statistics of the Joint Economic Committee, 87th Congress, 1st session, 1961.

[54] Tobin argues that the lower demand for black labor is the main reason why labor force participation rates are lower for black men and higher for black women than the corresponding rates for whites. While it would undoubtedly take a long period of high demand for black (male) labor for these racial differentials to diminish significantly, the racial differential for males might change faster than the one for females—assuming that one of the important reasons for the high participation rate of black women is that it acts as a sort of insurance against loss of income support by the husband. See Glen G. Cain, *Married Women in the Labor Force* (Chicago, Illinois: Univ. of Chicago Press, 1966), pp. 82–83.

yet persuasive, article by Rasmussen.[55] He obtains the following results (using annual data for 1948 to 1964) when he regresses the nonwhite–white male income ratio (Y_t) on the rate of growth of GNP $(\%\Delta\ GNP)$, the aggregate unemployment rate lagged one period (U_{t-1}),[56] and a time trend (T).

$$Y_t = 0.57 + .00984\ \%\ \Delta\ \text{GNP} - .0270\ U_{t-1} + .00323\ T$$
$$\quad\quad\quad\ (.0025) \quad\quad\quad\quad\quad (.0077) \quad\quad (.0015)$$

$$R^2 = .57$$

According to Rasmussen, "The relative income of nonwhites is clearly related to the level of aggregate demand, as both cyclical variables have the expected signs and are significant at the .01 level. . . . The trend variable . . . indicates that the income ratio increases about one percentage point every three years."[57]

The results for the cyclical variables support Tobin and suggest that maintaining a high level of aggregate demand is an important policy prescription for aiding the relative income position of blacks. To interpret the positive trend in Rasmussen's equation, we need to consider what factors may have been working to improve the black–white income ratio over the period from 1948 to 1964. Results by Gwartney suggest that,

[55] David W. Rasmussen, "A Note on the Relative Income of Nonwhite Men, 1948–1964," *The Quarterly Journal of Economics* 84 (February 1970). These results are updated in Chapter 6.

[56] Rasmussen does not explain why he uses the lagged value of unemployment. Certain parts of Tobin's argument, however, especially the migration argument, would clearly favor using the lag. Also, employers may not adjust very quickly to changes in the state of the labor market.

[57] Rasmussen, "Note on the Relative Income," pp. 169–170. These results differ from those of Ashenfelter ["Changes in Labor Market Discrimination Over Time," *The Journal of Human Resources* 5 (Fall 1970)], who found no positive trend and no effect of aggregate unemployment for the period 1950–1966. Ashenfelter does not explain why his results differ from those of Rasmussen. But he does indicate that the unemployment rate has a significant negative impact on the relative earnings of nonwhite families, a result he attributes to differential effects of labor-market conditions on the number of family earners. With this in mind, we note that Ashenfelter's male results are based on the ratio of median wage and salary income (for those with such income) rather than on the ratio of median total incomes. Therefore, Ashenfelter's results might be explained by a disproportionate number of black males dropping out of the labor force when jobs are scarce. If so, their absence might bias the trend as well as the unemployment coefficient since the unemployment rate was generally higher toward the end of this period. Note that, for females, Ashenfelter does find a positive trend and a significant unemployment effect.

for males, this trend disappears once an adjustment is made for the increase in the percentage of blacks living outside the South.[58] Therefore the trend is undoubtedly overstated since the results by Rasmussen (and others) are for money incomes, yet the cost of living is undoubtedly higher for blacks in the North than in the South.[59] Even with regard to the trend in relative money incomes, Rasmussen's results overestimate the long-term trend because they do not take account of the unusual civil rights activity of the early 1960s. For a further discussion of this issue and of changes since 1964, see our results in Chapter 6.

Prior to the late 1930s, income data were not available separately by race. To look at changes in the relative economic position of blacks prior to World War II, Becker uses an index of occupational position, defined as "fixed weighted averages of the proportion of Negroes or whites in different skill categories, the weights being the relative wages paid to whites in 1939."[60] Using these indices, Becker concludes that between 1910 and 1950 the relative occupational positions of blacks changed very little, increasing slightly in the North and decreasing slightly in the South.

Becker's approach has been refined by Heistand, who calculates indices for each decennial census from 1910 to 1960—based on seven occupational categories in contrast to the three used by Becker.[61] His results for males are presented in Table 2.2. They indicate a noticeable gain for blacks between 1940 and 1950 (probably as a result of very tight labor markets in World War II) but virtually no change during any other decade. With regard to the history of racial wage differentials within occupations, Fogel and Engerman maintain that "the gap between wage payments to blacks and whites in comparable occupations increased steadily from the immediate post Civil War decades down to the eve of

---

[58] James Gwartney, "Changes in the Nonwhite/White Income Ratio, 1937–1967," *American Economic Review* 60 (December 1970). For females, Gwartney finds that the black–white income ratio has improved since 1949, even after accounting for differences in the regional distribution. However, he finds that, after adjusting for regional composition, there is "little difference in the rate of increase in the median income of nonwhite males, white males, and nonwhite females during the entire 1949–1967 period [ibid., p. 877]." Consequently, the improvement in the black–white income ratio for females results mainly from the relatively low rate of increase in the income of white females.

[59] See Jean C. Brackett, "New BLS Budgets," *Monthly Labor Review* 92 (April 1969).

[60] Becker, *Economics of Discrimination*, 2d ed., 1971, p. 149. Also see Chapter 9.

[61] Dale L. Heistand, *Economic Growth and Employment Opportunities for Minorities* (New York: Columbia Univ. Press, 1964), pp. 51–55.

TABLE 2.2

*Changes in Relative Occupation Status of Black
and White Males over Time*

Year	Occupational position of black males relative to white males
1910	.780
1920	.781
1930	.782
1940	.775
1950	.814
1960	.821

SOURCE: Adapted from Dale L. Hiestand, *Economic Growth and Employment Opportunities for Minorities* (New York: Columbia Univ. Press, 1964), Table XII, p. 53.

World War II."[62] They also indicate that the relative occupational position of blacks declined over this longer period.

The results in this section suggest that, with the exception of the World War II period, there was no improvement, and indeed, probably a deterioration in the relative labor-market position of blacks in the period from slavery to 1960. As Becker indicates, these results do not prove that there has been no decline in labor-market discrimination. For example, the relative skill level of blacks may have fallen as a result of reduced immigration of unskilled whites. However, Gwartney's results do suggest that, since 1939, the effect of such counterbalancing factors probably has been neutralized by the effect of the northern migration of blacks. Thus, although the evidence is rather limited, there does not appear to have been any significant decrease in labor-market discrimination in the century following the Civil War. Changes in the recent past will be discussed in Chapter 6.

As we indicated in Chapter 1, the simple Becker theory of discrimination suggests that competitive pressures should lead to reductions in labor-market discrimination over time. On the other hand, the radical analysis implies that, at least until the 1960s, there was no reason to expect any decrease in labor-market discrimination. Once again, the

[62] Robert W. Fogel and Stanley L. Engerman, *Time on the Cross: The Economics of American Negro Slavery* (Boston, Massachusetts: Little, Brown, 1974), p. 261.

empirical results appear to provide at least as much support for the radical view of discrimination as they do for Becker's theory—although Welch and Arrow have modified Becker's model in an attempt to take account of this difficulty.[63]

V. A Preview of the Remaining Chapters

In the next three chapters, we present evidence on several hypotheses —each of which implies that labor-market discrimination may be relatively unimportant as an explanation for black–white income differentials in urban areas. Chapter 3 indicates that the low incomes of urban blacks cannot be attributed simply to low incomes received by black migrants to the northern cities. Using the 1/1000 sample of the 1960 Census, we show that although recent migrants (both black and white) from rural areas are at a minor disadvantage compared with long-term urban residents, the results for lifetime migration are quite different. Among blacks currently living in SMSAs outside the South, those born in the South are doing slightly better economically than those born in the North (with or without standardizing for differences in age, years of school, and a number of other factors).

In Chapter 4, we discuss the widely held view that housing segregation (combined with transportation problems and a shift in jobs from central city to suburb) has had an important effect on job opportunities for blacks. Our results, based on 1970 Census data for seventy-seven large SMSAs, indicate that the black–white male income ratio is not lower in cities where housing segregation is most pronounced. Moreover, there is also other evidence to suggest that housing segregation has little, if any, effect on the relative earnings of blacks.

In view of the results presented in Chapters 3 and 4, the two most likely remaining explanations for the low incomes of urban black males are differences in productivity (especially education) and labor-market discrimination. In Chapter 5, we try to estimate the relative importance of these two factors, using both the 1967 Survey of Economic Opportunity and the 1/1000 sample of the 1960 Census. The results indicate that differences in years of school have some effect on the racial

---

[63] Because the radical theory of discrimination has been developed since Becker's empirical analysis, one might argue that the theory has been tailored to fit the data. However, the criticism can be applied with at least as much validity to analyses of Welch and Arrow. Moreover, the principle of Occam's razor would give some support to the radical view.

earnings gap, but that the effect is small relative to the effect of labor-market discrimination. Although additional results suggest that differences in scholastic attainment per year of schooling may have more effect than differences in years of school per se, these results also indicate that labor-market discrimination remains high even when productivity differences are measured primarily in terms of predicted test scores rather than years of school.

In the last two chapters we turn to policy analysis. Chapter 6 analyzes the policy implications of the conservative, liberal, and radical views of discrimination. A test of the three perspectives is developed, which is based on their predictions of the effects of legislation such as the Civil Rights Act of 1964. Based on the experience thus far, we tentatively conclude that the liberal perspective is the most relevant, although all have valuable contributions to make.

Chapter 7 analyzes specific policies to combat labor-market discrimination and to improve the relative educational opportunities of blacks. The author gives high priority to affirmative-action requirements, maintaining tight labor markets, and enabling the black community to have greater control over schools in black areas.

3

The Effect of Migration on Black Incomes[1]

This chapter investigates one aspect of the migration of blacks from the South to the northern cities. Economists have often treated migration as an investment in human capital, an approach that seeks to evaluate whether the payoff to migrants is high enough to warrant its costs.[2] While a high monetary rate of return is usually found, very difficult problems occur whenever any attempt is made to treat such important issues as psychic costs (or benefits) of migration and differences in the cost of living between sending and receiving areas.[3] Therefore, it is not easy to judge whether more migration should be encouraged—even from the point of view of the potential migrant. Of course, this question becomes even more difficult once we take into account possible effects of migration on those who remain in the sending or receiving regions.

[1] The statistical part of this chapter was financed under a contract between Rutgers University and the United States Office of Economic Opportunity. A similar version appeared in the *Journal of Human Resources* 7 (© Fall 1972 by the Regents of the University of Wisconsin System), p. 411.
[2] For example, see Larry A. Sjaastad, "The Costs and Returns of Human Migration," *Journal of Political Economy* 70 (October 1962), Supplement.
[3] For example, see Richard F. Wertheimer II, *The Monetary Rewards of Migration Within the U.S.* (Washington, D.C.: The Urban Institute, 1970).

In this chapter we are concerned with a narrower aspect of the migration issue. We investigate whether the economic problems of blacks living in urban areas are concentrated among migrants from the South (often the rural South) or whether the problems are as bad or worse for those who have lived all their lives in the northern cities. To put the matter a little differently, we seek to evaluate whether Banfield is correct when he argues:

> Today the Negro's main disadvantage is the same as the Puerto Rican's and Mexican's: namely, that he is the most recent unskilled, and hence relatively low-income, migrant to reach the city from a backward rural area. The city is not the end of his journey but the start of it. He came to it not because he was lured by a cruel and greedy master but because he was attracted by job, housing, school, and other opportunities that, bad as they were, were nevertheless better by far than any he had known before. Like earlier immigrants, the Negro has reason to expect that his children will have increases of opportunity even greater than his.[4]

According to Banfield's view, we would expect recent black migrants from the South to be greatly disadvantaged.[5] However, we might also expect those who have lived longer in northern cities to have considerably improved their economic position—at least, on the average. In this case, black–white income differentials in the North might be explained primarily by the migration of blacks from the South to the northern cities. Certainly the size of this migration has been large enough to have had a major effect on the average income of blacks. Of all blacks over eighteen living in SMSAs outside the South in 1966, 65 percent were born in the South.[6] Most of this migration occurred in the 1940s and 1950s, while there has been no comparable urban immigration by whites since the restrictions imposed on foreign immigration in the 1920s.

If Banfield is correct in focusing on the importance of economic problems associated with migration, then antipoverty programs in the northern cities should probably be oriented more toward the problems facing recent immigrants (probably including whites as well as blacks).

[4] Edward C. Banfield, *The Unheavenly City* (Boston, Massachusetts: Little, Brown, 1968), p. 68.

[5] Although Banfield's general viewpoint is very conservative, his opinions on this matter are not very different from those of many who are far to his left politically. For example, see Charles Sackrey, *The Political Economy of Urban Poverty* (New York: W. W. Norton, 1973), pp. 39–46.

[6] This figure was calculated by the author from the 1/1000 sample of the 1960 Census.

New or expanded organizations could be established in the cities to help newcomers find jobs and housing; to provide information on health and welfare services, public transportation, and other complexities of urban life; and to offer emotional support during the difficult adjustment period. More emphasis could also be placed on certain kinds of rural programs. For example, greater efforts might be made to improve the quality of rural schools. New or improved urban orientation programs also could be developed for those rural areas where out-migration is especially heavy. Finally, greater efforts might be made to develop more and better jobs within commuting distance of the rural population in order to try to reduce the migration to urban areas.

The results presented below do not support Banfield's view. Instead they indicate that migrants are likely to have slightly higher incomes and less unemployment than nonmigrants, at least once an initial adjustment period has passed. Therefore, the low income of blacks in the urban North would appear to represent a long-run equilibrium position resulting mainly from white discrimination and not just a relatively short-run problem of dynamic adjustment resulting from migration difficulties. As a result, efforts to improve the situation of northern blacks should focus on the general issue of discrimination rather than on special programs to assist migrants. In addition, we should not be too optimistic that the position of northern blacks will automatically improve as the migration slows down. This last statement must be qualified, however, since a decrease in the size of the migration might still improve the position of northern blacks if the relative size of the black and white communities has an important effect on the opportunities available to blacks.[7]

I. The Data and the Measures of Migration Status

The results in this chapter are based on data from the 1/1000 sample of the 1960 Census.[8] With these data we can look at both lifetime and

---

[7] For example, if blacks are forced mainly into a few occupations, as Bergmann suggests, then a simple supply and demand analysis predicts that blacks will be worse off when they are a larger proportion of the total population. A similar analysis obviously applies to the housing market. Finally, the number of lower income black migrants may affect the ability of a city to provide welfare and other public services for its residents.

[8] Some earlier studies that have made somewhat similar comparisons, often as a side issue in connection with some other topic, are Karl E. and Alma F. Taeuber, *Negroes in Cities: Residential Segregation and Neighborhood Change* (Chicago, Illinois:

recent migration. Lifetime migrants are blacks[9] who were born in the
South, but who were living in Standard Metropolitan Statistical Areas
(SMSAs) outside the South in 1960. These migrants will be compared
with all blacks living in nonsouthern SMSAs who were born outside the
South.[10]

TABLE 3.1

Economic Status of Black Lifetime Migrants and Nonmigrants

	Lifetime migrants	Comparison group
For those in the labor force:		
Annual earnings	$2853	$2736
Earnings per week	$69.5	$67.5
Weeks worked	39.8	39.0
Unemployment rate	11.2	12.6
Sample size	1639	880
For the total sample:		
Family income	$4692	$4926
Percentage poor	27.9	28.5
Labor-force-participation rate	64.7	65.2
Sample size	2533	1349

SOURCE: Calculated from the 1/1000 sample of the 1960 Census.
NOTE: The unemployment rate and labor-force-participation rate are for the
survey week of 1960. The other figures are for 1959. Poverty status is determined on
the basis of the Orshansky definitions [see Mollie Orshansky, "Counting the Poor:
Another Look at the Poverty Profile," *Social Security Bulletin* 28 (January 1963): 3;
and "Who's Who Among the Poor: A Demographic View of Poverty," *Social Security
Bulletin*, 29 (July 1965): 3, adjusted for 1959 prices].

[9] We use the term blacks although the Census data refer to Negroes.
[10] This comparison group is limited to those born in the United States.

Aldine, 1965); John F. Kain and Joseph J. Perskey, "The North's Stake in Southern
Rural Poverty," *Rural Poverty in the United States* (Washington, D.C.: United States
Government Printing Office, 1968); Donald and Deborah Freedman, "Farm-Reared
Elements in the Non-Farm Population," *Rural Sociology* 21, no. 1 (March 1965):
50–61; Melvin Lurie and Elton Rayack, "Racial Differences in Migration and Job
Search: A Case Study," *Southern Economic Journal* 33, no. 1 (July 1966): 81–95;
John B. Lansing and James M. Morgan, "The Effect of Geographic Mobility on
Income, *Journal of Human Resources* 2 (Fall 1967): 449–460; Richard F. Wer-
theimer II, *The Monetary Rewards of Migration Within the U.S.* (Washington, D.C.:
The Urban Institute, 1970); Leonard Weiss and Jeffrey G. Williamson, "Black
Education, Earnings, and Interregional Migration, Some Recent Evidence," *American
Economic Review* 62 (June 1972); and A. Bradley Askin, "An Economic Analysis of
Black Migration," (Ph.D. diss., Massachusetts Institute of Technology, 1970).

Recent migrants are those who were living in an SMSA in 1960, but not in 1955. They will be compared with those who were living in SMSAs in both 1955 and 1960. For recent migration the analysis will be conducted for (*1*) blacks living in SMSAs outside the South, (*2*) blacks living in all SMSAs, and (*3*) whites living in all SMSAs.[11] For both recent and lifetime migration, the analysis is restricted to those who were at least eighteen years old in 1960, not students, not in the armed services, and not inmates of institutions.

Empirical results for lifetime migration are presented in the following section. In Section III we attempt to explain these findings. The results for recent migration are presented in Section IV.

II. Results for Black Lifetime Migration

Simple cross-tabulations for black lifetime migration are presented in Table 3.1. We see that lifetime migrants are generally better off than their comparison group. (The only exceptions are the figures for family income and possibly labor-force participation.)[12] On the other hand, as the first section of Table 3.2 indicates, lifetime migrants are usually older and have fewer years of school than the comparison group. To determine the net effect of migration, we use regression analysis with independent variables for years of school, age, sex, family status, region, and type of community as well as migration status.[13] For dependent variables we use each of the economic variables from Table 3.1.

The regression coefficients for lifetime migration are presented in Table 3.3. In all cases the dependent variable has been defined so that a positive coefficient for the migration variable means that the migrants are better off than the comparison group. The results indicate that the lifetime migrants are at least as well off in all respects except family income, where there is no appreciable difference between the two groups. The migrants are significantly better off than the nonmigrants (*1*) at the

[11] The first sample will allow the most direct comparison between results for black lifetime and recent migration. The other two samples allow us to compare results for blacks and whites, a comparison which need not be limited to those in northern SMSAs. Note that a black can be both a recent and a lifetime migrant.

[12] The interpretation of the results for labor-force participation and weeks worked depends on whether or not those who work less do so involuntarily. To keep the exposition simple, we will assume, somewhat arbitrarily, that all differences between migrants and the corresponding comparison group are at least partly involuntary.

[13] See Appendix 3A for a complete list of the independent variables.

TABLE 3.2

Percentage Distribution of Migrants and Nonmigrants, by Age and by Years of School

| | Blacks living in SMSAs outside the South | | | | Recent migration (all SMSAs) | | | |
| | Lifetime migration | | Recent migration | | Blacks | | Whites | |
	Migrant	Nonmigrant	Migrant	Nonmigrant	Migrant	Nonmigrant	Migrant	Nonmigrant
Years of school:								
0–7	35.3	17.4	22.7	29.4	28.7	36.1	9.8	15.4
8–11	40.0	44.0	39.0	41.5	38.0	38.2	30.4	36.6
12	17.9	27.9	27.3	21.1	24.1	18.2	35.9	29.2
Over 12	6.8	10.7	11.0	8.0	9.2	7.5	23.9	18.8
Age:								
18–25	11.5	22.1	44.2	13.8	45.5	13.9	30.5	10.4
26–45	48.1	50.2	37.2	49.4	39.3	48.0	46.3	43.0
46–65	32.1	22.1	18.0	29.1	14.9	29.4	16.9	33.6
Over 65	8.3	5.6	0.6	7.7	0.3	8.7	6.3	13.0

SOURCE: 1/1000 sample of the 1960 Census.

TABLE 3.3

Net Effect of Black Lifetime Migration on Economic Status

For those in the labor force:	
Annual earnings	.155
	(1.84)
Earnings per week	3.58
	(1.19)
Weeks worked	.754
	(1.09)
Unemployment (equals −1 if unemployed)	.012
	(.83)
Sample size	2519
For the total sample:	
Family income	−.003
	(.03)
Poverty status (equals −1 if poor)	.030
	(2.02)
Labor-force participation (equals −1 if not in labor force)	.033
	(2.25)
Sample size	3882

SOURCE: Calculated from the 1/1000 sample of the 1960 Census.

NOTE: This table shows regression coefficients (and *t*-values) for a dummy variable with a value of 1 for lifetime migrants. Other independent variables in the regression include dummies for age, education, and location. For a complete list, see Appendix 3A.

All the dependent variables are defined so that a positive value of the regression coefficient indicates that a person is better off if he is a migrant rather than a nonmigrant.

95 percent level for poverty status and labor-force participation[14] and (2) at the 90 percent level for annual earnings. These results are consistent with those of Weiss and Williamson, based on 1967 data, which show that, after standardizing for many variables including present location, black males who were living in the South at age 16 tend to have higher annual earnings than those who were living in the North at the same age.[15]

[14] This statement is true if the *t*-values are not biased upwards because these dependent variables are dummies. In fact, however, the *t*-values are likely to have a downward bias since ordinary least square regression estimates are inefficient when the dependent variable is a dummy.

[15] Weiss and Williamson, "Black Education," pp. 376–379.

III. Explaining the Results for Lifetime Migration

Other things being equal, we expect migrants to have lower incomes than nonmigrants because of adjustment problems.[16] For example, migrants are less likely to have the skills and experience for which employers are looking. In addition, the quality of schooling appears to be lower in the South.[17] Thus, we must seek explanations for why black lifetime migrants do as well or better than nonmigrants despite these apparent handicaps.

Three possible explanations will be discussed. First, migrants may choose to move to the more prosperous SMSAs. Second, there may be differences in the relationship between schooling and natural ability for those born in different regions. Finally, there may be differences in work effort between migrants and succeeding generations.

The first hypothesis is based on the fact that the migrants probably move in disproportionate numbers to areas in the North where economic opportunities are greatest. By moving to the most attractive areas, migrants may gain a significant advantage over nonmigrants. With regard to lifetime migration, however, this argument is not too convincing since the "nonmigrants" of the comparison group are likely to be quite mobile with regard to changing location in the North.

The second, more persuasive, hypothesis is based on differences in the relationship between schooling and natural ability for blacks born in the South versus those born in the North. Table 3.4 shows the percentages in the various schooling categories for those born in the South (whether they are now living in the North or South) and for those born and living outside the South. Note the much larger percentage in the lowest schooling category for those born in the South. If natural ability and years of school are correlated within each group, and if

[16] This expectation is confirmed in comparing foreign-born whites living in northern SMSAs with all other whites in such SMSAs. The net effect of lifetime migration on annual earnings is negative and statistically significant at the 95 percent level. See Stanley H. Masters, *A Study of Socio-Economic Mobility Among Urban Negroes,* United States Office of Economic Opportunity Research Contract Number B 99-4790, Final Report, 1970, Section 2.

[17] For example, see the data in the Coleman report, J. S. Coleman *et al., Equality of Educational Opportunity* (Washington, D.C.: United States Government Printing Office, 1966), especially pp. 274–275. Also see the data on the Armed Forces Qualifying Test presented in B.D. Karpinos, "The Mental Test Qualifications of American Youth for Military Service and Its Relation to Educational Attainment," *Proceedings of the American Statistical Association,* Social Statistics Section (Washington, D.C.: American Statistical Association, 1966), especially p. 111.

Percentage Distribution of Blacks, by Years of School, 1960

	0–7	8–11	12	Over 12	Total
Ages 18 and over:					
Born South	49.3	32.2	13.0	5.5	100.0
Born and live non-South	18.5	43.7	27.5	10.3	100.0
Ages 35–44:					
Born South	43.9	37.1	13.3	5.7	100.0
Born and live non-South	13.6	47.0	27.0	12.4	100.0

Years of school spans columns 0–7, 8–11, 12, Over 12.

SOURCE: Calculated from the 1/1000 sample of the 1960 Census.
NOTE: Students, inmates of institutions, and members of the armed services are excluded since they are not included in the rest of the analysis.
Similar results were obtained for age subgroups other than 35–44.

natural ability is fairly evenly distributed between those born in the two areas, then those with a given number of years of school will have higher ability, on the average, if they are southern born. This difference in ability could then account for the better performance of the lifetime migrants. If this hypothesis is correct, then the estimates for the net effect of lifetime migration are positively biased since natural ability could not be included as one of the independent variables.

If the quality of schooling is lower in the South, however, then the preceding argument can explain our findings only if differences in natural ability are greater than differences in the quality of the schools. Since the quality of schooling is probably most important for those with the most years of school, we can test our hypothesis of differences in natural ability per schooling level by looking at results for those with different amounts of schooling. These results are presented in Table 3.5. We see that the superior position of the migrants applies primarily (though not entirely) to those with less than twelve years of school. While this provides some support for our hypothesis, the support would be stronger if the results for those with less than eight years of school were larger relative to the results for those with eight to eleven years.

The final hypothesis starts with the assumption that many blacks migrate to the North to seek greater economic opportunities. Therefore,

TABLE 3.5

Net Effect of Lifetime Migration for Blacks, by Years of School

	Years of school			
	0–7	8–11	12	Over 12
For those in the labor force:				
Annual earnings	.303	.216	−.086	.227
	(1.17)	(1.02)	(.53)	(.75)
Earnings per week	3.78	4.15	−0.63	11.10
	(.41)	(.55)	(.11)	(1.03)
Weeks worked	0.02	2.58	0.47	−4.53
	(.01)	(1.48)	(.35)	(1.82)
Unemployment	.001	.034	−.001	−.031
	(.03)	(.97)	(.02)	(.62)
Sample size	658	1042	582	237
For the total sample:				
Family income	.155	.123	−.262	−.307
	(.44)	(.42)	(1.15)	(.70)
Poverty status	.066	.041	−.005	−.014
	(1.45)	(1.06)	(.15)	(.25)
Labor-force participation	.026	.049	.004	.046
	(4.63)	(1.32)	(.13)	(.83)
Sample size	1129	1608	829	316

NOTE: See Table 3.3 for the definition of the dependent variables and a discussion of the control variables.

The regressions were run with a set of joint dummies for migration status and education, with the reference group being nonmigrants with twelve years of school. For twelve years of school, the regression coefficient for migrants and its t-value are reported. For the other educational categories, the coefficient for the nonmigrants is subtracted from the coefficient for the migrants. In all cases, a positive number means the migrants are better off. Except for those with twelve years of school, the t-values represent the difference between the coefficients divided by the standard error of that difference.

they can be expected to work hard to take advantage of the better opportunities that probably do exist for blacks in the North. (See the results in Table 3.6.)[18] If we assume that these migrants are more ambitious than the average black and that there is little difference in

[18] The results in Table 3.6 indicate that the net effect of migration (holding age, years of school, and other factors constant) is to increase earnings and income by 15 to 20 percent. While these results are based on differences in money rather than real

TABLE 3.6

*Net Effect of Black Lifetime Migration on Economic Status
Relative to Those Left Behind in the South*

	Regression coefficient	*t*-value
Annual earnings	.477	(11.04)*a*
Earnings per week	13.50	(9.31)*a*
Weeks worked	−1.41	(3.11)*a*
Unemployment	−0.28	(3.97)
Family income	.765	(9.78)*a*
Poverty status	.121	(8.81)
Labor-force participation	−.034	(2.61)
Sample size	7980	

NOTE: The results in this table are regression coefficients (and *t*-values) for the lifetime migration dummy in various multiple regressions. In most respects, the procedures are the same as for Table 3.3 in the text. The exceptions are (*1*) the sample is all blacks born in the South and now living either in the South or in northern SMSAs and (*2*) due to financial constraints, the first four regressions were run for the total sample (with a dummy for labor-force participation added) rather than just for those in the labor force. If there were no relation between migration status and labor-force participation, the first four coefficients would be biased toward zero. However, since the migrants are less likely to be in the labor force, a negative bias is introduced. Therefore, the net bias for the first two coefficients is unclear. Results comparing black migrants with those already in urban areas, suggest that these biases are not large.

a Statistically significant at 99 percent level. For the three dummy dependent variables, it is not clear what the level of statistical significance is in this or any of the other tables.

ambition between black nonmigrants, North or South, then we have one explanation for the superior economic position of the migrants compared with the northern nonmigrants.

This argument has the advantage of simplicity, but the disadvantage that the assumption of similarity between southern and northern nonmigrants may be unrealistic. We can avoid this problem by noting that most northern blacks who are not first-generation migrants are

---

income, the differences in the cost of living are probably smaller. Cost-of-living figures for low-income families in various locations are available in Jean C. Brackett, "New BLS Budgets," *Monthly Labor Review* 92 (April 1969). These figures show that, in comparison with the large northern cities, the cost of living is 0 to 10 percent lower in the major southern cities, and 10 to 15 percent lower in urban centers of 2500 to 50,000 in the South. Slightly over 60 percent of southern black adults live in urban areas (mostly in the larger cities), but unfortunately no cost of living figures are given for the nonurban population. Most likely their cost of living is lower than for those in urban areas, but it is not clear how much lower.

second- or third-generation migrants.[19] Therefore, it makes sense to speculate on differences between migrants and their children (or grandchildren).

Although the economic opportunities for a black may be good in the North relative to his opportunities in the South, a northern black's opportunities (at least for males) are still quite small relative to those available to the average white.[20] While the black migrant may feel that his opportunities are better in the North than they were in the South and, therefore, work harder to take advantage of these opportunities, his children may react quite differently. Succeeding generations are likely to be much more conscious of how limited their opportunities are relative to those of whites. Consequently, a job that looks good to the migrant, relative to what he could get in the South, may look quite unattractive to his son, who compares this job with the jobs whites are able to get. Because of this difference in perspective, the extra income gained by working long hours, doing particularly strenuous physical labor, or participating in lengthy training programs may be much more important to the migrant than to succeeding generations. Consequently, the succeeding generations may not be willing to work as hard as the migrants.[21] If so, this lower work effort could explain why incomes are higher for black lifetime migrants than for nonmigrants.[22]

To the extent that racial discrimination in the North is greater against males than against females, this work-effort argument should

[19] In 1910, only 11 percent of the blacks in this country lived outside the South. In 1960, the figure was 40 percent. See Marion Hayes, "A Century of Change: Negroes in the U.S. Economy, 1860–1960," *Monthly Labor Review* 90 (December 1967): 1361. A somewhat similar difficulty occurs in our previous argument when we assume that natural ability is fairly evenly distributed among those born in the South and in the North, even though those with more ability probably had more incentive to emigrate from the South and thus are relatively more likely to be parents of children born in the North. (See the discussion in footnote 22.)

[20] For example, see the results in Giora Hanoch, "An Economic Analysis of Earnings and Schooling," *Journal of Human Resources* 2 (Summer 1967): 316–317.

[21] They may also be more willing (and able) to achieve illegal income, which presumably is not included in the Census data.

[22] If the typical migrant has more native intelligence than the average individual, then the principle of regression toward the mean implies that the migrant's children will be less intelligent than he is (on the average), but that they will still be above the general average. If we assume that the black migrants of each generation are about equal in natural ability and that they are above the black average, then the tendency for regression toward the mean could be at least a partial explanation for the finding that lifetime migrants do better economically than the nonmigrants. Note, however, that this argument can explain the regression results only to the extent that (1) migrants do have more natural ability than nonmigrants and (2) such differences do not lead to corresponding differences in years of school.

TABLE 3.7

*Net Effect of Lifetime Migration on Economic Status
for Black Males and Females*

	Males	Females
For those in the labor force:		
Annual earnings	.360	− .222
	(3.10)	(1.99)[a]
Earnings per week	9.01	−5.59
	(2.05)[a]	(1.64)
Weeks worked	1.00	−0.20
	(1.23)	(.16)
Unemployment	.015	.002
	(.82)	(.07)
Sample size	1548	971
For the total sample:		
Family income	.024	.032
	(.14)	(.21)
Poverty status	.044	.026
	(2.07)	(1.26)
Labor-force participation	.028	.017
	(1.72)	(.74)
Sample size	1802	2080

NOTE: See Table 3.3 for a discussion of how these estimates are derived.

[a] Statistically significant at 95 percent level.

apply more to males than to females.[23] Separate results by sex, presented in Table 3.7, indicate that the superior earnings position of migrants is due entirely to the results for males.[24] However, the most important explanation for the dramatic differences by sex may be a greater

[23] Among those with income in 1959, the ratio of black to white median income was .600 for females compared with .520 for males. On the other hand, the difference narrows considerably when the ratios are calculated only for the earnings of those who worked 50–52 weeks in 1959. In this case, the female ratio is .578 compared with .544 for males. Moreover, among these full-year workers the ratio for hours worked in the survey (of 1960) week was slightly higher for females (.934 versus .923). On balance, it appears that racial discrimination is only slightly less severe against black females than against black males. The first set of ratios were calculated from data in the "U.S. Census of Population: 1960, Detailed Characteristics," U.S. Summary Table 218. The others were calculated from the 1/1000 sample of the 1960 Census.

[24] The results for males will affect the female results for family income and poverty status.

TABLE 3.8

**Percentage Distribution of Occupations of Blacks,
Lifetime Migrants and Nonmigrants**

	Males		Females	
Occupation	Migrants	Nonmigrants	Migrants	Nonmigrants
Professional	3.3	6.3	6.6	7.9
Managers	2.4	3.1	0.8	0.8
Clerical workers	10.9	13.5	10.4	24.7
Sales workers	1.9	3.2	2.2	3.0
Craftsmen	12.5	10.8	1.6	1.2
Operatives	30.9	28.8	21.3	20.8
Nonfarm laborers	20.0	15.4	0.8	1.8
Private household workers	0.5	0.3	30.2	23.0
Other service workers	16.8	17.3	25.4	16.6
Farmers	0.0	0.6	0.0	0.0
Farm laborers	0.4	0.4	0.4	0.0

SOURCE: 1/1000 Sample of 1960 Census.

discrepancy between skills learned in the South and those in demand in the North for black females than for males. Data on occupation by sex, presented in Table 3.8, show little difference in the occupational distribution of black males between migrants and nonmigrants, although there is some tendency for migrants to be more heavily represented in blue-collar occupations and nonmigrants in white-collar ones. For black females, however, migrants are much more heavily concentrated in low-paying occupations like private household workers and less well represented in higher paying ones like clerical workers.

IV. Results for Recent Migration

If other factors are held constant, then the adjustment problems of migrants should be more serious the more recent their migration. The results are consistent with this view. Recall that, based on the 1960 Census data, we have defined recent migrants as those who were living in an SMSA in 1960, but who did not live in any metropolitan area in 1955. Cross-tabulations for the recent migrants and their comparison group, those living in SMSAs in both 1955 and 1960, are presented in Table 3.9. For all samples, the recent migrants are consistently worse off.

Regression results are presented in Table 3.10. After standardizing for differences in age, years of school, sex, family status, and type of community, the net effect of recent migration is almost always negative.[25] In other words, current residents of SMSAs are generally worse off economically if they are recent migrants from rural areas.[26]

In comparing the national results by race, note that recent migrants are at a greater relative disadvantage in weeks worked if they are black and in earnings per week if they are white. These findings on weeks worked are consistent with a queue theory of unemployment, with the average white not being too far back on the queue even if he is a recent migrant. The findings on earnings per week suggest that discrimination may be greater when good jobs are involved and that recent migrants may have trouble getting such jobs regardless of race. In this case, the adjustment problems of migration and the general problems resulting from discrimination would not be additive. Results on earnings per week, by sex, presented in Table 3.11, are also of interest in this regard. Recent migration is much more of a handicap for white males than for white females, which is consistent with the view that the handicaps of recent migration and sexual discrimination are not additive. While recent migration is more of a handicap for black females than black males, this result may stem from a greater discrepancy between skills learned in the South and those in demand in the North for black females than for black males. (See the discussion of this point in Section III.)

Our primary concern is with the effect of recent migration on the black–white earnings ratio. On the basis of the results in Table 3.9, this ratio is a little lower for the migrants (1778/4111 = .433) than for the nonmigrants (2510/5402 = .465).[27] Since the proportion of SMSA residents who are recent migrants is the same for both blacks and whites

---

[25] See Appendix 3A for a complete list of the independent variables. The black coefficients have lower t-values at least in part because of the much smaller sample size.

[26] Of course, they may still be better off than those who remained behind.

[27] We could obtain similar results standardizing for differences in years of school, age, and our other control variables by using the regression coefficients in Table 3.10. When we calculate the black–white earnings ratio for migrants, after adjusting for differences in years of school, age, and our other control variables (i.e., by subtracting the absolute value of the regression coefficients from the average earnings of the comparison group), we obtain a slightly larger figure (.438 instead of .433). Thus, the analysis in the test applies whether or not we use "standardized" or actual migrants.

TABLE 3.9

Economic Status of Recent Migrants and Nonmigrants

| | Non-South | | National | | | |
| | Black | | Black | | White | |
	Recent migrants	Comparison group	Recent migrants	Comparison group	Recent migrants	Comparison group
For those in the labor force:						
Annual earnings	$1827	$2863	$1778	$2510	$4111	$5402
Earnings per week	$54.4	$69.5	$49.0	$60.4	$95.8	$112.5
Weeks worked	30.0	40.0	33.4	40.4	45.1	46.5
Unemployment rate	16.1	11.5	12.8	9.6	5.7	4.3
Sample size	124	2395	219	4122	1939	34,412
For the total sample:						
Family income	$4380	$4791	$4066	$4301	$5950	$7334
Percent poor	36.0	27.7	39.6	35.3	14.2	11.6
Labor-force-participation rate	72.1	64.6	72.3	65.0	61.2	60.6
Sample size	171	3711	303	6337	3169	56,826

SOURCE: Calculated from the 1/1000 sample of the 1960 Census.
NOTE: See Table 3.1 for a discussion of some of these variables.

TABLE 3.10

Net Effect of Recent Migration

	Non-South	National	
	Black	Black	White
For those in the labor force:			
Annual earnings	−.557	−.324	−.410
	(3.04)[a]	(2.70)[a]	(7.17)[a]
Earnings per week	−.814	−4.49	−7.84
	(1.25)	(1.10)	(5.24)[a]
Weeks worked	−.640	−3.92	−0.64
	(4.23)[a]	(3.53)[a]	(2.98)[a]
Unemployment	−.027	−.012	−.008
	(.87)	(.55)	(2.83)
Sample size	2519	4341	—
For the total sample:			
Family income	−.281	−.156	−1.314
	(1.07)	(.88)	(14.96)[a]
Poverty status	−.054	.011	−.036
	(1.59)	(.40)	(6.37)
Labor-force participation	.065	.049	−.015
	(1.97)	(1.99)	(2.14)
Sample size	3882	6640	59,995

NOTE: See Table 3.3 for a discussion of how these estimates are derived.

The regression coefficients are now for the dummy variable representing recent migration. The variable for lifetime migration is dropped and (in the national samples) replaced by a dummy for the South.

[a] Statistically significant at the 99 percent level.

(5 percent), this migration does have a negative effect on the black–white earnings ratio of those living in metropolitan areas. However, the effect is very small due to the low percentage who are migrants. The black–white earnings ratio would have increased only from .463 to .465 if there had been no migration to metropolitan areas between 1955 and 1960.[28]

[28] The figure .463 was derived by taking a weighted average of the figures for migrants and nonmigrants (i.e., .463 = .465 × .96 + .433 × .05).

TABLE 3.11

Net Effect of Recent Migration by Sex for All SMSAs

	Blacks		Whites	
	Male	Female	Male	Female
For those in the labor force:				
Annual earnings	−.229	−.496	−.775	−.141
	(1.31)	(3.40)ᵃ	(6.94)ᵃ	(4.00)ᵃ
Earnings per week	−2.84	−7.39	−15.34	−2.35
	(.46)	(1.57)	(5.43)ᵃ	(1.83)
Weeks worked	−0.64	−8.37	−1.10	−0.50
	(.48)	(4.54)ᵃ	(3.81)ᵃ	(1.65)
Unemployment	.036	−.074	−.018	−.002
	(1.30)	(2.37)	(3.45)	(.51)
Sample size	2589	1752	—	—
For the total sample:				
Family income	−.185	−.097	−1.292	−1.315
	(.65)	(.43)	(9.88)ᵃ	(11.13)ᵃ
Poverty status	.016	.014	−.036	−.035
	(.41)	(.39)	(4.68)	(4.43)
Labor-force participation	.028	.052	−.013	−.026
	(.99)	(1.41)	(1.81)	(2.37)
Sample size	3025	3615	27,892	32,103

NOTE: See Table 3.10 for a discussion of how these estimates are derived.
ᵃ Statistically significant at the 99 percent level.

V. Conclusion

In proposing an outline for a federal urban policy in 1969, Daniel P. Moynihan presented ten propositions ranked "roughly to correspond to a combined measure of urgency and importance."[29] The first and sixth are relevant here.

[29] Daniel P. Moynihan, "Towards a National Urban Policy," *The Public Interest* (Fall 1969): 8, 14.

(1) The poverty and social isolation of minority groups in central cities is the single most serious problem of the American city today . . . .

(6) The federal government must assert a specific interest in the movement of people, displaced by technology or driven by poverty, from rural to urban areas . . . .

The results of this chapter strongly support Moynihan's conclusion that the poverty problems of the urban black are much more pervasive than simply the problems of adjustment facing black migrants from the rural South. While our data are for 1960, the migration of blacks out of the South has slowed down since that time.[30] Consequently, there should be less competition for those jobs available to the migrants (especially unskilled migrants), and less strain on governmental or other programs to assist disadvantaged migrants. As a result, the reduced migration stream should reduce the economic difficulties that recent migrants were experiencing in 1960.

Since recent migrants, both black and white, do not fare as well economically as long-term urban residents, there may be some role for the government to play in assisting such migrants. At least for blacks, however, the adjustment problems of migration do not remain important for very long. Among blacks currently living in SMSAs outside the South, those born in the South have higher earnings and less unemployment than those born in the North (especially for males). Therefore, programs aimed at easing the adjustment problems of migrants cannot be expected to lead to any major improvement in the income of urban blacks. If the policy goal is to reduce the economic problems of ghetto residents, then the alternative approach of fighting racial discrimination appears to have a much greater potential pay-off. As we shall demonstrate in the next two chapters, one of the major (if not *the* major) problem is labor-market discrimination.

---

[30] For example, the number of blacks born in the South and currently living in other regions increased by 664,000 (or over 25 percent) between 1950 and 1960, but by only 155,000 (less than 5 percent) between 1960 and 1970. (Figures calculated from the State of Birth Volumes of the 1950, 1960, and 1970 Census of Population.)

With regard to future trends, Beale concludes that the black urban migration will continue to be rather small relative to what it was in the recent past—largely because of the reduced population base in rural areas. See Calvin L. Beale, "Rural-Urban Migration of Blacks: Past and Future," *The American Journal of Agricultural Economics* 53 (May 1971).

APPENDIX 3A: Independent Variables
Used in the Regressions

In the regressions for lifetime migration, dummy variables were used for the following groups:

(1) Lifetime migrants
(2) Recent migrants
(3) Those with 0–7 years of school
(4) Those with 8–11 years of school
(5) Those with over 12 years of school
(6) Those 18–25 years old
(7) Those 46–65 years old
(8) Those over 65 years old
(9) Those in the Northeast
(10) Those in the West
(11) Those in the central cities of SMSAs of under 500,000 population
(12) Those in the central cities of SMSAs of 500,000 to 1,000,000 population
(13) Those not in a central city
(14) Males
(15) Those married with spouse present
(16) Those with children under the age of 6
(17) Those with children between 6 and 17

plus a variable (18) for the number of people in the family (maximum value of 12). For the recent migration regressions, the dummy for lifetime migrants is dropped and a dummy for those in the South is added for the national sample.

Since the values of some of these independent variables may be affected by a person's economic position (as reflected in the values of the dependent variables), other regressions were run with the variables for family status (15–18) eliminated and the variables for type of community combined into one dummy for those in SMSAs of less than 1,000,000. The results for these regressions are very similar to the results presented in the text.

4

The Effect of Housing Segregation
on Black–White Income Differentials

In the last few years there has been considerable discussion concerning the effect of housing segregation on the employment opportunities of urban blacks.[1] One of the first articles, and the one that has probably

[1] See John F. Kain, "Housing Segregation, Negro Employment and Metropolitan Decentralization," *Quarterly Journal of Economics* 82 (May 1968) and the "Note" on this article by Paul Offner and Daniel H. Saks, *Quarterly Journal of Economics* 85 (February 1971); John F. Kain and Joseph J. Persky, "Alternatives to the Gilded Ghetto," *The Public Interest* (Winter 1969); Edward Kalacheck, "Ghetto Dwellers, Transportation and Employment," paper delivered at a Transportation and Poverty Conference of the American Academy of Arts and Sciences (June 1968); John R. Meyer, John F. Kain, and Martin Wohl, *The Urban Transportation Problem* (Cambridge, Massachusetts: Harvard Univ. Press, 1965); Joseph D. Mooney, "Housing Segregation, Negro Employment and Metropolitan Decentralization," *Quarterly Journal of Economics* 83, no. 2 (May 1969); Dorothy K. Newman, "The Decentralization of Jobs," *Monthly Labor Review* 90 (May 1967); Roger Noll, "Metropolitan Employment and Population Distribution and the Conditions of the Urban Poor," in *Financing the Metropolis, The Urban Affairs Annual Review* 4, ed. John P. Crecine (Beverly Hills, California: Sage Publications, 1970); Bennett Harrison, "The Intrametropolitan Distribution of Minority Economic Welfare," *Journal of Regional Science* 12, no. 2 (April 1972); Benjamin I. Cohen, "Trends in Negro Employment within Large Metropolitan Areas," *Public Policy* 19 (Fall 1971); and Paul Offner, "Labor Force Participation in the Urban Ghetto," *Journal of Human Resources* 7 (Fall 1972).

attracted the most attention, is by John Kain, who argues:

> There are several reasons why housing market segregation may affect the distribution and level of Negro employment. The most obvious are: (1) The distance to and difficulty of reaching certain jobs from Negro residence areas may impose costs on Negroes high enough to discourage them from seeking employment there. (2) Negroes may have less information about and less opportunity to learn about jobs distant from their place of residence or those of their friends. (3) Employers located outside the ghetto may discriminate against Negroes out of real or imagined fears of retaliation from white customers for "bringing Negroes into all-white residential areas," or they may feel little pressure not to discriminate. (4) Similarly, employers in or near the ghetto may discriminate in favor of Negroes.[2]

In addition, he maintains (*1*) that the problem has become much more serious as a result of the "suburbanization of employment" since the end of World War II; and (*2*) that the situation can be expected to become more serious in the future, assuming that the trend toward greater suburbanization of jobs continues.[3]

Most of the studies in this area, including Kain's, are primarily empirical.[4] In general, the authors appear to start from two key assumptions: (*1*) that residential segregation by race is pervasive; and (*2*) that there are important employment opportunities available in areas that are hard to reach from black neighborhoods. Studies of the racial distribution of housing do indicate pervasive segregation, both between the central cities and surrounding suburbs and within central cities.[5] In addition, it

[2] Kain, "Housing Segregation," pp. 179–180.

[3] For a good discussion of probable future trends, see John F. Kain, "The Distribution and Movement of Jobs and Industry," in *The Metropolitan Enigma*, ed. James Q. Wilson (Cambridge, Massachusetts: Harvard Univ. Press, 1968).

[4] See Kalacheck, "Ghetto Dwellers," for a good theoretical discussion which utilizes both the traditional static theory of work effort and a dynamic analysis of the job-search process.

[5] For an extensive analysis of segregation, mainly within central cities, see Karl E. and Alma F. Taeuber, *Negroes in Cities: Residential Segregation and Neighborhood Change* (Chicago, Illinois: Aldine, 1965). Also, see the summary of this study in Chapter 2. For a comparison of central cities to suburbs, see Kain and Persky, "Alternative to the Gilded Ghetto."

Much of the discussion has also centered on transportation problems. In fact, the McCone Commission study of the Watts riot in Los Angeles, which stressed the role of poor public transportation in handicapping Watts residents, was perhaps instrumental in opening up the question of the effect of housing segregation on black employment opportunities. For a discussion of some of these issues see John F. Kain, and John R. Meyer, "Transportation and Poverty," *The Public Interest* (Winter 1970).

is also clear that in recent years employment has been growing more rapidly in the suburbs than in central cities.[6]

As Noll points out, however, it is very important to know why these differential growth rates have occurred.[7] Meyer, Kain, and Wohl stress the following factors:

> Containerization, the jet age, telecommunications, mechanized methods of materials handling, continuous processing, do-it-yourself deliveries, automation —all these connote recent technological changes that have had a decentralizing influence on the location of urban job opportunities.[8]

Alternatively, Noll argues that

> business location decisions are also affected by labor-market conditions. The argument that ghetto unemployment is caused by shifts in employment distribution assumes that the metropolitan area is comprised of several somewhat independent labor markets. It further assumes that, because more employment growth is occuring in the suburbs, labor markets must, perforce, be tighter there. But such differences in labor-market conditions will affect firm-locations decisions. A disproportionately large share of the metropolitan labor force works in the city (the ratio of employment to population is fifty percent higher than in the suburbs). It is possible that a much larger number of suburbanites working in the central city would prefer suburban jobs than can be filled by suburban employment growth, and that firms are locating in suburbs in response to tighter central-city labor markets.[9]

Noll suggests that we can distinguish between these two hypotheses by looking at wages and unemployment. If his view is correct, then, for workers of equal skill, wage rates should be higher in the central city than in the suburbs, and unemployment rates should be lower. The opposite should be true if changes in industrial technology are the main factors responsible for decentralization of employment. Noll does present some

---

[6] For evidence of this suburbanization (including some discussion disaggregated by skill level) see Meyer, Kain, and Wohl, *Urban Transportation Problem;* Mooney, "Housing Segregation"; Newman, "Decentralization of Jobs"; and John F. Kain, "The Distribution and Movement of Jobs and Industry."

[7] Noll, "Metropolitan Employment."

[8] Meyer, Kain, and Wohl, *Urban Transportation Problem*, p. 24.

[9] Noll, "Metropolitan Employment," p. 499. It should be noted that Meyer, Kain, and Wohl also indicate that "the ability of Americans to afford decentralized residential locations, private yards, and automobiles as their incomes have risen has of course strengthened the trend towards urban dispersal [Meyer, Kain, and Wohl, *Urban Transportation Problem*, p. 24]."

empirical analysis of this issue and concludes "that jobs, particularly for the less skilled, are easier to find in the central city."[10] But this conclusion depends rather heavily on the assumption that skill levels are higher in the suburbs than in central cities.

In summary, the housing segregation assumption appears valid, while the employment opportunities assumption remains open to at least some question. With this background in mind, let us look next at the two most important studies that seek to estimate the effect of housing segregation and the suburbanization of jobs on black employment. In the first, Kain attempts to test three hypotheses, "that racial segregation in the housing market (1) affects the distribution of Negro employment and (2) reduces Negro job opportunities and that (3) postwar suburbanization of employment has seriously aggravated the problem."[11] The data are for geographic areas in Detroit (1957) and Chicago (1956), with ninety-eight observations for each city. Regressions are run using the black percentage of total employment in the area as the dependent variable, w. The independent variables are R, the black percentage of employed residents in the area—used as a proxy for employers' propensity to discriminate— and d, the air distance from the area to either the nearest black residence area (more than 2 percent black) or to the nearest point in the black ghetto—used as a proxy for transportation costs and effects of such costs on job information. The regression coefficients have the correct signs and are statistically significant. Seventy-five percent of the total variance is explained for Chicago and 35 percent for Detroit.

Our interest centers on Kain's estimates of the effect of housing

---

[10] Noll, "Metropolitan Employment," p. 501. Rees also reports results on geographic wage differentials in the Chicago labor market that appear consistent with Noll's hypothesis. See Albert Rees, "Spatial Wage Differentials in a Large City Labor Market," *Proceedings of the 21st Annual Winter Meeting of the Industrial Relations Research Convention* (Madison, Wisconsin: Industrial Relations Research Association, 1969).

Of the authors arguing that blacks have been seriously hindered by the suburbanization of employment, Newman is the only one who presents any evidence on the relative tightness of central-city and suburban labor markets. She writes, "For every major industry and occupational group, whether involving relatively low paid repair services or higher paid professions, median family income in 1964 was lower among city than suburban residents [Newman, "Decentralization of Jobs," p. 9]." However, this evidence is very weak since the more highly paid city workers in any occupation may be more likely to move to the suburbs and commute to their city jobs. Therefore, it is necessary to look at relative earnings of those *working* in different areas rather than of those *living* in different areas.

[11] Kain, "Housing Segregation," p. 176.

segregation on the level of black employment.[12] He obtains these estimates by assuming that, with no housing segregation, the proportion of nonwhite workers would be the same, $\bar{R}$, for each geographical area. Consequently, for each area $R = \bar{R}$ and $d = O$. Substituting these values into the regression equation

$$w = aR + bd + c \quad \text{gives} \tag{1}$$

$$\hat{w} = a\bar{R} + c, \quad \text{for all areas.} \tag{2}$$

If $\hat{w}$ were the black proportion of employment in the absence of segregation and if E is the total employment of the SMSA, then the expected *level* of black employment in the absence of housing segregation would be $\hat{w} \times E$, a level considerably higher than the actual nonwhite employment level.

To evaluate this conclusion note that a regression line goes through the point representing the mean values of its variables. Therefore,

$$\bar{w} = a\bar{R} + b\bar{d} + c, \tag{3}$$

where $\bar{w}$, $\bar{R}$, and $\bar{d}$ are the mean values for w, R, and d. Substituting from Equation (2) and rearranging terms, we obtain

$$\hat{w} - \bar{w} = -b\bar{d} . \tag{4}$$

Now $(\hat{w} - \bar{w})$ is Kain's measure of the effect of housing segregation on the relative job opportunities of blacks. Since $b < 0$ and $\bar{d} > 0$, we see that Kain's estimate will be larger, the larger the absolute values of b and $\bar{d}$. But $\bar{d}$, the distance from the ghetto to the average area, will be larger the greater the extent of housing segregation, and the absolute value of b will be larger the greater the costs of transportation and reduced job information per unit of distance. However, the values of b and $\bar{d}$ do *not* depend on whether labor markets are tighter in suburban or central-city areas. In fact, b and $\bar{d}$ could be quite large even if the central-city labor market were very tight relative to the suburban market. Consequently, Kain has demonstrated no more in this part of his analysis than he had already indicated in his first conclusion—namely

[12] While his results are probably consistent with each of the following three interpretations—*(1)* housing segregation affects the distribution of employment; *(2)* employment segregation leads to housing segregation; or *(3)* tastes for discrimination lead simultaneously to segregation in employment and housing—we have no quarrel with Kain's choice of the first interpretation. Note that he obtains similar results when he disaggregates by occupation and industry, thus guarding against the possibility that his aggregate results occur mainly because of an increase in skill requirements for jobs as the distance from the ghetto increases.

that housing segregation and transportation costs probably affect the *distribution* of black employment. He has *not* demonstrated that housing segregation and transportation problems hurt the relative employment position of blacks.[13] Moreover, while this difficulty is most obvious in assessing Kain's estimate of the effect of housing segregation on the level of black employment, it also invalidates his test of the effect of increases in the suburbanization of employment over time, since changes over time in the values of R and d might only affect the geographical distribution and not the level of black employment.

In a second study, more interesting empirical results have been presented by Mooney, using 1960 data for twenty-five large SMSAs.[14] For his dependent variable, Mooney uses the employment–population ratio of nonwhite males (or females) in low-income, nonwhite census tracts. His independent variables are (*1*) the unemployment rate for the SMSA, (*2*) the ratio of central-city jobs to total SMSA jobs (for various industries), and (*3*) the proportion of nonwhite males (or females) in the central city and working in the SMSA who have jobs outside the central city. The second variable is designed to measure the suburbanization of employment while the third is an attempt to measure the accessibility of suburban jobs for central-city blacks. For males, the coefficients all have the expected signs and are statistically significant, although Mooney emphasizes that the unemployment variable has the greatest effect. For females, the same general pattern of results applies, but the statistical fit is not as good. Mooney's analysis will be discussed further when we present our empirical results.

I. Empirical Results Concerning the Effect of Housing Segregation on Black–White Earnings Ratios

In this section we use 1970 Census data for seventy-seven large SMSAs to examine the relation between housing segregation and

---

[13] Working within Kain's general framework, Offner and Saks ["Note," *Quarterly Journal of Economics* 85 (February 1971)], argue that Kain should have included R^2 as well as R in his set of independent variables and that $w = a\bar{R} + b\bar{R}^2 + c$ is less than the actual percentage of employment that is black—thus indicating that segregation might not reduce black job opportunities. Note that $a\bar{R} + b\bar{R}^2 + c \neq \bar{w} - b\bar{d}$ since $\overline{(R^2)} \neq (\bar{R})^2$—except in a very special case.

It also should be noted that $\bar{R}$, the mean value of R for the geographic areas, need not equal the city-wide mean calculated across individuals. Since Kain focuses on the latter and we concentrate on the former, our critique of Kain implicitly assumes that the two means will be highly correlated.

[14] See Mooney, "Housing Segregation."

black–white income differentials.[15] In contrast to the work of Kain and Mooney discussed in the introduction, these results provide a more direct test of the relationship between housing segregation and black job opportunities.

For our dependent variable, we give primary emphasis to the relative earnings (or income) of blacks rather than to employment measures, since we want to concentrate on the quality of jobs available to the average black, while employment rates are determined primarily by workers with a marginal attachment to the labor force. In Appendix 4A, however, we do present some analogous results for employment.

For our earnings variable, we use relative earnings rather than just black earnings since many factors—such as the balance between demand and supply, industrial mix, and location—should have a significant effect on both black and white earnings while our interest is in factors related to discrimination. Specifically, we would like to use the ratio of median earnings for all black males (or those aged 35–44) divided by the corresponding median for whites. Unfortunately, such data are not available from the published census documents. Three alternative variables can be used:[16] (*1*) the median earnings of black males divided by the median earnings of all males (BE/TE); (*2*) the median income of black males, ages 40–44, divided by the median income of all males, ages 40–44, $(BI/TI)_{40-44}$; and (*3*) the median income of black males divided by the median income of white males (BI/WI). The first measure is used since the hypothesis relating housing segregation to employment opportunities predicts that such segregation should affect earnings but says nothing about effects on unearned income. The second measure is valuable for two reasons. First, it provides a convenient way to standardize for age effects. Second, the combination of using this age–sex group and total income should minimize the problem that arises, since the census medians are calculated only for those who have income (or earnings) greater than zero.[17] However, the third measure will be given primary emphasis since we are interested in measuring the effects

---

[15] The sample consists of all SMSAs, with at least 250,000 total population, where data are available separately for blacks, with the exception of Jacksonville, Florida, which is omitted since the central city and the SMSA are synonymous.

[16] See Appendix 4B for means and standard deviations of these variables and all others used in the study. All three dependent variables have moderate standard deviations (.09 to .07 for the national sample).

[17] Note data on median earnings are not available by age.

of housing segregation on the black–*white* income ratio. More specifically, we are concerned that the level of black income and the percent of the population who are black will affect the median income for the total population (and thereby also affect variables that have the overall median in the denominator). We restrict the analysis to males since (*1*) Mooney's results suggest that the suburbanization of jobs is more of a problem for nonwhite males than females, (*2*) there generally is a negative relationship between a group's male income and the amount of time females spend in the labor force,[18] and (*3*) cases of zero earnings and income probably are more important for females than for males. In all cases we use the term "black" as synonymous with the census use of Negro rather than nonwhite.

Next, we turn to our measures of housing segregation. First, we shall use an index (Ta) that is similar to the Taeubers' measure of segregation. While the Taeubers' index measures "the minimum percentage of nonwhites who would have to change the block in which they live in order to produce an unsegregated distribution—one in which the percentage of nonwhites living in each block is the same throughout the city,"[19] our index measures the minimum percentage of blacks who would have to change the *census tract* in which they live in order to produce an unsegregated distribution. We use tracts rather than blocks as our unit of analysis because the larger unit appears more appropriate for testing the effects of housing segregation on labor-market opportunities.

In addition to using the (Ta) index of segregation, we also need to know whether the tracts that are predominately black are concentrated in one large ghetto or whether they are spread out in a number of smaller clusters. To measure ghettoization, we begin by defining a black census tract to be any tract that is at least 50 percent black. Then a ghetto is defined as a contiguous group of black tracts, and the average size of the ghettos in an SMSA is defined to be a weighted average of the size of each ghetto with the relative black populations used as weights. This measure of average size represents the expected value one would obtain by picking a person at random from the population of blacks living in

---

[18] See Bowen and Finegan, *The Economics of Labor Force Participation* (Princeton, New Jersey: Princeton Univ. Press, 1969); and Glen G. Cain, *Married Women in the Labor Force* (Chicago, Illinois: University of Chicago Press, 1966).

[19] Taeuber and Taeuber, *Negroes in Cities*, p. 30.

black tracts and then determining the size of the ghetto in which he lives.[20]

In our regression analysis we use three variables based on average ghetto size. One (GS/N) is basically a segregation measure, since we divide the average ghetto size by the number of blacks living in black census tracts, thus giving us a measure of the *relative* extent of clustering. However, an absolute measure of ghetto size (GS) is also used since it appears to be the most appropriate variable for testing Kain's transportation and job information arguments. Alternatively, our measures of relative segregation (Ta) and (GS/N) may be more appropriate for testing the arguments based on employer discrimination. Finally we use an interaction variable $GS^2/N = (GS/N) \times GS$ to see if the greatest effect occurs where relative and absolute ghettoization are both high. Both (GS) and (GS^2/N) are measured in 100,000s so that the means for these variables will be similar to those of our other variables. (For means and standard deviations of all variables see Appendix 4B.)

While the Kain–Mooney view is based partly on the prevalence of housing segregation per se, their view also emphasizes differences between central cities and suburbs. Thus we need to consider ways of testing this aspect of their hypothesis. To do so, we shall use two variables that are modifications of those used by Mooney. The first $(CC/SMSA)_{J/P}$ represents the percentage of SMSA jobs that are in the central cities divided by the percentage of the SMSA population living in the central cities. If most blacks are forced to live in the central city, and thus housing segregation has an important effect on their job opportunities, then their relative incomes should be higher the greater the relative number of central-city to suburban jobs. Thus the Kain–Mooney hypothesis suggests a positive relation between $(CC/SMSA)_{J/P}$ and our relative income measures. The second variable $(NCC/SMSA)_{B/W}$ represents the relative percentages of black and white (actually nonblack) males living and working in the SMSA who have suburban jobs. This variable is designed to measure the relative accessibility of surburban jobs to blacks and whites. If the Kain–Mooney

---

[20] Admittedly this approach is more complicated than simply taking an unweighted average of ghetto sizes, a procedure which gives us the expected value we would obtain if we picked a ghetto at random instead of an individual. Since this study is concerned with the effect of segregation on the average black (rather than on the average ghetto), our weighted average approach appears appropriate.

view is correct, then there should be a positive relation between $(NCC/SMSA)_{B/W}$ and our relative income measures.[21]

In Table 4.1 we present regression coefficients and t-values for simple regressions where there is only a single independent variable. Of the fifty-four regressions run, only five have the sign expected under the Kain–Mooney hypothesis (a negative sign for the four segregation measures and a positive sign for the two "central-city" variables), and none of these five even approaches ordinary standards of statistical significance. On the other hand, several of the coefficients are statistically significant in the opposite direction. Thus, these initial results suggest that, if housing segregation and the suburbanization of jobs have had an impact on the relative income of blacks, that impact is small relative to the total impact of other factors. Consequently, we must turn next to the issue of what other variables are likely to affect black–white income ratios. Once other variables have been identified, they can be added to our regressions as control variables.

First, differences in the relative years of school of blacks and whites are likely to be important: (*1*) because they should reflect differences in relative productivities; and (*2*) because differences in relative years of school may reflect differences in white tastes for discrimination across SMSAs.[22] Therefore, we include a variable (YS) which represents the median years of school for black males divided by the median years of school for white (or total) males.[23] We also include a dummy variable (S)

---

[21] Recall that the analogous variables used by Mooney are the ratio of central-city jobs to total jobs in the SMSA and the portion of nonwhites living in the central city and working in the SMSA who have jobs outside the central city. Although Mooney does not seem aware of the problem, the relative size of the central city should have an important positive effect on the first ratio and a corresponding negative effect on the second. If some central cities contain a much higher proportion of the population of their SMSAs due to historical and political rather than economic factors, then the relative size of the central city should have little effect on our dependent variables. However, for Mooney's variables there will be a bias leading toward coefficients of opposite size and equal absolute value. We modified Mooney's variables in an effort to avoid such difficulties.

[22] This second argument is based on the assumption that discrimination against blacks is greatest for those with the most schooling. (For example, many studies, starting with Becker's *Human Capital*, have found that, at least until very recently, additional schooling yields a lower rate of return for blacks than for whites.) If this assumption is correct, those blacks who do not migrate would have less of an incentive to continue their education if they live in a city where there is much discrimination. In addition, for blacks who do migrate, differences in discrimination across SMSAs would be a more important consideration for those with above average schooling.

[23] When the dependent variable is (BE/TE), we use corresponding medians for all men over 25. When it is (BI/TI) ₃₅₋₄₄, we use the medians for those 35–44. When the

TABLE 4.1

Results from Simple Regressions

Independent variables	Dependent variables		
	BI/WI	$(BI/TI)_{40-44}$	BE/TE
National sample ($N = 77$)			
Ta	.220 (1.8)	.182 (1.9)	.106 (1.1)
GS/N	.074 (1.8)	.079 (2.5)^a	.053 (1.7)
GS	.011 (1.5)	.007 (1.2)	.013 (2.3)^a
GS^2/N	.016 (1.7)	.011 (1.5)	.017 (2.5)^a
$(CC/SMSA)_{J/P}$	.000 (0.0)	−.013 (0.5)	−.004 (0.2)
$(NCC/SMSA)_{BIW}$	−.208 (4.1)^b	−.203 (5.2)^b	−.162 (4.2)^b
Non-South sample ($N = 40$)			
Ta	.163 (1.1)	.080 (0.6)	.206 (1.7)
GS/N	.011 (0.3)	.005 (0.2)	−.017 (0.5)
GS	.004 (0.8)	.000 (0.0)	.007 (1.4)
GS^2/N	.006 (0.8)	.001 (0.1)	.008 (1.4)
$(CC/SMSA)_{J/P}$	−.036 (1.1)	−.033 (1.2)	−.020 (0.7)
$(NCC/SMSA)_{BIW}$	−.120 (1.7)	−.063 (1.0)	−.115 (1.9)
South sample ($N = 37$)			
Ta	−.003 (0.0)	.040 (0.4)	−.125 (1.3)
GS/N	.059 (1.2)	.099 (2.7)^b	.076 (2.0)^a
GS	.002 (0.1)	.015 (1.0)	.019 (1.4)
GS^2/N	.006 (0.2)	.032 (1.7)	.030 (1.5)
$(CC/SMSA)_{J/P}$	.023 (0.7)	−.002 (0.1)	.005 (0.2)
$(NCC/SMSA)_{BIW}$	−.081 (1.4)	−.151 (3.6)	−.076 (1.6)

^{a} Statistically significant at 95 percent level.
^{b} Statistically significant at 99 percent level.

dependent variable is (BI/WI), we use the median schooling of blacks and whites for men over 25 with the latter estimating from the black and white figures assuming the means and medians are equal and that all men are either blacks or whites. A complicated procedure like this is necessary since there are no data available on the median schooling of whites.

It is appropriate to use YS as a control variable since differences in relative productivities and in tastes for discrimination across SMSAs should be factors that affect black–white income ratios, independently of any effects caused by housing segregation. For a more extended discussion, see the concluding section, especially footnote 38.

for South in our national regressions since tastes for discrimination against blacks appear to be greater in the South than in the rest of the country. Moreover, we shall continue running separate regressions for SMSAs in the South and non-South.

Since changes in the aggregate unemployment rate have a significant effect on the black–white income ratio (as discussed in Chapter 2), we include a variable (U) for the male unemployment rate. We also include a variable (B) for the black population divided by the white (or total)[24] population, since Becker's theory of discrimination predicts greater market discrimination when there are relatively large numbers of blacks. (See Chapter 1.)[25]

Finally we include two variables for industrial structure. First, the negative results for $(NCC/SMSA)_{B/W}$ suggest the possibility that blacks may have ready access to some jobs outside the central city—namely low-paying agricultural jobs. To test this hypothesis, we include a variable (Ag) for the percentage of employed males with jobs in agriculture. Second, Franklin has indicated that the black–white income ratio should be positively correlated with interurban variations in the capital–labor ratio. In his words:

> Urban economies which are dominated by capital-intensive modes of production have large-scale enterprises guided by impersonally oriented managers who have little need to form "coalitions" with consumers for the purpose of discrimination. Capital-intensive modes of production generally separate the product and/or service from the worker. Moreover, the technical conditions of production, such as big assembly plants and/or machines which are operated by one person and involve a repetitive process, tend to require a minimum of personal interaction on equal terms or interaction on terms in which the Negro has jobs vested with authority over whites. Therefore, the employer in capital-intensive operations has less reason to be concerned with the product-color connection which is made by the consumer or the breakdown of the dominant–subordinate human relations pattern which tends to operate as a barrier to the Negro's occupational mobility.[26]

[24] We use the total population when the dependent variable is (BE/TE) or $(BI/TI)_{35-44}$.

[25] Recall that Becker's analysis on this point assumes that tastes for discrimination are similar in each SMSA (or greater in SMSAs with relatively more blacks), that there is at least some competition in each local economy, and that there is some dispersion in tastes for discrimination. None of these assumptions appears unreasonable.

[26] Raymond S. Franklin, "A Framework for the Analysis of Interurban Negro–White Economic Differentials," *The Industrial and Labor Relations Review* 21 (April 1968): 370.

While Franklin makes no attempt to test his hypothesis empirically, we can make such a test if we assume that the capital–labor ratio is higher in manufacturing than in most other industries. Moreover, even if this assumption is incorrect, Franklin appears to be talking about manufacturing rather than any other potentially capital-intensive sectors. Thus we include a variable (Man) for the proportion of employed males with jobs in manufacturing.[27]

Results for regressions that include all of these potential control variables simultaneously are presented in Table 4.2. The first three columns show regression results for the total sample. These results show that when an SMSA has a relatively large percentage of its male employment in agriculture the relative income of blacks generally declines—a result which makes sense if many of the nonagricultural workers are black and receive very low wages.[28] To gauge the relevance of this finding, we need to know where the agricultural workers live—especially the black workers. If many black agricultural workers live in the central city, then we would have evidence that, contrary to the Kain–Mooney hypothesis, many blacks are able and willing to hold jobs even when these jobs are low-paying and the distance from home is considerable. On the other hand, if most agricultural workers reside in the outlying rural part of the SMSA, such workers should be excluded from our analysis since we want to treat SMSAs as urban labor markets.[29] Unfortunately the census data do not enable us to determine where these workers live. Thus, it appears desirable to present results where the sample is limited to SMSAs where nonagricultural employment is relatively unimportant for both blacks and whites. As a result, the last three columns in Table 4.3 present results based on a sample that is restricted to SMSAs where

[27] Reder suggests that a high percentage of employment in manufacturing will reduce wage differentials by skill since (*1*) manufacturing involves a high proportion of semi-skilled labor and (*2*) such labor allows for greater substitution (and competition) between workers of different skill levels. If this theory is correct, and if blacks are primarily in low-skilled groups, then we have another argument supporting the expectation that the black–white income ratio is positively related to the percentage of employment in manufacturing. See Melvin W. Reder, "The Theory of Occupational Wage Differentials," *American Economic Review* 45 (December 1955): 833–852.

[28] Similar (though slightly weaker) results were obtained when we used a variable for the percentage of blacks employed in agriculture.

[29] Since an SMSA consists of a central city (or cities) and surrounding counties whose economies are interconnected, a county may be included in an SMSA since it is partly suburban, but a considerable portion may still be rural. Ideally, our unit of analysis would not include those living in rural areas. However, census data for "urbanized areas" are much less complete than for SMSAs.

TABLE 4.2

Regression Results for Potential Control Variables
(Dependent Variables and Sample)

Independent variables	Total sample			Nonagricultural sample		
	BI/WI	$(BI/TI)_{40\text{-}44}$	BE/TE	BI/WI	$(BI/TI)_{40\text{-}44}$	BE/TE
	National					
	$N = 77$			$N = 65$		
Ag	−.013 (2.2)[a]	−.009 (2.1)[a]	−.013 (2.6)[a]	−.023 (2.4)[a]	−.008 (1.2)	−.018 (2.0)[a]
U	−.001 (0.1)	.004 (0.8)	.001 (0.3)	−.003 (0.5)	−.001 (0.1)	.000 (0.0)
B	−.165 (2.2)[a]	−.034 (0.4)	.032 (0.3)	−.021 (0.2)	.117 (2.0)[a]	.153 (1.4)
YS	.255 (2.4)[a]	.401 (4.8)[b]	.254 (2.6)[a]	.372 (3.2)[b]	.549 (5.9)[b]	.295 (2.6)[a]
Man	.167 (2.6)[a]	.248 (5.2)[b]	.162 (2.9)[b]	.195 (3.0)[b]	.290 (6.3)[b]	.165 (2.8)[b]
S	−.040 (2.0)[a]	−.029 (2.1)[a]	−.034 (2.0)[a]	−.056 (2.8)[b]	−.043 (3.3)[b]	−.049 (2.7)[b]
$\bar{R}^2$	.63	.70	.53	.63	.69	.48

Non-South

	N = 40			N = 37		
Ag	−.021 (2.8)[b]	−.006 (0.9)	−.016 (2.8)[b]	−.027 (2.6)[a]	−.010 (1.0)	−.019 (2.5)[a]
U	.004 (0.6)	.000 (0.0)	.007 (1.4)	.003 (0.4)	−.003 (0.5)	.005 (1.2)
B	−.042 (0.3)	.018 (0.1)	.124 (0.9)	.009 (0.1)	.086 (0.5)	.219 (1.7)
YS	.476 (3.9)[b]	.564 (3.4)[b]	.318 (3.0)[b]	.354 (2.7)[b]	.523 (3.2)[b]	.202 (1.9)
Man	.305 (4.5)[b]	.317 (4.9)[b]	.278 (5.1)[b]	.275 (3.9)[b]	.311 (4.6)[b]	.249 (4.8)[b]
$\bar{R}^2$	.53	.43	.58	.44	.43	.57

South

	N = 37			N = 28		
Ag	−.015 (1.8)	−.013 (2.3)[a]	−.014 (1.8)	−.007 (0.3)	−.008 (0.7)	−.009 (0.4)
U	−.024 (1.8)	.007 (0.7)	−.019 (1.5)	−.026 (1.7)	.009 (1.0)	−.019 (1.3)
B	.268 (2.8)[b]	−.112 (1.1)	−.023 (0.2)	−.104 (0.7)	.275 (2.2)[a]	.078 (0.4)
YS	.033 (0.2)	.312 (2.7)[b]	.173 (1.1)	.192 (0.9)	.672 (4.9)[b]	.221 (0.9)
Man	−.116 (1.1)	.163 (2.1)[a]	−.075 (0.7)	−.039 (0.3)	.298 (4.0)[b]	−.063 (0.5)
$\bar{R}^2$	.42	.51	.20	.14	.50	.14

[a] Statistically significant at the 95 percent level.
[b] Statistically significant at the 99 percent level.

agricultural workers account for less than 4 percent of either black or total male employment. In these regressions the percent in agriculture still has a strong negative effect, especially outside the South. Since the magnitude of the coefficients remains so large [e.g., a 1 percentage point increase in (Ag) leads to as much as a 2.7 percentage point decline in relative incomes], the results suggest that the percent in agriculture has indirect as well as direct effects on the black–white income ratio.[30] For example, the size of the agricultural sector may affect the composition of black migrants to the SMSA.[31]

Turning next to the results for the other independent variables, we see that the results for the unemployment rate are consistently insignificant. The discrepancy between these results and the time-series results discussed in Chapter 2 appears reasonable, if we assume that blacks have fewer firm-specific skills than whites and that firms want to hold workers with firm-specific skills during *temporary* slack periods so that they will be available when demand increases. While changes in the unemployment rate from year to year do represent such temporary changes, differences in unemployment rates across SMSAs are likely to represent relatively long-term differences where this human capital argument would be much less relevant.

The other variable that is generally, though not always, statistically insignificant is the relative size of the black population. Here we do find one significant negative relation in the results for the total samples, but, when the agricultural SMSAs are excluded, the results become generally positive and sometimes significantly so. The discrepancy between the total and nonagricultural samples can be explained by relatively large numbers of blacks living in SMSAs where employment opportunities in agriculture are plentiful. The positive results in the nonagricultural samples may indicate either that migration patterns by race are influenced by relative incomes or that blacks have more economic and political power in SMSAs where they constitute a relatively large percentage of the population.[32] In any event, the data do not support the

[30] Recall that although most of our variables are in ratio form, (Ag) and (U) are in percentage terms since otherwise their values would be much smaller than those of the other variables.

[31] The agriculture variable does become insignificant when we eliminate all SMSAs with more than 1 percent of black employment in agriculture—although the t-values are often as high as 1.6. In our judgment such a cutoff is too severe (*1*) because the agriculture variable may represent legitimate indirect effects and (*2*) because too few observations would remain, especially in the South. We based the cutoff on black employment in agriculture for reasons discussed in footnote 40.

[32] I am indebted to William K. Tabb for suggesting the latter of these hypotheses.

prediction, based on Becker's theory, of greater market discrimination when the black population is large relative to the white.

Our other independent variables do have the expected signs and are generally statistically significant. For example, the black–white income ratios are lower in the South, ceteris paribus.

The results for relative educational levels are uniformly positive and almost always statistically significant, except sometimes in the South.[33] As indicated earlier, these results could reflect differences in relative productivities by race. On the other hand, differences in relative years of school may reflect differences in white tastes for discrimination across SMSAs.

Perhaps the most striking results are the strong positive relation between the percentage of employment in manufacturing and the black–white income ratio, especially outside the South. While these results appear to offer some support to Franklin's view, which stresses the relative impersonality of relations in manufacturing, there are other possible explanations. For example, much manufacturing may require large firms and thus more formal personnel policies, including hiring and promotion policies. If so, then such formal procedures may have made racial discrimination relatively more difficult, especially in the North.[34]

Unionization may also be responsible for these results because (*1*) unions are relatively strong in manufacturing, especially outside the South; and (*2*) Ashenfelter's interstate analysis indicates that unionization has a positive effect on black–white income ratios—probably because of its influence in narrowing occupational skill differentials.[35]

[33] Perhaps in the South there is more discrepancy between the relative educational levels of all male workers and all males over 25 (e.g., because of relative improvements in black schooling). This hypothesis could explain why we do get significant results from the educational variable in the South when the analysis is restricted to males 40–44, but not in the other cases. On the other hand, none of the independent variables are significant in the southern nonagricultural regressions except when $(BI/TI)_{40-44}$ is the dependent variable.

[34] For example, see the discussion in Alfred W. Blumrosen, *Black Employment and the Law* (New Brunswick, New Jersey: Rutgers Univ. Press, 1971), pp. 166–169. While conditions in the South may have changed by 1970, the effects of earlier formal discrimination undoubtedly continue.

[35] See Orley Ashenfelter, "Racial Discrimination and Trade Unions," *Journal of Political Economy* 80 (May–June 1972), Part I. After the rest of the analysis had been completed, data on unionization for the majority of SMSAs were found in Area Wage Surveys, Selected Metropolitan Areas, 1970–1971 BLS Report no. 1685–91. When the unionization variable was added to the total and non-South nonagricultural regressions in Table 4.2, the manufacturing variable remained significant in all cases (despite the smaller sample size) while the unionization variable was never significant.

Of course, the unionization variable is a rather crude measure of union power, since

The main use of our results in Table 4.2 is to identify control variables to add to the analysis in order to make better tests of the net effect of housing segregation on the black–white income ratio. Based on our analysis of the results in Table 4.2, it appears reasonable to restrict the analysis to our sample of nonagricultural SMSAs. Moreover, in each equation we add, as control variables, each variable that is statistically significant in the nonagricultural regressions in Table 4.2 (except we omit the racial composition variable, since here the causation appears likely to run from the black–white income ratio to the racial composition variable). The coefficients and t-values for the segregation variables from these multiple regressions are presented in Table 4.3.

The results in Table 4.3 do provide a little more support for the Kain–Mooney hypothesis than did the simple regressions presented in Table 4.1. Except for the $(CC/SMSA)_{J/P}$ coefficients, almost all the results for the two relative income measures do have the correct sign in the national and non-South samples. Of the coefficients with the sign predicted by the Kain–Mooney theory, however, only one is statistically significant at the 95 percent level.

The strongest results are for (Ta), our modified version of the Taeubers' segregation index. Since this variable should have relatively little bearing on transportation difficulties, the Kain–Mooney view does not suggest that it should generate the best results. On the other hand, the relative strength of this variable appears more reasonable if we assume that differences in tastes for discrimination simultaneously affect both the black–white income ratio and housing segregation.[36]

The only other results that are statistically significant are two of the negative coefficients for $(CC/SMSA)_{J/P}$, the percentage of SMSA jobs that are in the central city divided by the percentage of the SMSA

---

[36] The only other variable that provides any real hint of potential statistical support for the Kain–Mooney view is $(NCC/SMSA)_{B/W}$, the variable representing the relative percentages of black and white males living and working in the SMSA who have suburban jobs. None of the coefficients are statistically significant, however, and the results do not agree with those of Harrison, which are discussed in the concluding section.

---

it is simply a percentage of plant workers employed in establishments where the majority of such workers are under a union contract. On the other hand, we should emphasize that this is the same unionization variable that Ashenfelter used and that he did not include any variable for the importance of manufacturing in his interstate analysis. Thus, his positive results for unionization across states may result, at least in part, from the correlation between unionization and manufacturing.

TABLE 4.3

Results from Multiple Regressions, Nonagricultural Sample

Independent variables	Dependent variables		
	BI/WI	$(BI/TI)_{40-44}$	BE/TE
	National sample ($N = 65$)		
Ta	$-.200$ (2.4)[a]	$-.060$ (0.9)	$-.122$ (1.5)
GS/N	$.028$ (1.0)	$-.002$ (0.1)	$.015$ (0.6)
GS	$-.002$ (0.3)	$-.002$ (0.5)	$.002$ (0.5)
GS^2/N	$-.001$ (0.2)	$-.002$ (0.6)	$.003$ (0.6)
$(CC/SMSA)_{J/P}$	$-.013$ (0.7)	$-.033$ (2.6)[a]	$-.015$ (0.9)
$(NCC/SMSA)_{BI\,W}$	$.071$ (1.6)	$.012$ (0.4)	$.061$ (1.4)
	Non-South sample ($N = 37$)		
Ta	$-.138$ (1.2)	$-.201$ (1.9)	$-.047$ (0.5)
GS/N	$.010$ (0.3)	$-.015$ (0.6)	$-.012$ (0.5)
GS	$-.002$ (0.5)	$-.003$ (1.0)	$.001$ (0.3)
GS^2/N	$-.003$ (0.5)	$-.005$ (1.1)	$.001$ (0.2)
$(CC/SMSA)_{J/P}$	$-.027$ (1.2)	$-.039$ (2.0)[a]	$-.021$ (1.3)
$(NCC/SMSA)_{BI\,W}$	$.066$ (1.1)	$.059$ (1.1)	$.056$ (1.1)
	South sample ($N = 28$)		
Ta	$-.079$ (0.7)	$.005$ (0.1)	$-.108$ (1.0)
GS/N	$.082$ (1.7)	$.023$ (0.7)	$.065$ (1.4)
GS	$.003$ (0.2)	$.011$ (1.1)	$.013$ (0.9)
GS^2/N	$.010$ (0.4)	$.021$ (1.6)	$.023$ (1.1)
$(CC/SMSA)_{J/P}$	$.009$ (0.3)	$-.024$ (1.4)	$-.003$ (0.1)
$(NCC/SMSA)_{BI\,W}$	$-.014$ (0.2)	$-.020$ (0.5)	$.013$ (0.2)

[a] Statistically significant at 95 percent level.

population living in the central city. Recall that we used this variable as a proxy for the relative tightness of the central-city labor market. Since the black population is generally concentrated in the central city,[37] we expected a positive sign for this variable under the Kain–Mooney hypothesis. Since we obtain negative coefficients, it may be that the

[37] For example, see the figures cited in Kain and Persky, "Alternatives to the Gilded Ghetto."

variable really serves more as a proxy for the degree of political and social fragmentation in an SMSA (e.g., the extent to which most of the better residential areas lie outside the central cities). In this case, such fragmentation may be either a partial cause or a result of race–class animosities.

On the basis of the results in Table 4.3, together with our earlier criticism of Kain's work, we conclude that there is very little support for the hypothesis that housing segregation affects the relative money incomes of blacks. Additional support for this conclusion, together with various qualifications, will be discussed in the next section.

II. Conclusion and Qualifications

Our basic conclusion is that we have found no support for the hypothesis that housing segregation, together with the suburbanization of jobs, has had a significant effect on the black–white income ratio. While we have not attempted to test alternative explanations for this finding, two obvious possibilities are (*1*) Noll's hypothesis that central-city labor markets are tighter than suburban ones and (*2*) the hypothesis that blacks can find suburban jobs without undue difficulty when such jobs are open to blacks.

With regard to qualifications, we should begin by emphasizing that we have not directly tested Kain's view that housing segregation affects the amount of employment among blacks. In Appendix 4A, however, we do present a few results in which the dependent variable represents relative employment rates. While these results provide a little support for Kain's view, the results are still generally quite weak. Moreover, our relative income measures are much more relevant to the concerns in this book.

Even if we restrict our attention to the results for relative income, a number of possible qualifications must still be discussed. First, housing segregation may have an indirect effect on relative black incomes as a result of its effect on the education of blacks. Since it is not known where a person attended school, there is no satisfactory way to deal with this problem using our cross-section data. Unless housing and school desegregation leads to reduced tastes for discrimination against blacks, it does not seem likely that such desegregation would have any appreciable impact on black educational opportunities.[38] For example, blacks

---

[38] Since housing segregation might possibly affect relative years of school, it is not clear if our results should standardize for schooling differences. However, we suspect that there is enough migration to prevent the schooling of an SMSA's present population from being too closely related to previous, let alone current, housing segregation in that SMSA. Moreover, our simple regression results are less favorable to the Kain–Mooney results than are the results from the multiple regressions.

can be subject to considerable discrimination even within desegregated schools.

On the other hand, housing and school segregation may affect white tastes for discrimination. If there were no migration and no changes in segregation over time, then this effect of housing segregation would be adequately reflected in the results for our segregation variables. While the effects of migration may bias these results toward zero, we doubt that the bias is strong enough to make our segregation coefficients completely insignificant, if segregation really does have a strong effect on tastes for discrimination. Migration may also bias our results toward zero, since SMSAs where segregation is relatively low may attract the most black migrants, and these migrants may have lower incomes than long-term urban residents. However, it is not clear that segregation has any appreciable effect on black migration[39] and our results in Chapter 2 suggest that migrants are not dramatically worse off than nonmigrants.

The importance of the agriculture variable, even in the "nonagricultural" samples, suggests that our results may be affected by the experience of blacks who live outside the regular urban labor market. Moreover, the presence of such blacks may simultaneously reduce both the segregation measures and the black–white income ratios, thus leading to a positive bias in the coefficients for the segregation variables. However, the general pattern of the results in Table 4.3 was unchanged when we reran these regressions for a sample where we imposed the additional restriction that less than 1 percent of the black employment be in agriculture.[40]

With regard to more general qualifications, we note that, in addition to measuring the relative quality of jobs, our relative income measures are also designed to give us some idea of the relative economic well-being

---

[39] In an earlier study using 1960 Census data, we tested this hypothesis and found that segregation had no significant effect on the relative migration ratio. See Stanley H. Masters, "The Effect of Housing Segregation on Black–White Income Differentials," in *Perspectives on Poverty*, ed. Dennis J. Dugan and William H. Leahy (New York: Praeger, 1973). Due to an oversight, we were not able to obtain similar results for 1970, but we know of no reason to expect stronger results in 1970 than in 1960.

[40] In this case, we imposed the restriction on the basis of black (rather than total) employment in agriculture, since this approach appears more relevant in testing the specific bias hypothesis mentioned in the text. (Because only eight observations remained in the South, we only obtained new results for the national and non-South samples.)

The main difference between the results in these more restrictive nonagricultural samples and those reported in Table 4.3 is larger, more significant coefficients for $(CC/SMSA)_{J/P}$ in the national sample. The results for Ta are weaker (and never significant) when the dependent variable is BI/WI, but stronger (and significant in the non-South sample) when the variable is (BI/TI) [40–44].

of blacks and whites. As a result of housing segregation, however, our measures of relative money income may not be a good indication of differences in real income. For example, there is considerable evidence that blacks must pay more for housing as a result of discrimination.[41]

Another general difficulty with our empirical results is the relatively small variation in some of our segregation measures. As Appendix 4B indicates, however, the standard deviation is at least 10 percent of the mean values in almost all cases and is often much larger. Therefore, although we obviously cannot estimate what would happen if there were no segregation, our results are probably relevant when considering the effect of any desegregation likely to occur in the next few years.

Despite the need for some qualifications, our results do suggest that *if* housing segregation has *any* effect on the relative money income of black males, its effect is too weak to be demonstrated by standard empirical techniques. Recently some significant independent evidence has been presented in support of our conclusion. On the basis of data from the 1966 Survey of Economic Opportunity for individuals living in the twelve largest SMSAs, Harrison looks at weekly earnings, annual unemployment, and occupational status for white and nonwhite males living (*1*) in poverty neighborhoods of the central city, (*2*) in other areas of the central cities, and (*3*) in the suburbs.[42] He concludes that

> The white levels improve monotonically with "distance" from the core, while nonwhite opportunity increases somewhat with the "move" from the ghetto to the central city, but falls again with the further "move" out to the suburban ring. . . . Nor are the marginal returns to nonwhite education significantly greater in the suburbs than in the ghetto.[43]

In contrast, those blacks who do live in the suburbs should have a significant advantage over their brethren, if we accept the hypothesis that the average black is significantly handicapped in the labor market because it is difficult for him to find housing near suburban job opportunities. Although these results of Harrison are still subject to some of our qualifications (e.g., the possible effect of housing segregation on

---

[41] Recall the discussion of this issue in Chapter 2.

[42] See Harrison, "Intrametropolitan Distribution."

[43] The quote is taken from an earlier version of Harrison's work, "Education and Underemployment in the Urban Ghetto," in *Problems in Political Economy: An Urban Perspective*, ed. David M. Gordon (Lexington, Massachusetts: Heath, 1971), pp. 187–188. Also, see his article of the same title in *American Economic Review* 62 (December 1972).

quality of schooling), they do strengthen our confidence in our conclusion that housing segregation is not one of the major factors accounting for the relatively low earnings of urban blacks.

To conclude this chapter, let us look more carefully at some of the policy issues involving housing segregation. Kain and Persky, and other proponents of the view that housing segregation has a significant effect on black employment opportunities, have put primary emphasis on the importance of reducing housing segregation.[44] Contrary to their view, our results suggest that there is little reason to stress housing desegregation *as a means of increasing the relative money incomes of blacks*.[45] On the other hand, we should emphasize that housing desegregation may still be a valid means toward a number of other important objectives, such as improving social and other relations between the races (including reducing the chance of riots)[46] or reducing the cost of interurban transportation (e.g., the costs of building expressways and the daily transportation cost of many commuters both white and black).[47] To explain black–white income differentials, however, we need to consider other factors such as labor-market discrimination and racial differences in educational attainment. The relative importance of these two factors will be investigated in Chapter 5.

APPENDIX 4A: Results for Relative Employment Ratios

In the text, we have attempted to relate housing segregation to the relative income and earnings of blacks and have found very little

---

[44] Kain and Persky, "Alternatives to the Gilded Ghetto."

[45] While the effect of housing segregation on black job opportunities may become serious in the future, it appears reasonable to focus present policies primarily on present problems rather than on hypothetical future problems. Of course, a complete analysis would require a discussion of relative benefits *and costs* of alternative programs. The author suspects that pay-offs may be higher, and political costs lower, for policies aimed at (*1*) maintaining high aggregate demand and (*2*) combating discrimination in employment. These issues are discussed in Chapter 7.

[46] For example, see the discussion in Anthony Downs, "Alternative Futures for the American Ghetto," *Daedalus* 99 (Fall 1968).

[47] See Kain and Persky, "Alternatives to the Gilded Ghetto."

evidence of any negative relationship. However, most of the previous literature on this topic has focused on the relation between housing segregation and black employment rather than black earnings. To express the distinction a little differently, other studies of this issue have focused on the relative quantity rather than the relative quality of black jobs.

The relative quality and quantity of jobs available to blacks should be closely related. For example, if blacks are severely handicapped by the inaccessibility of good suburban jobs, there should be a direct effect on the quantity of jobs available to blacks. However, this handicap should also increase the relative supply of blacks competing for the limited jobs available in the central city. Therefore, as long as wage rates are at least somewhat affected by supply and demand considerations, housing segregation should affect relative wage rates as well as relative employment rates. Moreover, employment rates presumably depend, at least in part, on the quality as well as the quantity of available jobs. Consequently, our earlier results on relative earnings should be of some relevance in testing the hypothesis that housing segregation affects the quantity of jobs available to blacks.

A more direct test of the quantity hypothesis is available, however. To estimate the impact of housing segregation on black male employment, we can begin by calculating the percentage of males over 14 who are employed for blacks and for whites.[48] As a result of various kinds of discrimination, we expect this percentage to be lower for blacks than for whites. Our concern is whether the racial differential varies with housing segregation. To test this hypothesis, we run results where the dependent variable is $BJ\%/WJ\% = [(BJ/BP)/(WJ/WP)]$, where J = employed, P = population, B = black, and W = white.

While this variable for relative employment rates has the advantage of being closely related to the concerns of Kain and Mooney, it does have some important disadvantages as a measure of the relative job opportunities available to blacks and whites. Employment, like earnings, is determined by supply as well as demand. While the effect of supply on earnings is limited, since we control for relative years of school and ignore those with no earnings in 1959, there is no equally promising method to reduce the effect of supply on our employment measures. Three specific difficulties arise. First, the relative employment measure may be heavily affected by those who have enough income or wealth to

[48] Due to data limitations, whites are defined here as the total nonblack population.

retire early or to devote their time exclusively to schoolwork while they are young. This difficulty might be reduced by limiting the analysis to prime-age males. The Kain–Mooney hypothesis, however, might apply with greatest force to the young and the old, since they may suffer the most serious transportation difficulties. Moreover, the other difficulties would still remain. Perhaps the most important problem of the relative employment measure is that it will be heavily affected by the behavior of those with a marginal attachment to the labor force, while we should probably be at least equally concerned with the opportunities of those who will find some job, no matter how little it pays or how unattractive it may appear. Finally, the Census has traditionally undercounted the number of black males, and it seems likely that many of those who are missed are men without regular employment.

Because of these difficulties with the relative employment measure and because our main concern in this book is with income differentials, we present only a few very simple results for relative employment. Specifically, in Table 4A.1, we present standardized regression coefficients and t-values for simple regressions for each of the six independent variables we have been using to test the Kain–Mooney hypothesis. Thus, these regressions are analogous to those presented in Table 4.1 of the text, except that the sample is limited to those SMSAs where agricultural employment is relatively unimportant (as in Table 4.3 and the second half of Table 4.2). On the basis of these regressions we hope to see whether housing segregation and the suburbanization of jobs has had

TABLE 4.A1

Results for Relative Employment Rates

Independent variables	National	Non-South	South
		Samples	
Ta	.077 (0.6)	.111 (0.8)	.168 (0.8)
GS/N	−.106 (2.6)[a]	−.039 (1.1)	−.158 (2.1)[a]
GS	−.002 (0.1)	.003 (0.5)	−.009 (0.3)
GS^2/N	−.004 (0.4)	.002 (0.3)	−.028 (0.7)
$(CC/SMSA)_{J/P}$	.010 (0.3)	−.013 (0.4)	.032 (0.6)
$(NCC/SMSA)_{B/W}$	.058 (1.0)	−.087 (1.3)	.063 (0.7)

[a] Statistically significiant at 95 percent level.

any *major* impact on the relative employment of blacks—an impact large enough to appear when no standardization is made for other factors.

The only significant results are for GS/N, the relative extent of ghettoization. Although the negative coefficients for this variable do support the Kain–Mooney hypothesis, it is rather surprising that the strongest results occur in the South and that the coefficients are all insignificant in the North, where Kain and many supporters of his view have focused their attention and concern. Thus, we conclude that, on the basis of our very simple test, the Kain–Mooney hypothesis does not appear to be very much more useful in explaining relative employment rates than in explaining relative incomes.

APPENDIX 4B: Means and Standard Deviations for the Variables

	National Total		National NonAg		Non-South Total		Non-South NonAg		South Total		South NonAg	
	$\bar{X}$	S_x	$\bar{X}$	S_x	$\bar{X}$	S_x	$\bar{X}$	S_x	$\bar{X}$	S_x	$\bar{X}$	S_x
BI/WI	.632	.093	.648	.084	.692	.066	.700	.058	.568	.072	.579	.060
$(BI/TI)_{40-44}$	.640	.075	.655	.065	.687	.054	.691	.052	.590	.060	.608	.048
BE/TE	.708	.071	.721	.065	.748	.055	.755	.049	.664	.059	.676	.056
$BJ\%/WJ\%$	.886	.094	.878	.072	.863	.059	.872	.051	.910	.118	.885	.093
Ta	.781	.087	.783	.085	.800	.071	.810	.063	.760	.099	.746	.098
GS/N	.671	.257	.703	.251	.713	.260	.710	.265	.626	.249	.693	.234
GS	.876	1.422	.969	1.519	1.098	1.842	1.178	1.895	.636	.692	.692	.736
GS^2/N	.630	1.129	.707	1.204	.831	1.472	.892	1.515	.412	.498	.463	.517
$(CC/SMSA)_{J/P}$	1.44	.351	1.44	.362	1.44	.329	1.44	.329	1.43	.378	1.44	.408
$(NCC/SMSA)_{B/W}$	.721	.190	.688	.165	.650	.143	.643	.129	.798	.620	.747	.191
Ag	1.89	1.31	1.54	0.69	1.63	1.11	1.43	0.75	2.18	1.44	1.68	5.75
U	3.48	1.16	3.43	1.15	3.91	1.32	3.82	1.25	3.01	.71	2.90	0.73
$B(B/W)$	.193	.133	.177	.111	.119	.062	.120	.060	.272	.144	.254	.118
$B(B/T)$	.151	.086	.143	.076	.103	.049	.103	.047	.204	.086	.194	.076
$YS(B/W)$	.799	.110	.820	.089	.872	.066	.871	.060	.721	.093	.754	.077
$YS(B/T)_{40-44}$	.841	.081	.857	.066	.885	.051	.882	.049	.794	.082	.823	.071
$YS(B/T)$	.823	.091	.841	.074	.882	.060	.881	.055	.760	.076	.788	.062
Man	.301	.113	.321	.110	.341	.116	.354	.111	.258	.092	.278	.094
S	.481	.503	.431	.499	.000	.000	.000	.000	1.00	.000	1.00	.000

5

Estimating the Relative Importance of Labor-Market Discrimination versus Differences in Productivity between Blacks and Whites[1]

In Chapters 3 and 4, we showed that, subject to some qualifications, the earnings gap between black and white urban males does not result either from handicaps facing migrants to the large cities or from problems associated with housing segregation. In this chapter, we shall attempt to estimate the relative importance of the two most obvious possible explanations for the racial earnings gap: (1) labor-market discrimination, and (2) differences in education and other variables related to productivity.

Numerous studies have been done on this topic. Therefore, we start with a selective review of the literature. Stephan Michelson's work is a convenient starting point, valuable for its end results and also for its excellent review of literature.[2] Michelson seeks to determine how much of the racial earnings gap should be attributed to differences in age, years of school, occupation, and job within an occupation. In order to facilitate the analysis of interaction effects, Michelson uses a matrix mul-

---

[1] A similar version of this chapter appeared in the *Journal of Human Resources* 9 (© Summer 1974 by the Regents of the University of Wisconsin System), pp. 342–360.
[2] Stephan Michelson, "Incomes of Racial Minorities," (Washington, D.C.: The Brookings Institution, 1968). (Also, Ph.D. diss., Stanford University, 1968.)

97

TABLE 5.1

Michelson's Results for Racial Earnings Gap

	Percent of racial earnings gap accounted for by each factor	
	Ages 21–36	Ages 45–60
1) Age	0.0	0.0
2) Years of school	6.3	8.7
3) Occupation	5.5	8.2
4) Job within occupation	61.4	50.2
5) Interactions	26.8	32.9
2, 3	−4.1	−3.4
2, 4	1.6	6.0
3,4	19.4	18.6
2, 3, 4	9.9	11.7

SOURCE: Stephan Michelson, "Income of Racial Minorities," (Washington, D.C.: The Brookings Institution, 1968).

tiplication approach. His main results, based on data for white and black males from the 1/1000 sample of the 1960 Census, are presented in Table 5.1.[3] For both age groups, discrimination is most important within occupations, while interaction effects are more important than the separate effects of schooling or occupation.

TABLE 5.2

Revised Version of Michelson's Results

	Percent of racial earnings gap accounted for	
	Ages 21–36	Ages 45–60
1) Age	0.0	0.0
2) Schooling	6.3	8.7
3) Employment (occupation and job + their interaction)	86.3	91.3
4) Interaction	7.4	0.0

SOURCE: Calculated from figures in Table 5.1 by the author.

[3] Ibid., Chapter 4, p. 15.

Since our major interest is in the relative effects of education versus labor–market discrimination, with the latter including both occupation and job components,[4] we have combined the occupation and job effects in Table 5.2.

These results indicate that, if years of school are an adequate measure of education, then labor-market discrimination is much more important than differences in education as an explanation for the black–white income gap. Michelson indicates that these results are consistent with other results on black–white differentials (provided one interprets these results properly).[5] Thus, he comments:

> Economists and sociologists in and out of the government have presented measures of the amount of the white–nonwhite income differential (not always defined the same way) which is attributable to differences in nominal schooling, as compared with that attributable to labor market discrimination and real differences in the quality of labor at equal schooling levels. Regression analysis and simpler forms of standardization have been employed. The major fault with the procedures used lies in their failure to account for interactions of the causal mechanisms. The measures employed by the Council of Economic Advisers (via Katzner), the Department of Commerce, Paul Siegel and Lester Thurow, all were shown to be substantially in error. More importantly, when each was corrected the amount of the income difference attributable to different years of school was "small"—under 20 percent. Lassiter's equations, though assuming linearity of the schooling effect, produced equally low estimates of the education's effect on nonwhite income.[6]

Duncan has also dealt with these issues.[7] As part of his study, he calculates separate regressions for whites and blacks (using 1962 data for

[4] Also note that the results for occupation depend on the number of occupational categories. Michelson used eighteen, a fairly large number, but if he had used more his results for occupation would probably have been larger.

[5] Using somewhat similar techniques applied to 1960 data for those in certain states, Fogel compares results for various minority groups. He finds that, in comparison with blacks, differences in years of school account for more of the "ethnic income gap" for Puerto Ricans, others with Spanish surname, and Chinese, but less of the gap for Indians, Filipinos, and Japanese. Only for those with a Spanish surname in the Southwest do years of school account for a majority of the gap. Walter Fogel, "The Effect of Educational Attainment on Incomes," *Journal of Human Resources* 1 (Fall 1966).

[6] Michelson, "Incomes of Racial Minorities," Chapter 2, p. 37.

[7] Otis Dudley Duncan, "Inheritance of Poverty or Inheritance of Race?" in *On Understanding Poverty*, ed. Daniel P. Moynihan (New York: Basic Books, 1968). Note that Duncan's basic answer is that, aside from racial differences, family background has relatively little effect on a person's income.

TABLE 5.3

Duncan's Estimates for the Components of the Racial Income Gap
(in dollars)

White income	7070	
		940—Father's background
Estimate from Regression 1	6130	
		70—Number of siblings
Estimate from Regression 2	6060	
		520—Years of school
Estimate from Regression 3	5540	
		830—Occupation
Estimate from Regression 4	4710	
		1430—Income
Black income	3280	

SOURCE: Otis Dudley Duncan, "Inheritance of Poverty or Inheritance of Race?" in *On Understanding Poverty*, ed. Daniel P. Moynihan (New York: Basic Books, 1968). © 1968, 1969 by The American Academy of Arts and Sciences, Basic Books, Inc., Publishers, p. 98.

native men, 25–64, with nonfarm backgrounds)[8] with annual earnings as the dependent variable and with the following sets of independent variables: (*1*) father's education and occupation; (*2*) these two variables plus number of siblings; (*3*) these three variables plus years of school; and (*4*) these four variables plus occupation.[9] In each case, the mean black values for the independent variables are then substituted into the white regressions.[10] The results are presented in Table 5.3.

The differences between these results are Duncan's estimates of the effect of the various independent variables on the income gap. Of the total gap of $3790, the components that can be labeled discrimination in employment (occupation and income) account for $2260 (or about 60 per-

[8] These data are described in more detail in Peter M. Blau and Otis Dudley Duncan, *The American Occupational Structure* (New York: Wiley, 1967).

[9] Measured on Duncan's scale of occupational socio-economic status.

[10] As Duncan indicates ("Inheritance of Poverty," p. 102): "It follows, therefore, that the hypothetical calculations are to be taken to represent what would happen only if the Negro were allowed to play the same game as whites in addition to receiving a 'handicap score' bonus to compensate for the effects of impediments to achievement in present generations. The estimates exhibited here are based on the hypothesis that both types of handicaps are eliminated." Another way of putting it is to say that the estimates combine the effects of changes in the independent variables with interaction effects.

cent) while the components for family background and years of school account for only $1530.[11]

As Duncan and Michelson both recognize, an important problem with such studies is that years of school do not measure all aspects of educational attainment. Duncan deals with this problem by presenting an alternative set of results, which include mental ability as one of the variables. Unfortunately, however, correlations had to be estimated from a variety of data resources, a procedure which Duncan recognizes as quite risky.[12] Although a majority of the correlations were obtained from 1964 CPS data for men 25 to 34, where the measure of mental ability is a person's AFQT score, it appears that Duncan's main results, presented in Table 5.4, are based on estimates of early IQ as the measure of mental ability.

In comparing the results from Tables 5.3 and 5.4, we see that adding

TABLE 5.4

Duncan's Results with Component for Mental Ability
(in dollars)

White earnings	6730	
		560—Father's background
Estimate from Regression 1	6170	
		100—Siblings
Estimate from Regression 2	6070	
		650—Mental ability
Estimate from Regression 2a	5420	
		70—Education
Estimate from Regression 3	5350	
		350—Occupation
Estimate from Regression 4	5000	
		1200–1460—Earnings
Black earnings	3600–3800	

SOURCE: Otis Dudley Duncan, "Inheritance of Poverty or Inheritance of Race?" in *On Understanding Poverty*, ed. Daniel P. Moynihan (New York: Basic Books, 1968). © 1968, 1969 by The American Academy of Arts and Sciences, Basic Books, Inc., Publishers, p. 106.

[11] Recently, Blinder achieved similar results decomposing black and white differentials in hourly wages using data from the "Panel Study of Income Dynamics" of the Michigan Survey Research Center. See Alan S. Blinder, "Wage Discrimination: Reduced Form and Structural Estimates," *Journal of Human Resources* 8 (Fall 1973).

[12] Many of the details are presented in Otis Dudley Duncan, "Ability and Achievement," *Eugenics Quarterly* 15 (March 1968).

mental ability as a separate component has relatively little effect on the other results, except for education and, to a lesser extent, occupation. With regard to our main interest, more than half the racial earnings gap is still attributed to labor-market discrimination (occupation plus earnings components). However, including mental ability might have been more effective if it had been measured in terms of adult achievement (e.g., AFQT scores) rather than as childhood IQ. If so, then the estimate for labor-market discrimination, a residual, would have been lower. In addition, conclusions based on those under 35 may not apply for older workers. As a result of these difficulties, Duncan's mental-ability results must be treated cautiously.

Another recent study by Gwartney is relevant to the topic of this section. In Gwartney's words:

> This study seeks to break down the income differential between whites and nonwhites into two categories: (a) a differential resulting from differences in productivity factors not directly related to employment discrimination, and (b) a residual unaccounted for by differences in productivity factors and which may result largely from employment discrimination.[13]

Like Duncan, Gwartney also attempts to use test scores in his analysis, but his methods of calculation and data sources are quite different from Duncan's.[14]

Gwartney uses aggregate data for urban males—mainly from the 1960 Census with test-score results from the Coleman report—to calculate what he calls indices of income differences and distributional differences. The income indices, which are the most important for our purposes, are defined in Table 5.5.

In 1959, the median unadjusted nonwhite income was 58.3 percent of the white income. After adjusting for years of school, scholastic achievement, state, city size, and age, Gwartney obtains a value of 86.5 for the

[13] James D. Gwartney, "Discrimination and Income Differentials," *American Economic Review* 60 (June 1970): 396.

[14] While Duncan and Gwartney take account of the fact that years of school are not an ideal measure of educational attainment by using test-score data, Finis Welch tries a different approach. [See Finis Welch, "Labor Market Discrimination in the Rural South," *Journal of Political Economy* 75 (June 1967).] He estimates the effect of differences in school inputs on earnings and then calculates the effect that equalizing school inputs by race would have on racial earnings differentials. However, Welch's empirical analysis is limited to those in the rural South and is concerned primarily with explaining why nonwhites in that area receive a lower pay-off than whites for extra years of schooling.

TABLE 5.5

Gwartney's Income Indices

Laspeyres	$\displaystyle\sum \frac{Yn \times Dw}{Yw \times Dw}$
Paasche	$\displaystyle\sum \frac{Yn \times Dn}{Yw \times Dn}$

where Y is the median income of those with income within productivity categories (e.g., age, education, or region)

D is the percent of the population with income within the productivity category

n represents nonwhite

w represents white

SOURCE: James D. Gwartney, "Discrimination and Income Differentials," *American Economic Review* 60 (June 1970): 396.

Lespeyres index and 80.9 for the Paasche.[15] These results imply that (*1*) differences in these factors account for 68 percent of the racial income gap, (*2*) labor-market discrimination accounts for 33 percent, and (*3*) there is a negative interaction effect of 1 percent.[16] This estimate for

[16] Roughly similar results are obtained for median and mean earnings for those in nonfarm occupations using region, age, years of school, and scholastic achievement as the independent variables.

[16] Let Iw $\quad$ = white income

$\qquad In \quad$ = nonwhite income

$\qquad In(w) = \sum Yn \times Dw$

$\qquad Iw(n) = \sum Yw \times Dn$

$\qquad L \quad$ = Laspeyres income index = $100 \, In(w)/Iw$

$\qquad P \quad$ = Paasche income index = $In/Iw(n)$.

Then the proportion of the income gap due to differences in productivity characteristics is

$$\frac{In(w) - In}{Iw - In} = \frac{.01L - (In/Iw)}{1 - In/Iw} = \frac{.865 - .583}{.417} = .68 \text{ or } 68 \text{ percent,}$$

while the portion of the gap due to labor-market discrimination is

$$\frac{Iw(n) - In}{Iw - In} = \frac{(1/P) - 1}{(Iw/In) - 1} = \frac{(1/.809) - 1}{(1/.583) - 1} = .33 \text{ or } 33 \text{ percent.}$$

labor-market discrimination is considerably lower than the estimates derived from Michelson and Duncan.

When the only independent variable is years of school, this variable accounts for 21 percent of the gap with a positive interaction effect of 19 percent. Most of the difference between these results and the preceding set comes from the scholastic achievement variable. Gwartney accounts for differences in scholastic achievement (Coleman report test scores) in the following manner:

> The income ratio of nonwhites to whites after adjustment for both quantity of education and scholastic achievement was estimated by comparing the actual income of nonwhite urban males in an education cell with the income of white urban males equal in achievement level with the nonwhites of the education cell.[17]

We shall return to these results, and criticisms of them, after presenting our own test-score results in Section IV.

I. The Conceptual Framework

In this chapter, we follow a modified version of Duncan's approach, while incorporating some of Michelson's ideas. Separate earnings functions will be estimated for blacks and for whites. Let us assume, for the moment, that these earnings functions are specified perfectly (i.e., given a set of values for the independent variables, we can predict the individual's earnings with perfect accuracy). Then we shall define labor-market discrimination as the difference between black and white earnings that would exist if blacks and whites had the same average values for all the independent variables.

Operationally, we estimate the effect of labor-market discrimination by substituting the mean black values for the independent variables into our white earnings function. Let this result be represented by $f_W(\bar{B})$ and let the actual mean earnings of blacks be represented by $\bar{E}_B$. Then, if the earnings function were specified perfectly, $f_W(\bar{B}) - \bar{E}_B$ would

---

[17] Gwartney, "Discrimination and Income Differentials," pp. 400–401.

represent the effect of labor-market discrimination against blacks.[18] As we shall see, this approach is rather crude since it basically defines labor-market discrimination as a residual, despite the fact that our earnings functions are far from being specified perfectly (in considerable part because of the lack of data).[19] Given current limitations with regard to earnings functions, however, there does not appear to be any superior approach available.

The effect of differences in all the independent variables will be estimated by substituting the average white values for these variables into the black earnings functions and calculating $f_B(\bar{W}) - \bar{E}_B$. Note that this effect plus the effect of labor-market discrimination may not add up to the total racial earnings gap. Symbolically $[f_W(\bar{B}) - \bar{E}_B] + [f_B(\bar{W}) - \bar{E}_B]$ need not equal $\bar{E}_W - \bar{E}_B$. Intuitively, if labor-market discrimination were eliminated and if blacks were also given the white values for education and the other independent variables, the total effect might be greater or less than the individual effects since blacks with above average education may face greater or less discrimination in the labor market. Consequently, we will also need to be concerned with an interaction effect, defined as the residual

$$\bar{E}_W - \bar{E}_B - [f_W(\bar{B}) - \bar{E}_B] - [f_B(\bar{W}) - \bar{E}_B]$$

$$= \bar{E}_W + \bar{E}_B - f_W(\bar{B}) - f_B(\bar{W}).$$

In addition to looking at the effect of differences in all the independent variables, we are especially interested in estimating the effect of dif-

---

[18] This approach assumes that we could eliminate labor-market discrimination without changing the white earnings function. While this assumption is not likely to be strictly true, it appears reasonable as a first approximation. See Barbara R. Bergmann, "The Effect on White Income of Discrimination in Employment," *Journal of Political Economy* 79 (March–April 1971), for some results supporting this general view. Note, however, that Bergmann's model does not allow poorly educated whites to lose from discrimination as a result of extra competition from blacks with superior education (or other skills).

We could also measure labor-market discrimination as $E_W - f_B(W)$, but this approach involves the much more dubious assumption that we could give whites the black earnings function without changing that function. This assumption is less realistic than assuming no change in the white earnings function when it is given to blacks for the simple reason that blacks are only a small percentage of the total population.

[19] For example, according to this definition, differences in on-the-job training that are not correlated with our independent variables will be included in labor-market discrimination, since we have no independent variables for such training.

ferences in education, which will be defined both in terms of years of
school and predicted performance on tests. We are more interested in the
effects of education than the effects of some of the other variables,
mainly because educational differences are much more subject to governmental influence than differences in age or location.

II. Empirical Results from the 1960 Census

Earnings functions will be estimated using the 1967 Survey of Economic Opportunity (SEO) and the 1/1000 sample of the 1960 Census.
The results from the 1960 Census will be presented first since this data
source is older and better known. Also, these data do not permit some
interesting, but complicated, new approaches that can be attempted with
the SEO data.

For the 1/1000 analysis, separate earnings functions are obtained for
blacks (Negroes) and for whites who do not have a Spanish surname.
In each case the sample is limited to males 17 to 64 years old who are
not in the armed services, not students, and who worked for some period
during 1959.[20] Females are excluded mainly because the problem of voluntary leisure (discussed later) is much more serious for females than for
males.[21] Those under 17 and over 64 are excluded for the same reason
and also because the number in each educational category who are working is very small. Those in the armed services are excluded since many
are not serving voluntarily, while students are excluded since their labor-
market situation is likely to improve dramatically once they enter the
labor market on a full-time basis.

With regard to disabilities, such as health problems, the ideal approach
would probably be to use health status as a set of independent variables.
Unfortunately, however, health information is not included in the 1/1000
sample. We also want our earnings to be unaffected by any differences in
voluntary leisure. Therefore, we would like information on the amount of
time individuals spent looking for work, but this information is also

---

[20] For whites, 90 percent of the rest are also excluded (on a random basis) to reduce
costs. The total sample sizes are 3676 for whites and 3673 for blacks. The smallest
subsamples are southern whites (938) and non-SMSA blacks (1123).

[21] In addition, racial and sexual discrimination may not be completely additive.
If so, then racial discrimination would appear to be less for females than for males.
See the discussion in Chapter 3, especially Section IV.

missing from the 1/1000 sample. Given these data limitations, we shall simply exclude those who did not work at all in 1959 on the grounds that most able-bodied men who wanted to work presumably could have found at least some employment during the year. For those who worked for part, but not all, of the year these issues are more difficult to resolve since unemployment and temporary health disabilities are both probably important. Therefore, we ran our regression with and without a set of five dummy variables for the number of weeks worked in 1959.

For the dependent variable, we use annual earnings. Other possibilities would be weekly or hourly earnings, but these measures would not be very accurate since the data on weeks and hours worked are rather limited.

The primary independent variables will be a set of joint dummies for age and education. For years of school, we use eight categories and for age we use seven.[22] In addition, we shall use three dummy variables for geographic region and four for the degree of urbanization.

Although these are the kinds of variables that are most frequently included in earnings functions,[23] we do not include some other common variables (e.g., marital status) since we suspect that earnings have as much effect on marital status as marital status has on earnings. However, we shall use a dummy for those who are primarily self-employed since those who go into business for themselves are probably more ambitious and less adverse to taking risks than the average person.[24]

The actual regression results are presented in Appendix 5A. However, our primary interest is not in the earnings functions themselves, but in the magnitude of the racial earnings gap $(\bar{E}_W - \bar{E}_B)$ and in decomposing this gap into (1) a component (DIV) due to differences in the values of the independent variables $[f_B(\bar{W}) - \bar{E}_B]$, (2) a component (LMD) due to labor-market discrimination $[f_W(\bar{B}) - \bar{E}_B]$, and (3) a component $(INTER)$ that results from the interaction between (1) and (2). The results are presented in Table 5.6. The regressions on which they are

[22] The exact variables used, plus some of the regression results, are included in Appendix 5A.

[23] For example, see the earnings function, based on the same data, that Giora Hanoch presents in "An Economic Analysis of Earnings and Schooling," *Journal of Human Resources* 2 (Summer 1967).

[24] A person is considered to be a self-employed businessman if more than half of his earnings are from nonfarm self-employment income. Farm income is not included primarily because we did not want this variable to be highly correlated with our variable for farm status.

TABLE 5.6

Decomposing the Racial Earnings Gap:
Results from 1/1000 Sample, 1960 Census
(in dollars)

Sample	$\bar{E}_W$	$\bar{E}_B$	$\bar{E}_W - \bar{E}_B$	DIV	LMD	INTER
National	5366	2693	2673	457	1728	488
SMSA	6061	3160	2901	450	1949	502
Non-SMSA	4134	1631	2503	906	1141	456
Non-South	5512	3548	1964	−170	1783	351
South	4941	2036	2905	245	1632	1028

NOTE: $\bar{E}_W$ = mean white earnings
            $\bar{E}_B$ = mean black earnings
           DIV   = estimate of effects of differences in productivity in racial
                         earnings gap (see text for exact definition)
        LMD   = estimate of labor-market discrimination
    INTER   = the interaction term, $\bar{E}_W + \bar{E}_B - DIV - LMD$

based do not include the set of dummies for weeks worked. Moreover, the results are presented, not only for the total population, but also separately for those in and outside SMSAs and for those in the North and South. The results for those in SMSAs are of particular interest since this book is primarily concerned with black–white income differentials in metropolitan areas. These results, which are consistent with those of Michelson and Duncan, suggest that labor-market discrimination is much more important than differences in the values of our independent variables. There is also a rather pronounced positive interaction effect, especially in the South.

Again it should be emphasized, however, that these results depend on the assumption that our earnings functions are well specified. To be more concrete, these results are consistent with two quite different interpretations: (1) that labor-market discrimination is primarily responsible for the racial earnings gap; and (2) that variables related to productivity but not included in the earnings functions, such as the *quality* of schooling, are the primary factor. Later in this chapter we shall use data from the SEO and from the AFQT to try to assess the relative importance of education using test scores instead of years of school.

Before turning to the SEO analysis, however, we should examine the results based on regressions that include the set of dummies for weeks worked. Although we are inclined to assume that differences in weeks worked between blacks and whites are primarily the result of differences in the demand for their labor[25]—in which case our earlier results are more appropriate—there could also be important differences in labor supply (e.g., due to differences in health or tastes for leisure). If differences in supply should be more important than differences in demand, then we should standardize for differences in weeks worked in order to get the best estimates of differences in earnings potential. These results, along with our earlier figures, are presented in Table 5.7.

The results standardizing for differences in weeks worked still suggest that labor-market discrimination is more important than the effect of differences in our independent variables—even though labor-market discrimination undoubtedly has some effect on weeks worked and thus on DIV. The main effect of standardizing for differences in weeks worked is to make the interaction effects negative.

The greater importance of differences in the independent variables, DIV, is not surprising since blacks work fewer weeks than whites. The larger estimates for labor-market discrimination are surprising, however, since not only are blacks more likely to be employed for only part of the year but the costs of being employed for part of the year are greater in the white earnings function. Apparently controlling for differences in the amount of employment increases the rest of the earning function more for whites than for blacks. Moreover, this effect must be greater than the

TABLE 5.7

Decomposing the Racial Earnings Gap: With and without Standardization for Weeks Worked, Results from 1/1000 Sample (in dollars)

Sample	Without standardization			With standardization		
	DIV	LMD	$INTER$	DIV	LMD	$INTER$
National	457	1728	488	1608	2463	−1398
SMSA	450	1949	502	929	2638	−666
Non-SMSA	906	1141	456	1342	1937	−776
Non-South	−170	1783	351	547	2419	−1002
South	245	1632	1028	634	2384	−113

NOTE: For definitions of DIV, LMD, and $INTER$ see Table 5.6.

[25] See the results in the next section.

TABLE 5.8

**Decomposing the Racial Earnings Gap: The Effect of Differences
in Years of School, Results from 1/1000 Sample
(in dollars)**

| Sample | Without variables for weeks worked | | | With variables for weeks worked | |
	$\bar{E}_W - \bar{E}_B$	DE	DIV	DE	DIV
National	2673	319	457	286	1608
SMSA	2901	307	450	263	929
Non-SMSA	2503	291	906	293	1342
Non-South	1964	230	−170	177	547
South	2905	279	245	276	634

NOTE: DE = effect of differences in years of school.
For definitions of DIV and $\bar{E}_W - \bar{E}_B$, see Table 5.6.

direct effect of the employment-status variables on our estimates of
labor-market discrimination.

The positive interaction effects, using the first set of earnings functions,
suggest that labor-market discrimination is greater (or achievement
per school year is less) for those with more schooling. On the other hand,
the negative interaction effects when we add the employment-status
variables suggest that blacks with above average schooling *and* steady
jobs may be subject to relatively little wage discrimination.

To conclude this section, let us see how much of the total effect of the
independent variables can be attributed to differences in years of school
(DE). These results are presented in Table 5.8.[26] We see that, in all
cases, differences in schooling account for approximately 10 percent of
the racial earnings gap. Therefore, although young blacks are rapidly
approaching equality with young whites in terms of years of school, we
should not expect this narrowing of the schooling gap to have a major
effect on the earnings gap between blacks and whites.[27]

[26] For making this calculation, we assumed that blacks and whites each had the
same age distribution—specifically a weighted average of these two distributions. The
results are about the same if we use the white or the black distribution instead.

[27] For evidence of the narrowing of the schooling gap, see Marion Hayes, "A
Century of Change: Negroes in the U.S. Economy, 1860–1960," *Monthly Labor
Review* 85 (December 1962). For more recent evidence, see *Social and Economic
Conditions of Negroes in the United States*, a joint publication of the Bureau of Labor
Statistics and the Bureau of the Census, October 1967.

To summarize, we find differences in years of school to have much less effect on the racial earnings gap than "the residual component," which we have tentatively identified as labor-market discrimination but which could also represent other factors, such as differences in the quality of schooling. These results are quite consistent with those obtained by other authors.

In the next section, we shall compare these results, which are based on the 1/1000 sample of the 1960 Census, with results based on a more recent data source, the 1967 Survey of Economic Opportunity. Then, in Section IV, we shall attempt to measure the effect of differences in education using test-score results instead of years of school.

III. Empirical Results from 1967 Survey of Economic Opportunity

The Survey of Economic Opportunity contains data on fewer individuals than the 1/1000 sample, but it is more recent and it contains more information on each individual.[28] Before using this extra information, however, we begin by presenting results analogous to those presented in Section I. In this way we can examine what, if any, changes occurred between 1959 and 1966, a period during which labor markets tightened considerably and federal laws were passed outlawing many aspects of racial discrimination. This question is of particular interest given the results of Weiss and Williamson, who find that differences in education had a much greater effect on black earnings in 1966 than they

---

[28] We restricted the analysis to the "national" part of the SEO sample, where people are sampled from different areas in such a way as to approximate a random national sample. The total sample sizes that result are 10,149 for whites and 1092 for blacks, with "other" races excluded from the analysis. Although sample size is no problem for whites, it is for blacks where there are only 325 outside SMSAs and 527 outside the South. We could increase the sample size for blacks by including those in the "supplemental" sample, which resulted from oversampling poor Negro neighborhoods. However, the biases that could result from including the nonrandom sample appear likely to be more serious than the small sample sizes for the "national" sample. For a discussion of such biases, see Stanley H. Masters and Thomas I. Ribich, "Schooling and Earnings of Low Achievers: Comment," *American Economic Review* 62 (September 1972). When we did include the observations from the supplemental sample, there was little change in the results except that there was much less effect due to differences in AFQT tests (i.e., the figures for *DIV* in Table 5.13 were much smaller).

TABLE 5.9

Decomposing the Racial Earnings Gap:
Results from Survey of Economic Opportunity, 1967
(in dollars)

Sample	$\bar{E}_W$	$\bar{E}_B$	$\bar{E}_W - \bar{E}_B$	Without standardization for weeks worked			With standardization for weeks worked		
				DIV	LMD	INTER	DIV	LMD	INTER
National	7290	4018	3272	789	1755	728	1263	2428	−419
SMSA	7920	4716	3204	601	1828	775	1039	2503	−338
Non-SMSA	6070	2552	3518	1131	1631	756	1662	2293	−437
Non-South	7574	5121	2453	586	1595	272	1278	2239	−1064
South	6525	2989	3536	408	2026	1102	720	2690	126

NOTE: For definitions, see Table 5.6.

did in 1959.[29] In Table 5.9 we present results for 1966 that are analogous to the 1959 results presented in Tables 5.6 and 5.7.

The results from the SEO are basically similar to those from the 1/1000 sample. The effect of differences in our independent variables is substantially less important than the effect of labor-market discrimination while interaction effects depend heavily on whether we standardize for differences in weeks worked.

To make a closer comparison between the SEO and 1/1000 results, we need to observe that the average earnings have increased considerably for both blacks and whites between 1959 and 1966. Perhaps the best way to adjust for such changes is to look at the racial earnings gap and its components as a percentage of $\bar{E}_W$, the average white's earnings. These results are presented in Table 5.10—with no standardization for weeks worked.

We see that, as a percentage of mean white earnings, the racial earnings gap has declined modestly in all regions and that the most noticeable decline has occurred in labor-market discrimination in the SMSAs and in the non-South. Note, however, that these results could have occurred either as a result of tighter labor markets (see the discussion in Chapter 2) or as a result of less discrimination because of equal-employment

TABLE 5.10

Decomposing the Racial Earnings Gap: Comparative Results for 1/1000 and SEO Samples, All Results as Percentage of $\bar{E}_W$ (*in dollars*)

Sample	1/1000				SEO			
	$\bar{E}_W - \bar{E}_B$	DIV	LMD	INTER	$\bar{E}_W - \bar{E}_B$	DIV	LMD	INTER
National	49.8	8.5	32.2	9.1	44.9	10.8	24.1	10.0
SMSA	47.9	7.4	32.2	8.3	40.5	7.6	23.1	9.8
Non-SMSA	60.5	21.9	27.6	11.0	58.0	18.6	26.9	12.5
Non-South	35.6	−3.1	32.3	6.4	32.4	7.7	21.1	3.6
South	58.8	5.0	33.0	20.8	54.2	6.3	31.1	16.9

NOTE: For definitions, see Table 5.6.

[29] Leonard Weiss and Jeffrey G. Williamson, "Black Education, Earnings, and Interregional Migration: Some Recent Evidence," *American Economic Review* 62 (June 1972).

TABLE 5.11

**Decomposing the Racial Earnings Gap: Results from Persons
in the Labor Force All Year, SEO
(in dollars)**

Sample	$\bar{E}_W$	$\bar{E}_B$	$\bar{E}_W - \bar{E}_B$	DIV	LMD	INTER
National	7687	4350	3337	766	1867	704
SMSA	8347	5001	3346	618	1948	781
Non-SMSA	6382	2810	3572	1194	1672	706
Non-South	7960	5418	2542	503	1719	320
South	6940	3262	3678	400	2141	1137

NOTE: For definitions, see Table 5.6.

legislation, the war on poverty, and related social changes during the early 1960s.

The results in Table 5.10 are not standardized for differences in weeks worked. With the SEO data, we have information on a person's labor-force status when he is not working. Consequently we can standardize for differences in weeks worked as a result of being out of the labor force without simultaneously standardizing for differences in unemployment. We do so by eliminating from the sample all those who were not in the labor force for fifty to fifty-two weeks during 1966. In this way, we attempt to adjust for differences in supply factors (health, preferences for leisure) without adjusting for differences in demand. Unfortunately, however, differences in demand for black and white labor are likely to affect the relative supplies,[30] but there is no obvious way to adjust for this difficulty.[31] Results using this smaller sample are presented in Table 5.11.[32]

The results are quite similar to those in Table 5.9 where there is no standardization for weeks worked (especially given that we have eliminated more than 10 percent of the whites and more than 15 percent of

[30] For example, see William G. Bowen and T. Aldrich Finegan, *The Economics of Labor Force Participation* (Princeton, New Jersey: Princeton Univ. Press, 1969).

[31] Note that the results in Section II indicate that standardizing for differences in weeks worked had little effect on our main interest, the relative estimates for labor-market discrimination and the effect of the productivity variables. However, it did have an important effect on the interaction term.

[32] The sample sizes are reduced to 9023 for whites and 902 for blacks.

the blacks from our previous sample). The similarity between these two sets of results suggests that most of the differences in weeks worked occur because of unemployment. Consequently, for the 1/1000 sample, the results without standardizing for weeks worked probably are the most reliable. In the rest of our SEO analysis, we shall restrict the sample to those in the labor force all year (at least fifty weeks).

Next let us use the sample of full-year labor force participants to estimate the effect of differences in years of school. We use the same procedures here as were used in Table 5.8. The new results, together with some of the results from Table 5.8 for comparative purposes, are presented in Table 5.12.

The effect of differences in years of school appears slightly more important in this SEO analysis, but it still accounts for less than 20 percent of the racial earnings gap. These results reinforce our conclusion from Section II that, even though there has been a significant narrowing of the schooling gap between young blacks and young whites, we should not expect this narrowing to have a major effect on the earnings gap between blacks and whites.

The results presented thus far suggest that discrimination in the labor market may be the most important factor in accounting for the racial earnings gap. Before we can have much confidence in this conclusion, however, we need to give more attention to some of the limitations of our earnings functions.

TABLE 5.12

Decomposing the Racial Earnings Gap: Results for Effect of Differences in Years of School, 1/1000 and SEO (in dollars)

Sample	1/1000 (no weeks variables)			SEO (full-year sample)		
	$\bar{E}_W - \bar{E}_B$	DE	DIV	$\bar{E}_W - \bar{E}_B$	DE	DIV
National	2673	319	457	3337	561	766
SMSA	2901	307	450	3346	576	618
Non-SMSA	2503	291	906	3572	429	1194
Non-South	1964	230	−170	2542	487	503
South	2905	279	245	3678	364	400

NOTE: For definitions, see Table 5.8.

IV. Results Using Predicted Test-Score
Performance Instead of Years of School
to Measure Educational Attainment

Thus far, we have found that differences in the values of our independent variables account for relatively little of the racial earnings gap. As we have indicated earlier, however, these results are consistent with two quite different interpretations: (*1*) that labor-market discrimination is more important than productivity differences between blacks and whites, and (*2*) that important variables are left out of the earnings functions *and* that blacks have lower productivity as measured by these variables.

We can consider two factors that might account for additional portions of the racial earnings gap if they could be included in the earnings functions—differences in motivation and differences in ability. We shall not spend much time on differences in motivation—partly because we do not have the necessary data, and partly because differences in motivation are likely to be related to labor-market discrimination.[33] However, we shall try measuring ability in terms other than years of school completed.[34]

As a measure of potential productivity on the job, we shall use estimates based on data from the AFQT. O'Neill describes the AFQT data as follows:

> These data were obtained from a 50 percent sample of the records of all individuals who were called up for the draft or attempted to enlist during the period January 1953 to July 1958. The sample was composed of three-quarters of a million young men.
>
> The AFQT, which is given to every youth when he is initially examined for military service, contains 100 questions equally distributed among the four areas: vocabulary or verbal concept; arithmetic; spacial relations; and mechanical ability. . . .

---

[33] For example, blacks may have greater absenteeism and tardiness because of relatively low work motivation, but this lower motivation may occur because, historically, jobs that require worker stability (and that pay high wages) have not been open to blacks. For example, see the discussion of Arrow and Gordon presented in Chapter 1. Of course, differences in motivation may also be related to other factors, including discrimination in the schools. Ideally we would like to include independent variables for differences in motivation that are not caused by labor-market discrimination. However, the necessary data are unavailable.

[34] Note that discrimination may also affect ability, if it affects motivation.

The AFQT is *not* designed to measure only innate ability characteristics; it is an achievement-type test rather than an IQ-type. . . . Benjamin Karpinos, a medical statistician in the Office of the Surgeon General has succinctly stated the goals of the AFQT:

"The AFQT was delegated a dual objective: (a) To measure the examinee's general ability to absorb military training within a reasonable length of time, so as to eliminate those who do not possess such ability—a qualification device; and (b) to provide a uniform measure of the examinee's potential general usefulness in the service, if qualified in the test—a classification device. It was hence specifically intended to predict potential success in general military training and performance ('military trainability'). It has been validated for that purpose."[35]

This data source has a few disadvantages: (*1*) It obviously contains no information on those who were never tested by the Army; although this group is certainly not a random sample of all males, the problem is reduced once the data are cross-classified by race, region, and years of school. (*2*) At least some individuals probably tried to do poorly on this test. (*3*) The data are not available for the same individuals as are included in the 1/1000 or SEO samples. Although these problems may be relatively serious, the alternative data sources available to us appear to present difficulties that are at least as serious.[36]

As indicated earlier, AFQT scores are available by race, years of school, and region. Since the SEO data include location at age sixteen, a reasonable proxy for the location at which a young man would have taken the test, we can assign each individual in our SEO sample a predicted probability distribution of AFQT scores. However, we shall not attempt this kind of an analysis for the 1/1000 sample, mainly because its only data on region are current location, location five years ago, and place of birth.

For each race–location subgroup, Karpinos presents data on the distribution of individuals by years of school and five categories of AFQT

[35] From Dave M. O'Neill, "The Effect of Discrimination on Earnings: Evidence From Military Test Score Results," *Journal of Human Resources* 5 (Fall 1970): 479–481. © 1970 by the Regents of the University of Wisconsin.

[36] We could avoid the third problem (but not the other two), by using data sources like those used by Hansen, Weisbrod, and Scanlon or Griliches and Mason (see the discussion of these studies in Chapter 2). Unfortunately the first is limited to low achievers while the second contains only about 100 nonwhites. The test-score data from the Coleman report would enable us to avoid problems 1 and 2, but these data are not related to *terminal* years of schooling, do not cover those who completed more than twelve years of school, and include girls as well as boys. On balance, our aggregative AFQT data appear to be the best data source currently available.

scores.[37] Therefore, we can take an individual of given race,[38] region at age sixteen (nine categories), and years of school (nine categories), and we can assign him a probability distribution for being in each of the five AFQT score categories.[39]

Using this information, we shall define a set of variables for age and expected AFQT score. For each age category, we create five new variables—one for each category of AFQT scores. If the individual is in the given age group, then he is assigned a value for each variable corresponding to his probability of being in that range of AFQT scores. If he is not in the appropriate age group, then all the variables are given a value of zero.

When these variables are included in the regressions instead of the dummies for age and years of school, we can predict the earnings effect of a change in the AFQT probabilities.[40] Specifically, we can proceed as we did earlier and calculate how much of the racial earnings gap is due to (*1*) differences in AFQT score and the other independent variables, (*2*) labor-market discrimination, and (*3*) the interaction effects. These results are presented in Table 5.13. The corresponding results using years of school (taken from Table 5.11) are also presented to facilitate comparisons.

The results in Table 5.13 indicate that differences in the values of the independent variables (mainly the AFQT score variables) are now the most important component of the racial earnings gap. However, our estimates for the effect of labor-market discrimination are still substantial—about 30 percent of the total earnings differential between the races.[41] Moreover, we can show that these estimates for the effect of labor-market discrimination are probably too low.

[37] B. D. Karpinos, "The Mental Qualification of American Youths for Military Service and its Relationship to Educational Attainment," *Proceedings of the American Statistical Association*, Social Statistics Section (Washington, D.C.: American Statistical Association, 1966).

[38] In this case, whites are defined as nonblacks. Since nonwhite nonblacks are a very small percentage of all nonblacks, there is no serious problem of data comparability with regard to race.

[39] On first glance, it would appear much simpler to assign to each individual his mean expected score rather than a distribution of such scores. However, no data on means (or medians) were presented. While we could have interpolated a mean, this procedure would have involved an equally complicated procedure, and we would also have destroyed some potentially valuable information.

[40] The statistical fit for these earnings functions (as measured by the R^2 and the standard error of estimate) is about the same as for the earlier ones.

[41] Note that the interaction effects are now generally negative, except for the national sample. These results suggest that *labor-market* discrimination may *not* be greatest against blacks with the most ability. Also note the comment in footnote 48.

TABLE 5.13

Decomposing the Racial Earnings Gap: Results Using Predicted AFQT Scores Compared with Results Using Years of School SEO (*in dollars*)

Sample	$\bar{E}_W - \bar{E}_B$	AFQT scores				Years of school			
		DIV	(DE)[a]	LMD	INTER	DIV	(DE)	LMD	INTER
National	3337	2234	(2032)	1010	93	766	(561)	1867	704
SMSA	3346	2926	(2854)	965	−544	618	(576)	1948	781
Non-SMSA	3572	b	b	923	b	1194	(429)	1672	706
Non-South	2542	2405	(2428)	793	−657	503	(487)	1719	320
South	3678	4008	(4420)	1174	−1504	400	(364)	2141	1137

NOTE: For definitions of *DIV*, *LMD*, and *INTER* see Table 5.6. For the AFQT section of the table, our primary independent variables are now variables for age and expected AFQT score instead of age and years of school.

[a] The results in this column were calculated in the same manner as our earlier results for the effect of differences in years of school. However, now we are calculating the effect of differences in test scores.

[b] The black regression included one very large coefficient of no statistical significance (one observation in the cell). As a result, the numbers for *DIV*, *DE*, and *INTER* appeared to be very unreasonable and too unreliable to report.

119

Recall from our review of the literature that Gwartney uses test-score score data from the Coleman report to attempt to answer the same questions that have been addressed in this chapter.[42] His results, for the whole nation, are quite similar to ours. However, these results have been criticized by Ashenfelter and Taussig on four counts.[43] They argue that Gwartney's approach could exaggerate the effect of differences in test scores on the racial earnings gap *(1)* if schooling has an effect on learning that is independent of its effect on test scores, *(2)* if cultural factors give whites an advantage in taking tests that is independent of advantages in productivity, *(3)* if dropouts at a given grade have lower test scores than all students who take the test at that grade and if this difference declines at higher grade levels, and *(4)* if labor-market discrimination leads blacks to obtain less education. Since we are using test scores for the AFQT rather than for the Coleman report, we do not have to be concerned with objection three, but the other difficulties all could be as applicable to this study as to Gwartney's. While these criticisms all appear to be potentially valid, in our view the main issue is an empirical one—are any of these biases large enough to be important?[44]

In Chapter 2, we discussed two studies that showed that schooling does have a reasonably important positive effect on earnings even after

[42] Gwartney, "Discrimination and Income Differentials."

[43] Orley Ashenfelter and Michael K. Taussig, "Discrimination and Income Differentials: Comment," *American Economic Review* 61 (September 1971) and Gwartney's "Reply" in the same issue.

[44] In replying to Ashenfelter and Taussig, Gwartney points out that, if cultural factors do give whites this extra advantage on tests (and thus on earnings) but *not* on productivity, then there is discrimination based on test-score (or possibly class) differences rather than simply on race. Although Gwartney's distinction between these two kinds of discrimination appears valid theoretically, in practice the distinction becomes blurred because of the strong correlation between test scores and race, thereby enabling people to use test scores as a proxy if they want to discriminate on the basis of race but feel constrained from doing so in a blatant manner.

As this goes to press, Kiker and Liles have responded to several of the Ashenfelter and Taussig criticisms by using data on men recently separated from the Army. They find that when schooling and AFQT scores are considered *simultaneously*, AFQT scores have a much greater effect on earnings than schooling and employment. Unfortunately, however, their data are for a very unrepresentative sample of the total population. Not only are these men very young, but their Army occupation and training (presumably determined in part by AFQT score) are probably the main factors affecting their employment and earnings the first year after they leave the military—thus giving an upward bias to these estimates of the effect of AFQT scores as a general measure of "scholastic achievement." See B. F. Kiker and W. Pierce Liles, "Earnings, Employment, and Racial Discrimination: Additional Evidence," *American Economic Review* 64 (June 1974).

standardizing for differences in AFQT scores.[45] These results appear open to at least three possible interpretations—all of which appear plausible. First, years of school may be a good measure of characteristics other than scholastic achievement which do influence a person's productivity (e.g., dependability, willingness to submit to authority, and ability to adjust to one's social environment).[46] Second, employees may use years of school as a somewhat arbitrary screening device.[47] Third, schooling may affect earnings almost entirely as a result of the effect of schooling on scholastic achievement, but AFQT scores may not reflect some important aspects of scholastic achievement.

Regardless of the relative importance of these three factors, our results in Table 5.13 using the AFQT-related variables should overestimate the effect of these variables on the racial earnings gap since, for a given predicted AFQT score, a black will have had more years of school than a corresponding white.[48] Moreover, the overestimate may be compounded as a result of the two other factors suggested by Ashenfelter and Taussig. Of particular importance for our purposes, these considerations also suggest (see the formal argument in Appendix 5B) that our results in Table 5.13 underestimate the importance of labor-market discrimination, as we have defined it.

Even though our earnings functions are still quite imperfectly specified,[49] we are now in a position to conclude that, after standardizing for

---

[45] W. Lee Hansen, Burton A. Weisbrod, and William J. Scanlon, "Schooling and Earnings of Low Achievers," *American Economic Review* 60 (June 1970); and Z. Griliches and W. Mason, "Education, Income, and Ability," *Journal of Political Economy* 86 (May–June 1972), Supplement.

[46] For example, Doeringer and Piore show that years of school has a positive effect on job tenure, an effect which they attribute to some combination of the following: (*1*) the effect of schooling on "habits of stability;" (*2*) those with more education being able to obtain better jobs; or (*3*) schools acting as a screening device to weed out those who are not likely to be stable workers. Since, for most jobs, productivity depends on stability or dependability as well as on mental or other skills, all these arguments (with the possible exception of number two) suggest that schooling is likely to be positively related to productivity even after standardizing for differences in skill levels. See Peter B. Doeringer and Michael J. Piore, *Internal Labor Markets and Manpower Analysis* (Lexington, Massachusetts: Heath, 1971), Appendix to Chapter 8. With regard to the effect of schooling on "habits of stability," see the interesting analysis in Herbert Gintis, "Education, Technology, and the Characteristics of Worker Productivity," *American Economic Review* 61 (May 1971).

[47] For example, see Ivar Berg, *Education and Jobs: The Great Training Robbery* (New York: Praeger, 1970).

[48] If this bias is more serious for those with higher predicted AFQT scores, it might account for the negative interactions in Table 5.8.

[49] The $\bar{R}^2$s are never greater than 0.5.

differences in education, there is still a substantial earnings differential between blacks and whites. While this differential is essentially a residual, it appears that it probably results in large part from labor-market discrimination.[50]

V. Conclusion

The results in Sections II and III suggest that differences in years of school have some effect on the racial earnings gap, but that the effect is small relative to the effect of labor-market discrimination and/or differences in scholastic attainment per year of school. Then in Section IV we saw that, although differences in scholastic attainment may have much more effect than differences in years of school, the estimates of labor-market discrimination remain high even when productivity differences are measured primarily in terms of predicted test scores rather than years of school. Because the statistical estimates are subject to various biases and because interaction effects are likely to be important, it is not possible to give a clear ranking of the relative effect of each factor on the magnitude of the racial earnings gap. However, labor-market discrimination and differences in scholastic attainment both appear to have important effects.

In the next two chapters, we conclude the study by examining some of the policy issues that are involved in attempting to reduce labor-market discrimination and educational inequalities. On the basis of our previous analysis, these appear to be the most promising ways of reducing the black–white earnings gap.

Although the analytical approach of this chapter emphasizes the distinction between productivity differences and labor-market discrimination, we shall see that the dichotomy is less clear cut when we turn to policy considerations. Reductions in labor-market discrimination, especially for the better jobs, should provide blacks with a greater incentive to obtain a good education. At the same time, improvements in black education might reduce white tastes for discrimination and thus lessen labor-market discrimination.

---

[50] Of course, there are also other possibilities. For example, we have not been able to standardize for differences in health. If we had, perhaps our estimates of labor-market discrimination would have been reduced. Differences in difficulties with the law might also be a factor.

APPENDIX 5A: Variables Used Plus National Regression Results

I. National Regressions

For the national regressions the following variables were used:

A. Joint Dummies for Age and Education

	Age	Years of school		Age	Years of school
1.	17–19	0–7	23.	30–34	16+
2.	″	8	24.	35–44	0–4
3.	″	9–11	25.	″	5–7
4.	″	12+	26.	″	8
5.	20–24	0–7	27.	″	9–11
6.	″	8	28.	″	13–15
7.	″	9–11	29.	″	16+
8.	″	12	30.	45–54	0–4
9.	″	13+	31.	″	5–7
10.	25–29	0–4	32.	″	8
11.	″	5–7	33.	″	9–11
12.	″	8	34.	″	12
13.	″	9–11	35.	″	13–15
14.	″	12	36.	″	16+
15.	″	13–15	37.	55–64	0–4
16.	″	16+	38.	″	5–7
17.	30–34	0–4	39.	″	8
18.	″	5–7	40.	″	9–11
19.	″	8	41.	″	12
20.	″	9–11	42.	″	13–15
21.	″	12	43.	″	16+
22.	″	13–15		reference group	
				35–44	12

B. Joint Variables for Age and Predicted AFQT Score

Age		AFQT score	Age		AFQT score
44.	17–19	0–9	62.	30–34	65–92
45.	″	10–30	63.	″	93–100
46.	″	31–64	64.	35–44	0–9
47.	″	65–92	65.	″	10–30
48.	″	93–100	66.	″	65–92
49.	20–24	0–9	67.	″	93–100
50.	″	10–30	68.	45–54	0–9
51.	″	31–64	69.	″	10–30
52.	″	65–92	70.	″	31–64
53.	″	93–100	71.	″	65–92
54.	25–29	0–9	72.	″	93–100
55.	″	10–30	73.	55–64	0–9
56.	″	31–64	74.	″	10–30
57.	″	65–69	75.	″	31–64
58.	″	93–100	76.	″	65–92
59.	30–34	0–9	77.	″	93–100
60.	″	10–30	reference group		
61.	″	31–64		35–44	31–64

C. Other Variables

		Weeks worked	
78.	Northeast		
79.	South		
80.	West	86.	1–13
81.	Farm	87.	14–26
82.	Rural nonfarm	88.	27–39
83.	Urban, not SMSA	89.	40–47
84.	SMSA under 500,000	90.	48–49
85.	Self-employed		

II. Subregion Regressions

For the subregions, we combined dummies for age and years of school so that there would always be at least three observations per cell. At least, this was our original intention. Due to an oversight, we had fewer observations in a few cells for the SEO full-time samples. Due to computer problems we also had to combine variables 47 and 48 for those not in SMSAs. The combined variables are presented in the table below.

South	Non-South	SMSA	Non-SMSA
1, 2	1, 2, 3	1, 2	8, 9
14, 15, 16	5, 6	5, 6	10, 11
35, 36	10, 11, 12	10, 11	14, 15, 16
41, 42, 43	17, 18	17, 18	22, 23
	22, 23		28, 29
	35, 37		35, 36
			40, 41, 42, 43
			47, 48

III. National Regression Results Using 1/1000 and Comparable SEO Samples
(Regression Coefficients and *t*-values)

Variable	1/1000				SEO—comparable to 1/1000			
	Black		White		Black		White	
1.	−2251	(7.5)	−4467	(2.5)	−2647	(3.6)	−5678	(5.9)
2.	−2388	(5.7)	−3830	(2.9)	−3236	(3.9)	−5458	(6.2)
3.	−2638	(9.0)	−4543	(5.4)	−3054	(6.0)	−5795	(11.2)
4.	−2431	(7.6)	−4518	(7.9)	−3349	(7.1)	−5445	(13.3)
5.	−1446	(7.0)	−2901	(2.9)	−1340	(2.3)	−4339	(6.1)
6.	−1992	(6.9)	−3470	(4.0)	−1974	(2.6)	−4113	(5.9)
7.	−1657	(7.9)	−2663	(5.3)	−1934	(4.6)	−3183	(8.8)
8.	−1601	(7.8)	−2710	(6.7)	−907	(2.3)	−2531	(9.0)
9.	−2242	(6.0)	−2828	(5.2)	−714	(0.9)	−3382	(9.4)
10.	−1113	(4.0)	−3707	(2.5)	−1755	(1.8)	−4356	(3.2)
11.	−1032	(4.5)	−2462	(3.3)	−510	(0.8)	−3317	(4.9)
12.	−1224	(4.2)	−1962	(2.6)	−1146	(1.9)	−2522	(4.2)

(continued on p. 126)

Variable	1/1000 Black		White		SEO—comparable to 1/1000 Black		White	
13.	−719	(3.5)	−1831	(3.6)	−599	(1.4)	−1623	(4.5)
14.	−636	(3.1)	−1321	(3.1)	540	(1.3)	−1141	(4.5)
15.	−818	(2.5)	173	(0.2)	1017	(1.8)	−933	(2.3)
16.	−634	(1.7)	−900	(1.5)	3265	(3.3)	139	(0.4)
17.	−969	(3.8)	−3413	(3.2)	−1242	(1.5)	−4149	(4.1)
18.	−997	(4.8)	−1666	(2.3)	−1276	(2.4)	−2856	(4.7)
19.	−878	(3.5)	−1908	(3.4)	−1298	(2.2)	−1757	(3.2)
20.	−996	(4.9)	−768	(1.7)	−249	(0.6)	−1395	(3.9)
21.	−678	(3.0)	−522	(1.2)	−326	(0.8)	−110	(0.4)
22.	−596	(1.8)	781	(1.2)	680	(1.1)	203	(0.5)
23.	1516	(3.5)	2406	(4.5)	1481	(1.9)	2887	(8.5)
24.	1076	(5.8)	−2908	(3.9)	−936	(2.0)	−3420	(6.1)
25.	−868	(4.9)	−1613	(3.3)	−816	(2.2)	−1875	(4.8)
26.	−713	(3.7)	−953	(2.3)	−646	(1.5)	−1527	(4.7)
27.	−412	(2.3)	−853	(2.5)	49	(0.1)	−549	(2.1)
28.	217	(0.7)	1505	(3.3)	975	(1.8)	2012	(6.2)
29.	1891	(5.4)	3744	(8.8)	3295	(5.8)	4157	(15.4)
30.	−1156	(6.5)	−3342	(4.8)	−1478	(3.7)	−3326	(6.1)
31.	−776	(4.4)	−2390	(5.7)	−550	(1.5)	−2212	(6.4)
32.	−567	(2.8)	−1258	(3.4)	263	(0.6)	−1619	(5.5)
33.	−446	(2.2)	−903	(2.5)	−38	(0.1)	−591	(2.3)
34.	−119	(0.5)	185	(0.5)	90	(0.2)	469	(2.1)
35.	48	(0.1)	1664	(3.0)	1246	(2.2)	2702	(8.5)
36.	490	(1.3)	4773	(9.6)	2194	(2.7)	6876	(23.3)
37.	−1272	(6.8)	−2802	(4.8)	−1393	(3.7)	−3509	(6.5)
38.	−960	(4.8)	−1927	(4.8)	−807	(1.9)	−2751	(8.3)
39.	−594	(2.2)	−1742	(4.4)	−1484	(3.0)	−1940	(6.7)
40.	−339	(1.2)	−1155	(2.6)	−771	(1.4)	−1021	(3.5)
41.	−765	(2.1)	828	(1.6)	104	(0.2)	202	(0.7)
42.	52	(0.1)	1343	(2.3)	614	(0.6)	2746	(6.9)
43.	1726	(2.1)	4850	(6.8)	−307	(0.3)	4194	(11.6)
78.	−96	(1.1)	−305	(1.8)	−683	(3.7)	−426	(3.4)
79.	−896	(11.1)	−229	(1.3)	−1729	(10.0)	−577	(4.7)
80.	−158	(1.2)	−228	(1.4)	−985	(4.0)	−33	(0.2)
81.	−1414	(12.0)	−2291	(9.2)	−1599	(5.5)	−2000	(10.2)
82.	−791	(9.0)	−1152	(6.9)	−1190	(5.7)	−1433	(10.4)
83.	−626	(6.6)	−1228	(6.0)	−767	(4.0)	−1106	(7.7)
84.	−129	(1.7)	−255	(1.5)	−76	(0.4)	−770	(6.1)
85.	−877	(6.6)	800	(3.8)	−1055	(2.8)	1431	(9.0)
Constant	4465		6874		6103		8395	
N	3673		3676		1092		10149	
$\bar{R}^2$	.29		.23		.42		.27	
SE of E	1621		3899		1872		4529	

IV. National Regression Results for Full-Time SEO Sample (Regression Coefficients and *t*-values)

	Years of school			AFQT	
Variable	Black	White	Variable	Black	White
1.	−2450 (3.3)	−5257 (4.4)	44.	−1801 (1.4)	−12281 (2.5)
2.	−2916 (3.6)	−5270 (5.0)	45.	−8423 (2.5)	−7439 (1.4)
3.	−3936 (6.1)	−5533 (9.4)	46.	9009 (0.9)	−14664 (1.8)
4.	−2390 (3.7)	−4568 (7.3)	47.	−74232 (1.0)	1689 (0.1)
5.	−1158 (2.1)	−4057 (5.3)	48.	373010 (1.0)	−30302 (0.9)
6.	−2462 (3.1)	−3762 (4.8)	49.	−1878 (2.2)	−8513 (3.2)
7.	−1479 (3.4)	−2904 (7.2)	50.	−1186 (0.8)	−10110 (4.4)
8.	−555 (1.3)	−2218 (7.3)	51.	−2148 (0.8)	−5776 (2.3)
9.	−480 (0.7)	−2829 (7.0)	52.	7467 (0.7)	−7006 (1.9)
10.	−1702 (1.8)	−3712 (2.1)	53.	−36525 (1.1)	−9216 (2.0)
11.	−362 (0.6)	−2968 (4.0)	54.	−1169 (1.3)	−9740 (4.6)
12.	−1080 (1.7)	−2404 (3.7)	55.	−2488 (1.9)	−7206 (5.2)
13.	−712 (1.7)	−1592 (4.2)	56.	5132 (2.1)	−526 (4.6)
14.	492 (1.2)	−1160 (4.4)	57.	−15345 (1.6)	−6834 (3.8)
15.	850 (1.5)	−976 (2.5)	58.	44874 (1.6)	−1560 (0.7)
16.	3068 (3.2)	559 (1.4)	59.	−1625 (2.0)	−9652 (6.2)
17.	−749 (0.7)	−4003 (3.7)	60.	−1112 (0.9)	−7498 (5.8)
18.	−1357 (2.4)	−2866 (4.3)	61.	−1457 (0.6)	−3070 (2.9)
19.	−1300 (2.2)	−1753 (3.1)	62.	16207 (1.6)	−8967 (5.6)
20.	−291 (0.7)	−953 (2.4)	63.	−39610 (1.0)	6061 (3.3)
21.	−375 (0.9)	−99 (0.4)	64.	−1017 (1.7)	−7179 (8.4)
22.	895 (1.5)	34 (0.1)	65.	−1246 (1.4)	−9146 (8.3)
23.	2169 (2.5)	2719 (8.0)	66.	16928 (3.7)	−12814 (8.2)
24.	−968 (2.1)	−3458 (5.9)	67.	−33136 (1.9)	13462 (11.5)
25.	−583 (1.5)	−1609 (3.8)	68.	−1314 (2.1)	−6409 (6.6)
26.	−561 (1.3)	−1497 (4.4)	69.	−118 (0.1)	−10341 (11.3)
27.	190 (0.5)	−563 (2.1)	70.	16 (0.0)	1826 (1.9)
28.	1136 (2.0)	2018 (6.0)	71.	3769 (0.6)	−15918 (11.3)
29.	4092 (6.8)	4336 (15.4)	72.	20113 (1.0)	21768 (13.5)
30.	−1457 (3.2)	−2938 (4.7)	73.	−1699 (2.6)	−7958 (8.0)
31.	−539 (1.4)	−2073 (5.6)	74.	73 (0.1)	−8332 (8.7)
32.	39 (0.1)	−1574 (5.0)	75.	−598 (0.4)	−2371 (2.2)
33.	177 (0.4)	−496 (1.8)	76.	−1856 (0.5)	−7956 (4.5)
34.	51 (0.1)	494 (2.1)	77.	48163 (1.7)	9971 (4.7)
35.	1451	2675 (8.2)	78.	−686 (3.4)	27 (0.2)
36.	2085 (2.2)	6764 (22.0)	79.	−1594 (8.3)	−225 (1.7)
37.	−1154 (2.9)	−3294 (5.4)	80.	−533 (2.0)	2 (0.0)
38.	−665 (1.5)	−2536 (6.8)	81.	−1565 (4.5)	−2206 (10.5)

(continued on p. 128)

	Years of school			AFQT	
Variable	Black	White	Variable	Black	White
39.	−1102 (1.9)	−1645 (5.2)	82.	−1282 (5.6)	−1590 (10.7)
40.	−435 (0.7)	−764 (2.4)	83.	−676 (3.2)	−1255 (8.2)
41.	637 (1.0)	499 (1.6)	84.	22 (0.1)	−829 (6.2)
42.	510 (0.5)	2907 (7.0)	85.	−1268 (2.8)	1613 (9.3)
43.	−254 (0.3)	4488 (11.7)	Constant	6436	13053
78.	−757 (3.9)	−449 (3.4)	N	902	9023
79.	−1828 (9.9)	−534 (4.1)	$\bar{R}^2$	.39	.24
80.	−847 (3.3)	77 (0.5)	SE of E	1856	4589
81.	−1541 (4.4)	−2209 (10.5)			
82.	−1299 (5.8)	−1536 (10.4)			
83.	−622 (2.9)	−1213 (8.0)			
84.	−71 (0.4)	−791 (5.9)			
85.	−1398 (3.1)	1595 (9.3)			
Constant	6230	8546			
N	902	9023			
$\bar{R}^2$	.42	.26			
SE of E	1816	4554			

APPENDIX 5B: Demonstration That the Results in Section IV Are Likely to Underestimate Labor-Market Discrimination

We defined labor-market discrimination as $LMD = f_W(B) - \bar{E}_B$. In Section IV the independent variables in the earnings function are the AFQT variables plus a set of variables unrelated to years of school (with schooling variables excluded due to problems of multicollinearity). In this appendix we show that the results in Section IV underestimate labor-market discrimination given the following assumptions:

A. Schooling has an effect on earnings that is partly (but not completely) independent of its effect on AFQT scores.[51]

[51] See Hansen, Weisbrod, and Scanlon (HWS) and Griliches and Mason (GM), both referred to in text footnote 45.

B. For given years of school, the average black has lower AFQT score than the average white.[52]

C. Our earnings functions are correctly specified except for the omission of variables for schooling.

To simplify the exposition, we shall compare $f_W(\bar{B}) - \bar{E}_B$ for the following two white earnings functions.

$$E = a_0 + a_1 TS + u_1 \tag{1}$$

$$E = b_0 + b_1 TS + b_2 Ed + u_2, \tag{2}$$

where E is annual earnings, TS is expected test score, Ed is years of school, and the u_i are error terms. On the basis of assumption A, we expect that $b_2 > 0$, $a_1 > b_1 > 0$ and

$$TS = c_0 + c_1 Ed + u_3 \text{ with } c_1 > 0. \tag{3}$$

Assuming that there is a fairly strong positive correlation between TS and Ed,[53] we expect the effect of Ed on E to be approximately the same whether it is estimated from Equations (1) and (3) or from (2) and (3). In other words, we can make assumption D that

$$a_1 c_1 \cong b_1 c_1 + b_2. \tag{4}$$

We want to show that $f_W(B) - \bar{E}_B$ will be smaller when based on Equation (1) than when based on Equation (2). Assuming that $\bar{E}_W > f_W(\bar{B}) > \bar{E}_B$, this is equivalent to showing that $\bar{E}_W - f_W(\bar{B})$ is larger when based on Equation (1). Let $\bar{E}_W - f_W(\bar{B}) = X$. Then the value of X based on Equation (1) will be X_1 and the value based on Equation (2) will be X_2.

To prove that $X_1 > X_2$, we start by noting that $E_W \cong f_W(\bar{W})$. Therefore,

$$X_1 \cong a_1(\overline{TS}_W - \overline{TS}_B) \quad \text{while} \tag{5}$$

$$X_2 \cong b_1(\overline{TS}_W - \overline{TS}_B) + b_2(\overline{Ed}_W - \overline{Ed}_B). \tag{6}$$

---

[52] See the Karpinos article referred to in footnote 37.

[53] HWS find this correlation to be about 0.4, while GM find a correlation of about 0.5 between AFQT and schooling prior to entrance into the armed forces.

Therefore,

$$X_1 - X_2 \cong (a_1 - b_1)(\overline{TS}_W - \overline{TS}_B) - b_2(\overline{Ed}_W - \overline{Ed}_B). \qquad (7)$$

From assumption B, it follows that[54]

$$\overline{TS}_W - \overline{TS}_B > c_1(\overline{Ed}_W - \overline{Ed}_B). \qquad (8)$$

However, from assumption D [Equation (4)], we have $c_1 \cong b_2/(a_1 - b_1)$. Substituting this in Equation (8), we have

$$\overline{TS}_W - \overline{TS}_B > [b_2/(a_1 - b_1)](\overline{Ed}_W - \overline{Ed}_B) \quad \text{or}$$
$$(a_1 - b_1)(\overline{TS}_W - \overline{TS}_B) - b_2(\overline{Ed}_W - \overline{Ed}_B) > 0. \qquad (9)$$

Consequently, $X_1 > X_2$ and labor-market discrimination is underestimated by the earnings function in Equation (1). Therefore, given the preceding assumptions—all of which appear reasonable—our results in Section IV underestimate labor-market discrimination.

[54] For the proof, note that

 (a) $\overline{TS}_W = c_0 + c_1\overline{Ed}_W$ and
 (b) $TS_W(\overline{B}) = c_0 + c_1\overline{Ed}_B$.

Subtracting (b) from (a), we obtain

 (c) $\overline{TS}_W - TS_W(\overline{B}) = c_1(\overline{Ed}_W - \overline{Ed}_B)$.

However, from assumption B, $TS_W(\overline{B}) > \overline{TS}_B$. Therefore,

 (d) $\overline{TS}_W - \overline{TS}_B > \overline{TS}_W - TS_W(\overline{B}) = c_1(\overline{Ed}_W - \overline{Ed}_B)$.

6

Alternative Policy Perspectives

In the last three chapters, we showed that migration from the South and housing segregation appear to have relatively little effect on the earnings opportunities of urban black males. On the contrary, labor-market discrimination together with skill differentials appear to be the main factors responsible for the lower incomes of blacks. In this chapter, three alternative policy perspectives will be presented and evaluations attempted; in the concluding chapter specific policy recommendations will be discussed.

While most agree that racial discrimination is bad, there is no such agreement on what, if any, policies are desirable for reducing such discrimination. In discussing policy questions, we shall begin by looking at the following general approaches: (1) the conservative, as represented by Friedman; (2) the liberal, as represented by Myrdal and by Allport; and (3) the radical, as represented by Baran and Sweezy and by Sherman.

I. The Conservative View

The conservative position emphasizes efforts to change tastes for discrimination, as indicated by Milton Friedman:

I believe strongly that the color of a man's skin or the religion of his parents is, by itself, no reason to treat him differently; that a man should be judged by what he is and what he does and not by these external characteristics. I deplore what seem to me the prejudice and narrowness of outlook of those whose tastes differ from mine in this respect and I think the less of them for it. But in a society based on free discussion, the appropriate recourse is for me to seek to persuade them that their tastes are bad and that they should change their views and their behavior, not to use coercive power to enforce my tastes and my attitudes on others.[1]

In addition the conservatives believe that the forces of competition automatically help combat such discrimination, an argument that was discussed at some length in Chapter 1 in connection with Becker's theory of discrimination.[2] While the conservatives hope to combat racial discrimination by changing people's tastes through persuasion and by making the economy more competitive, they are strongly opposed to legislation prohibiting discrimination.

First, such legislation is regarded as an unnecessary violation of the freedom of individuals to enter into voluntary contracts. Second, businessmen may be hurt if they are forced to hire blacks when their present customers or employees have discriminatory preferences. Finally, conservatives fear that government intervention may ultimately lead to more discrimination rather than less. Friedman argues:

If it is appropriate for the state to say that individuals may not discriminate in employment because of color or race or religion, then it is equally appropriate for the state, provided a majority can be found to vote that way, to say that individuals must discriminate in employment on the basis of color, race or religion.

If one takes a broad sweep of history and looks at the kind of things that the majority will be persuaded of if each individual case is to be decided on its merits rather than as part of a general principle, there can be little doubt that the effect of a widespread acceptance of the appropriateness of government action in this area would be extremely undesirable, even from the point of view of those who at the moment favor [fair employment legislation]. If, at the moment, [such] proponents are in a position to make their views effective, it is only because of a constitutional and federal situation in which a regional majority in one part of the country may be in a position to impose its views on a majority in another part of the country.[3]

[1] Milton Friedman, *Capitalism and Freedom* (Chicago, Illinois: Univ. of Chicago Press, 1962), p. 111. © 1962 by The University of Chicago Press.
[2] Also see ibid., pp. 109–110.
[3] Ibid., pp. 113–114.

II. The Liberal View

In contrast to the conservatives, the liberals place great emphasis on legislation to combat discrimination. In part, the liberal view may be simply a special case of the general liberal inclination for the government to "do something" whenever society appears to face a serious problem. However, a more serious liberal must come to grips with the conservative view. From a liberal perspective, two of Friedman's assumptions appear open to question: (*1*) the view that the forces of competition are sufficiently strong in our society to significantly reduce racial discrimination and to subvert fair employment legislation; and (*2*) the implicit assumption that legislation will have little effect on the public's tastes for discrimination or prejudice.

The first of these two key conservative assumptions was criticized in Chapters 1 and 2, where it was shown that there has been relatively little improvement in the economic position of blacks in the past several generations. To the extent that competitive forces are relatively weak, Marshall's bargaining model of discrimination becomes more important. Under this theory, which was summarized in Chapter 1, civil rights legislation should aid the bargaining power of blacks since it increases the potential costs of discrimination for firms and other institutions. The neglect by conservatives of the effect of legislation on racial attitudes is criticized by Allport:

> Legislation, if enforced, may be a sharp tool in the battle against discrimination. So too may court decisions that invalidate discriminatory legislation left over from the past. Legal action, however, has only an indirect bearing upon the reduction of personal prejudice. It cannot coerce thoughts or instill subjective tolerance. It says, in effect, "your attitudes and prejudices are yours alone, but you may not act them out to a point where they endanger the lives, livelihood, or peace of mind, of groups of American citizens." Law is intended only to control the outward expression of intolerance. But outward action, psychology knows, has an eventual effect upon inner habits of thought and feeling. And for this reason we list legislative action as one of the major methods of reducing, not only public discrimination, but private prejudice as well.[4]

While conservatives, liberals, and radicals all argue that tastes for racial discrimination should be changed, liberals such as Myrdal and Allport have discussed how such tastes might be changed in much

[4] Gordon W. Allport, *The Nature of Prejudice* (Reading, Massachusetts: Addison-Wesley, 1954), p. 442. By permission of Addison-Wesley.

greater detail than conservatives such as Friedman. The liberals emphasize that few whites are prepared to openly discriminate against blacks since such attitudes conflict with our egalitarian values.[5] According to this view, whites begin by assuming that blacks are either innately lazy or genetically and culturally inferior. Thus, whites can treat blacks as inferiors, not because of a difference in skin color, but because of other characteristics. A vicious cycle develops since limiting opportunities for blacks because of their assumed inferior nature means that blacks will not be as economically successful as whites, which in turn reinforces the white view that blacks are inherently inferior.

Myrdal has developed this analysis quite extensively in his classic book, *An American Dilemma*, written in 1944. Concerning the relation of racial prejudice to our egalitarian ideals, he writes:

> The influences from the American Creed thus had, and still have, a double-direction. On the one hand, the equalitarian Creed operates directly to suppress the dogma of the Negro's racial inferiority and to make people's thoughts more and more "independent of race, creed or color," as the American slogan runs. On the other hand, it indirectly calls forth the same dogma to justify a blatant exception to the Creed. The race dogma is nearly the only way out for a people so moralistically equalitarian, if it is not prepared to live up to its faith. A nation less fervently committed to democracy could, probably, live happily in a caste system with a somewhat less intensive belief in the biological inferiority of the subordinate group. The need for race prejudice is, from this point of view, a need for defense on the part of the Americans against their own national Creed, against their own most cherished ideals. And race prejudice is, in this sense, a function of equalitarianism. The former is a perversion of the latter.[6]

Thus, to reduce white tastes for discrimination, liberals claim that it is important to combat the view that blacks are inferior. Myrdal suggests three specific strategies for improving white beliefs about blacks: (*1*) showing whites that they are mistaken in their belief that blacks are inferior; (*2*) improving the objective position of blacks (e.g., income, education, and housing); and (*3*) "strengthening the American Creed in its primary function of bending people's minds toward equalitarianism."

As Myrdal recognizes, the first strategy must try to overcome beliefs that serve important, opportunistic interests.

---

[5] Recall Arrow's discussion of this issue which we quoted in Chapter 1.

[6] Gunnar Myrdal, *An American Dilemma*, 20th anniversary ed. (New York: Harper, 1944), p. 89.

People want to be rational, to be honest and well informed. This want, if it is properly nourished, acts as a competing force among the opportunistic interests. To a degree the desire to be rational slowly overcomes the resistance of the desire to build false rationalizations. The resistance is, however, keen.[7]

This issue of correcting erroneous racial beliefs is also discussed cogently by Allport:

It always has been thought that planting right ideas in the mind would engender right behavior. Many school buildings still display the Socratic motto, Knowledge Is Virtue. But the student's readiness to learn facts, it is now pretty well agreed, depends upon the state of his attitudes. Information seldom sticks unless mixed with attitudinal glue.

This frequent segregation of knowledge from conduct is revealed in a few investigations that have tested both beliefs and attitudes. Intercultural instruction may have the power of correcting erroneous beliefs without appreciably altering attitudes. Children may, for example, learn the facts of Negro history without learning tolerance.

Yet there is an argument to be made on the opposite side. Perhaps students may in the short run show no gains or may twist the facts to serve their prejudices. But, in the long run, accurate information is probably an ally of improved human relations. To take one example: Myrdal has pointed out that there is no longer any intellectually respectable "race" theory that can justify the position of the Negro in this country. Since people are not wholly irrational, the fact that scientific evidence fails to support the theory of racial inferiority can scarcely fail gradually to penetrate into the marrow of their attitudes. . . .

Some evidence indicates that films, novels, and dreams may be effective, presumably because they induce identification with minority group members. There is indication that this approach may be, for certain children, more effective than the informational approach. If this finding stands up in future research, we shall be confronted with an interesting possibility. It may be that strategies of realistic discussion constitute too strong a threat to some people. A milder invitation to identification at the fantasy level may be a more effective first step. Perhaps in the future we shall decide that intercultural programs should start with fiction, drama, and films, and move gradually into more realistic methods of training.[8]

If Allport is correct on this latter point, then the treatment of blacks on television and in ordinary reading assignments at school may be of particular importance in changing the discriminatory attitudes of whites. In fact, it is quite possible that such school reforms may be more important than attempts at desegregation—especially if the contact as a

[7] Ibid., p. 109.
[8] Gordon W. Allport, *The Nature of Prejudice* (Reading, Massachusetts: Addison-Wesley, 1954), pp. 451, 453. By permission of Addison-Wesley.

result of "desegregation" does not take place on the basis of complete equality between the races.

While changes in the schools are likely to be important in changing tastes for discrimination, television may be even more important. In addition to the treatment of blacks in standard programs, the television news coverage (and photographs in newspapers and magazines) of racial events may have a great impact. For example, the response to Martin Luther King's marches by Bull Connor and similar southern whites apparently made whites (especially northern whites) much more sympathetic to civil rights issues. However, the rioting in northern cities from Watts in 1965 to Detroit in 1967 helped increase white hostility.

Myrdal's second and third strategies for changing white beliefs about blacks involve improving the objective position of blacks and strengthening the American creed of equalitarianism. These issues are closely interrelated. As Myrdal indicates, the difficulty in trying to change beliefs by improving the objective position of blacks is that white beliefs have played an important role in keeping blacks from improving their position. Thus, we have the vicious cycle. However, if this cycle is once broken (e.g., by a strengthening of the American creed or by improved information), then improvements in the economic status of blacks should affect white (and black) beliefs about black capabilities, and this change in attitude should lead to further economic improvements. As Myrdal puts it:

> Every improvement of the actual level of Negro character will increase the effectiveness of both the intellectual and moral education of white people in racial matters and vice versa. It is this mechanism of mutual and cumulative dynamic causation which explains the actual situation in theory, and, at the same time, affects the basis for constructive practical policy.[9]

Thus, once change can be instituted, Myrdal presents a very rosy view of future progress. Since initial improvements have occurred (e.g., the change in attitudes that led to passage of the Civil Rights Act of 1964), Myrdal's view suggests that the economic status of blacks should continue to improve, while white tastes for discrimination should continue to decline.[10]

[9] Myrdal, *American Dilemma*, p. 109.

[10] In the twentieth anniversary edition of *An American Dilemma*, Myrdal and one of his collaborators, Arnold Rose, indicate that this snowballing effect has been very important in the twenty years from the early forties to the early sixties. Also see the discussion of this issue in Paul A. Baran and Paul M. Sweezy, *Monopoly Capital* (New York: Monthly Review Press, 1966), p. 250.

III. The Radical View

Before accepting this conclusion, we should consider whether there are any countering forces that would tend to keep this cumulative snow-balling effect from occurring. In this regard, we must return to the radical theory of discrimination that was discussed in Chapter 1. Recall that, according to the radical view, racial discrimination is inherent in the capitalist system for two important reasons. First, capitalists can exploit racial tensions as a means of dividing and weakening the working class. Second, capitalism leads to psychological as well as economic insecurity among workers, and white workers are in a position to allay some of this psychological insecurity by emphasizing their superiority over blacks.

Although radicals are skeptical that any fundamental improvement in the relative position of blacks will occur under capitalism, they do concede that blacks can make some gains by successfully threatening the interests of the capitalist class. In the words of Baran and Sweezy:

> It seems clear that with respect to the race problem in the United States capitalists have come to understand that the very existence of their system is at stake. Either a solution will be found that ensures the loyalty, or at least the neutrality, of the Negro people, or else the world revolution will sooner or later acquire a ready-made and potentially powerful Trojan horse within the ramparts of monopoly capitalism's mightiest fortress.[11]

Another possibility, that of straightforward repression, is ruled out since that would give the United States a bad image abroad and thus hinder the imperialism of United States capitalists. Given this perspective, tokenism and co-optation appear to be the most effective ways of dealing with black demands. As a result the black bourgeoisie has been able to make significant gains (e.g., access to the best restaurants and hotels now depend only on money and not on color), but there has been little reason to appease the majority of blacks who have little money or education. In fact, one of the main purposes of tokenism is "to detach the ablest young men and women from their own people and thus to deprive the liberation movement of its best leadership material."[12]

Given this framework, the critical question is what effect tokenism will have on the economic conditions of the average black. In discussing whether the civil rights reforms of the 1960s are likely to lead to signifi-

[11] Ibid., pp. 270–271. Copyright © 1966 by Paul M. Sweezy. Reprinted by permission of Monthly Review Press.
[12] Ibid., p. 277.

cant gains for the average black, Baran and Sweezy argue:

> It seems clear to us that the answer is negative; that the chief beneficiaries of reforms of this type are the black bourgeoisie; and that, regardless of the intentions of their sponsors, their objective effect is merely to supplement the policy of tokenism.
>
> This might be thought not to be the case with prohibitions against discrimination in the hiring of labor, which unquestionably helped open up many new jobs to Negroes during the war. In a period of heavy and growing unemployment, however, no such effect can be expected. Even if color is not the reason, Negroes will be discriminated against because of their inferior qualifications. Only those with special talents or training will benefit, and they are already set apart from the ghettoized masses . . . .
>
> There is really no mystery about why reforms which remain within the confines of the system hold out no prospect of meaningful improvement to the Negro masses. The system has two poles: wealth, privilege, power at one; poverty, deprivation, powerlessness at the other. It has always been that way, but in earlier times whole groups could rise because expansion made room above and there were others ready to take their place at the bottom. Today, Negroes are at the bottom, and there is neither room above nor anyone ready to take their place. Thus only individuals can move up, not the group as such: reforms help the few, not the many. For the many nothing short of a complete change in the system—the abolition of both poles and the substitution of a society in which wealth and power are shared by all—can transform their condition.[13]

Thus, they suggest that most blacks will remain very disadvantaged until there is a revolution (or until some other group that can be viewed as inferior to blacks comes along). While Baran and Sweezy emphasize the importance of revolutions in the Third World and their possible effects on monopoly capitalism, such upheavals might lead to facism in this country rather than to socialism. Therefore, although the Baran and Sweezy policy perspective appears to be the predominant radical position, other more domestically oriented radical proposals deserve attention. A particularly interesting proposal along these lines has been developed by Howard Sherman.[14] He defines the ultimate social goal as a state of pure communism where each produces according to his ability and receives according to his need. In other words, all goods would be free. However, Sherman agrees with the standard economic analysis that, given present tastes, such a system is impractical because the demand for goods would be infinite and there would be little, if any, labor supply. Therefore, the question becomes how can tastes be changed to

[13] Ibid., pp. 278–279. Copyright © 1966 by Paul M. Sweezy. Reprinted by permission of Monthly Review Press.

[14] Howard Sherman, *Radical Political Economy* (New York: Basic Books, 1972), Chapter 23.

decrease the demand for goods and increase the labor supply, given the existence of free goods. As a side effect, Sherman and other radical economists indicate that racism would be much reduced, if not completely eliminated, in such a noncompetitive communist society.

Sherman's proposal is to start by making a few goods free and then to increase their number little by little.[15] People would become gradually less money oriented as money would be needed only for buying luxury goods. For necessities, the price would be measured in terms of time or inconvenience of storage rather than money. In Sherman's view:

> The communist dream . . . seem[s] to be satisfied sufficiently by the provision of a free supply of basic consumer necessities. Free consumer necessities may be sufficient because the point of the change is to increase socialist consciousness and the feeling for social cooperation and to remove the ethos of competition. If all the basic necessities are free . . . eventually there would be a large change in the basic attitudes towards work and consumption.[16]

Although necessities would be free to consumers, the government would pay firms to produce these goods, and wages would be paid to all workers.[17]

Sherman believes that this proposal would only be feasible if the state first owned the means of production. However, some initial steps might be taken in our present economy.[18] Specifically, we could begin by making a few basic foods available to everyone. Perhaps powdered milk and flour would be appropriate as a starting point. This suggestion can be viewed simply as an extension of our present Commodity Distribution Program. Instead of limiting the quantity of the commodities and restricting eligibility to certain people with low incomes, everyone could have as

---

[15] While Sherman's proposal is exceptionally well presented from an economic viewpoint, many others have made similar proposals. For example, see Michael Harrington, *Socialism* (New York: Saturday Review Press, 1972), Chapter 14; and Eric Fromm, "The Psychological Aspects of the Guaranteed Income," in *The Guaranteed Income*, ed. Robert Theobald (Garden City, New York: Doubleday, 1966).

[16] Sherman, *Radical Political Economy*, p. 342.

[17] As a precondition for the proposal, Sherman assumes an affluent country where productivity is high and little labor supply is needed. However, people would still be expected to work, for several reasons. First, money would still be necessary to buy luxury goods. Second, social pressures would be exerted on those who were not eager to do any work, while doing a few hours of work a week would not be regarded as much of a chore by most people. Finally, much of the work might be made more interesting and challenging so that many people would be willing to work long hours voluntarily. For example, this situation should prevail in research work, thus leading to continued productivity improvements in the economy.

[18] This modification of Sherman's plan is more along the lines of Fromm's proposal.

much as they wanted.[19] At least once the novelty wore off, the demand probably would not be enormous.[20] In this way we could not only move a small step toward Sherman's objectives, but we could also economically assist the poor without having to be too concerned with either stigma problems[21] or the work incentive effects of high marginal tax rates.

Before discussing policy proposals in greater detail, we should look next at empirical evidence in an attempt to determine the relative validity of the conservative, liberal, and radical approaches to the problem of racial discrimination.

IV. Empirical Evidence on the Three Views

According to the conservative view, competition should gradually reduce racial discrimination. As we suggested in Chapter 2, however, there has been little apparent decrease in discrimination against blacks during this century. In fact, as we saw in Chapter 1, traditional economists such as Welch and Arrow have devoted much ingenuity to attempting to explain why our economy, which is at least somewhat competitive, has *not* led to greater improvement in the relative economic position of blacks. While the conservative viewpoint appears relevant on some issues (as we shall see in the next chapter when we discuss the issue of school integration), it does not appear particularly helpful as a general guide to policies for reducing racial income differentials.[22]

Although the time-series evidence (discussed in Chapter 2) does not provide much support for the simple conservative view, the evidence prior to 1964 could be consistent with either the liberal or radical view. However, a test of all three competing viewpoints can be developed based on the experience since the Civil Rights Act of 1964. This landmark

[19] Such commodities would also be made available free to firms. If competitive forces are not strong enough to force such firms to reduce their output prices, then the government should require such reductions so that the firms do not gain a windfall profit.

[20] For example, the present cost of powdered milk is only about half the cost of regular milk, yet relatively little powdered milk is consumed.

[21] Of course, there could be a stigma problem if the well-to-do never took advantage of the free commodities. While some might do so in the beginning, this is one of many attitudes that might eventually change.

[22] Of course, Friedman might conclude from this evidence that we should concentrate on making the economy more competitive. As argued in Chapter 1, however, it seems unlikely that an additional economic argument for competition is likely to have much effect in the political arena.

legislation prohibited most discrimination in employment, public accommodations, and all federally assisted activities, including education. Together with the Voting Rights Act of 1965, it provided significant new opportunities for blacks to vote, especially in the South.

Given the conservative perspective, this legislation might be expected to have little effect on the economic position of blacks, except in the South.[23] According to the liberal view, the act—and the attitude changes that both led to and resulted from the act—should have led to continued improvements in the relative position of blacks since 1964.[24] Finally, the radical view suggests that the act should have had some initial impact, but that the gains resulting for the average black will not withstand a recession.[25]

Although there have been only a relatively few years since the passage of the act, the available data can give us some guidance in choosing among the conservative, liberal, and radical views. A regression is specified with a dummy variable (D) for the period since 1964 and with separate trend variables $(T_1$ and $T_2)$ for the period before and after 1964. If the conservative view is correct and the act has had little effect (at least in the North) then the coefficient of D should not be significantly greater than zero and the coefficient of T_2 should not be significantly greater than that of T_1, unless black gains have been heavily concentrated in the South. If the liberal view is correct and the relative position

[23] In the passage quoted earlier, Friedman appears to be saying that antidiscrimination laws are unlikely to be passed and enforced for any appreciable time period if they conflict with the tastes for discrimination of the average voter, although a national majority, based in the North, may succeed in forcing southern whites to desist from blatant, overt forms of discrimination. While logrolling might enable antidiscrimination laws to be passed despite the absence of majority support (as Becker indicates), logrolling is less likely to result in such legislation being enforced vigorously for an extended period of time if a majority is strongly opposed to the effects of such legislation. On the other hand, logrolling might have a long-term effect if the majority is not strongly opposed. Partly for this reason and partly because Friedman is talking mostly about very long time periods, our test of the conservative view based on the experience since 1964 is rather weak.

Although Friedman wrote *Capitalism and Freedom* shortly before the Civil Rights Act of 1964, no conservative work of equal stature has addressed these issues since that time. Therefore, although to our knowledge Friedman has not made specific predictions about the effects of this act, we shall attempt to apply Friedman's earlier analysis to extrapolate conservative predictions about the effectiveness of such legislation.

[24] According to this view (which is derived from the analysis of both Myrdal and Allport), the cumulative effects of the act can include further legislation and federal affirmative-action requirements.

[25] Here we are following the predictions of Baran and Sweezy. Sherman's analysis does not lead to any relevant predictions.

of blacks has improved at a faster rate after passage of the act, then the coefficient of T_2 should be greater than the coefficient of T_1 and the coefficient of D may also be positive. Finally, if the radicals are correct, then the coefficient of T_2 should not be significantly greater than that of T_1 although the coefficient of D may be positive.

Since it appears appropriate to standardize for differences in aggregate demand,[26] we shall obtain our regression estimates for the effect of cyclical and trend factors on the male black–white income ratio by updating Rasmussen's results.[27] Thus our regression model is given by the following equation:

$$Y_t = a\%\Delta GNP + bU_{t-1} + cT_1 + dT_2 + eD + u, \qquad (1)$$

where Y_t = the ratio of nonwhite to white median male income,[28] $\%\Delta GNP$ = the percentage rate of growth of GNP, U_{t-1} = the aggregate unemployment rate lagged one year, T_1 = the time trend prior to 1964, T_2 = the time trend beginning in 1964,[29] D = a dummy for the peroid beginning in 1964, u = the error term.

[26] It is appropriate to standardize for changes in aggregate labor-market conditions to the extent that such changes occur for reasons that are unrelated to concern about the relative employment opportunities available to blacks. While many factors affecting fiscal and monetary policy are unrelated to any such concern about blacks (e.g., the widespread concern about inflation and the balance of payments), one reason for favoring tight labor markets, at the expense of moderate inflation, is concern about the economic position of blacks and other disadvantaged groups. Thus, in evaluating the conflicting views of the liberal, Myrdal, and the radicals, Baran and Sweezy, it is not entirely clear whether we should standardize for differences in aggregate labor-market conditions, as we have done in Equation (2). In our view, however, concern for the employment opportunities of blacks is a relatively minor factor in determining fiscal and monetary policies so that standardized results are the most appropriate ones for our purposes.

[27] See David Rasmussen, "A Note on the Relative Income of Nonwhite Men, 1948–1964," *Quarterly Journal of Economics* 84 (February 1970). Also recall the discussion of these results in Chapter 2.

[28] We use data for males rather than for families since we do not want the results to be altered by differences in family composition that may occur as a result of economic changes. Moreover, annual earnings of wives will be affected by husbands' income. We use relative income rather than relative earnings primarily because income appears to be a better measure of economic status. In addition, the only earnings data available annually for blacks and whites are median wage and salary income for those with such income, a measure that excludes many more individuals than are excluded from our relative income measures (which exclude only those with no income of any kind). However, we did run a regression using relative wage and salary income and obtained very similar results.

[29] The values for T_1 go from 1 in 1948 to 16 in 1963 and then become zero. For T_2, the values are zero through 1963, 1 in 1964 and then up to 8 in 1971. We use 1964 as the dividing point, rather than 1965, since the legislation is likely to affect both specific employer practices and general attitudes as soon as it is passed rather than just when it becomes legally effective.

When this model is applied to annual data for the period 1948 to 1971, we obtain the results reported in Equation (2) (standard errors are in parentheses).

$$Y_t = \underset{(.0023)}{0.565} + \underset{(.0023)}{.0056\%\Delta GNP} - \underset{(.0069)}{.0153U_{t-1}} + \underset{(.0015)}{.0005T_1} + \underset{(.0033)}{.0112T_2} \tag{2}$$

$$+ \underset{(.0207)}{.0077D} \quad \bar{R}^2 = .73 \quad \text{D.W.} = 2.3$$

These results indicate that the trend has significantly increased since 1964,[30] thus supporting the liberal view that there should be a continuous improvement in the relative position of blacks once some precipitous event like the Civil Rights Act and the pressures that led to it have occurred. The findings are particularly impressive since the black migration to the North has increased the relative income of blacks, and this migration has slowed down quite dramatically since 1960.[31]

Using these results, we can estimate the effects of the act as of 1971, at least if we are willing to assume that (*1*) the legislation has had a greater effect than the attitude changes that led to the act and (*2*) changes in legislation and attitudes since 1964 have resulted in large part from the 1964 act. While both of these assumptions are rather strong, they enable us to obtain an upperbound estimate for the effects of the legislation.

To obtain such an estimate, we must add the coefficient of the dummy variables to the effect of the difference in the trend estimates. Let the total effect be Δz, then

$$\Delta z = e + 8.0(d - c) = .0079 + 8.0(.0112 - .0005) = .0935. \tag{3}$$

According to this model, the act and the pressures that led to it have

[30] Since the dummy variable allows the two trend coefficients to be independent, the relevant *t*-value is $(.0122 - .0005)/\sqrt{.0015^2 + .0033^2} = 3.4$, which indicates that the difference between the two trend coefficients is statistically significant at the 99 percent level. The trend estimate for 1948 to 1963 is much lower than Rasmussen's estimate for 1948 to 1964, which suggests that Rasmussen's figure might have been considerably lower if he had adjusted for the effects of the act. We obtain similar results when the dependent variable is the ratio of median wage and salary incomes. Our findings appear quite consistent with those of Richard B. Freeman, expressed in his recent article, "Changes in the Labor Market for Black Americans," *Brookings Papers on Economic Activity*, No. 1 (January 1973). Freeman generally finds even greater relative gains for black females during the period since the Civil Rights Act of 1964.

[31] Recall the discussion of this issue in Chapter 3.

TABLE 6.1

Changes in the Nonwhite–White Male Income Ratio, 1960–1971

	Median income of males			
Year	Nonwhite	White	Nonwhite/ White	Unemployment rate
1960	$2369	$4511	52.5%	5.5%
1961	2378	4610	51.6	6.7
1962	2359	4785	49.3	5.5
1963	2558	4880	52.4	5.7
1964	2798	4936	56.7	5.2
1965	2672	5135	52.0	4.5
1966	3097	5592	55.4	3.8
1967	3448	5862	58.8	3.8
1968	3829	6267	61.1	3.6
1969	3992	6765	59.0	3.5
1970	4240	7011	60.5	4.9
1971	4401	7237	60.8	5.9

SOURCE: The income figures are taken from the P-60 Series, *Current Population Reports*, United States Census Bureau.

already increased the black–white income ratio by more than nine percentage points (e.g., without the act, the ratio would have been about 0.52 instead of 0.61 in 1971). Thus the act and its accompanying pressures appear to have had a sizeable as well as a statistically significant effect on the relative income of black males.

This analysis requires several qualifications. First, it is not clear whether we should have standardized for differences in aggregate labor-market conditions, thereby treating such differences as exogenous.[32] Even if such a standardization is not made, however, the results in Table 6.1 indicate that blacks have at least maintained their relative position during the recession of the early 1970s.

Second, the results might have been different if we had standardized for other factors such as age, schooling, and location. In addition, we should examine whether the results primarily reflect class rather than racial changes (e.g., whether poor whites have improved their relative position as much as blacks).

[32] Recall the discussion of this issue in footnote 26.

In Table 6.2 calculations based on the 1960 and 1970 Census are presented which can help us evaluate these issues. First, we see that the relative improvement of nonwhite males increases slightly when we restrict the analysis to prime-age males (25–54), but that the improvement is still substantial. It is also considerably greater than the relative improvement of prime-age white males in the bottom quintile of the white income distribution. Both results increase our confidence that the civil rights legislation may have had an important effect on the relative income of blacks. The figures by years of school indicate that blacks have improved their relative position at all schooling levels, although blacks with the most schooling have made the greatest gains.

Next, we need to test Friedman's view that the effects of the act will have been mainly limited to the South.[33] In contrast, the liberals and

TABLE 6.2

Median Black–White Male Income Ratios, 1959–1969,
by Age and Years of School

	1959	1969	Difference
All males,	.534	.601	.067
Males, 25–54	.558	.639	.081
White males, 25–54			
bottom quintile/median	.604	.617	.013
Years of school			
0–4	.780	.806	.026
5–7	.726	.807	.081
8	.729	.775	.046
9–11	.659	.677	.018
12	.676	.707	.031
13–15	.660	.783	.123
16+	.571	.717	.146

NOTE: All figures have been calculated from data in the 1960 and 1970 Census of Population. For 1959 black means nonwhite and for 1969 it means Negro. Since for all men the 1959 Negro–white ratio was lower than the nonwhite–white ratio (.520 versus .534), all the racial differences would probably have been greater if we could have used a consistent definition.

[33] The results could also support the conservative position if there had been a significant increase in competition during this period. However, there does not appear to be any evidence of such an increase. For example, concentration ratios in manufacturing increased slightly from 1963 to 1967. For a good summary of opinion on recent trends, see Jerry E. Pohlman, *The Economics of Wage and Price Controls* (Columbus, Ohio: Grid, Inc., 1972), pp. 96–97.

TABLE 6.3

Changes in the Black–White Income Ratio, by Location

Location	1969	1959	1959–1969
Nation	.601	.575	.026
Region			
Northeast	.753	.719	.034
North Central	.798	.766	.032
West	.719	.711	.008
South	.558	.466	.092
Regional urbanization			
Northeast—urban	.744	.707	.037
North Central—urban	.762	.703	.059
West—urban	.714	.703	.011
South—urban	.573	.510	.063
South—rural nonfarm	.485	.402	.083
South—rural farm	.474	.420	.054
SMSAs in North and West			
(over 200,000 blacks)			
Chicago	.713	.678	.035
Cleveland	.718	.701	.017
Detroit	.738	.685	.053
Los Angeles	.726	.684	.042
New York	.712	.678	.034
Newark	.695	.671	.024
Philadelphia	.689	.663	.025
San Francisco	.686	.722	− .036
Median change			.030
SMSAs in South			
(over 200,000 blacks)			
Atlanta	.531	.481	.050
Birmingham	.515	.488	.027
Dallas	.550	.476	.074
Houston	.551	.511	.040
Memphis	.483	.467	.016
New Orleans	.507	.511	− .004
Median change			.034
SMSAs in border areas			
(over 200,000 blacks)			
Baltimore	.631	.626	.005
St. Louis	.583	.581	.002
Washington	.610	.573	.037
Median change			.005

SOURCE: These figures have been calculated from data in the 1960 and 1970 Census of Population.
NOTE: For both years black means Negro.

radicals apparently believe that the effects will be felt throughout the nation—although perhaps with greatest force within the South.

Regional results, based on the 1960 and 1970 Census, are presented in Table 6.3. While the increases are generally greatest in the South, some improvements can also be observed in the North. Moreover, the regional differentials diminish once we disaggregate by rural–urban location, a finding that can be partially explained by the rapid urbanization of southern blacks. In fact, when we disaggregate still further and look at individual SMSAs, we see that, among SMSAs with over 200,000 blacks, the median increase in the black–white income ratio over this period is almost as great in the North as in the South and greater than in the border states.[34] Since these SMSAs account for about two-thirds of the black population outside the South (and about one-quarter of those in the South), our results support the liberal and radical view that blacks would improve their relative position in all areas as a result of the act.[35] Although the relative gains attained by blacks do not appear very dramatic, once we disaggregate by location, they compare very favorably with the decline in the relative position of blacks within each region during the 1960s.[36]

To further evaluate the validity of the model used in Equation (2) and to compare the liberal view of continuing progress with the radical

[34] In Table 6.3 we depart from the census definition of South and include only the states of the old Confederacy in this region. The border areas are defined to include other areas allowing slavery prior to the Civil War. In contrast, in the census definition, Washington and Baltimore are in the South and St. Louis is in the North Central region.

[35] While these results do not standardize for other factors, such as changes in relative educational levels or changes in aggregate demand, there do not appear to have been major variations in these factors between the South and the rest of the country. We can look at changes in relative male earnings beween 1959 and 1969, standardizing for differences in age, years of school, and degree of urbanization, using our earnings functions of Chapter 5. These results suggest somewhat greater gains in the North than in the South. With regard to the tightness of labor markets, the unemployment rate fell between 1960 and 1970 in all but three of our SMSAs. While increases in the unemployment rate may explain the decline in the black–white income ratio in San Francisco–Oakland and the small increases in St. Louis and Memphis, the unemployment rate fell substantially in the other three SMSAs (New Orleans, Baltimore, and Cleveland) where the racial income ratio either declined or only increased slightly during the 1960s.

[36] See Alan B. Batchelder, "Decline in the Relative Income of Negro Men," *Quarterly Journal of Economics* 78 (November 1964): 525–548, for an excellent discussion of the experience in the 1950s. Of course, the improvements in the 1960s are attributable to tighter labor markets as well as the effects of legislation against discrimination.

TABLE 6.4

The Residuals for Equation (2), Where the Dependent Variable (Y)
Is the Black–White Income Ratio

Year	Actual Y	Predicted $\hat{Y}$	Residual $Y - \hat{Y}$
1960	0.525	0.504	0.021
1961	.516	.502	.014
1962	.493	.510	−.017
1963	.524	.514	.010
1964	.567	.530	.037
1965	.520	.554	−.034
1966	.554	.577	−.023
1967	.588	.577	.011
1968	.611	.600	.011
1969	.590	.603	−.013
1970	.605	.598	.007
1971	.608	.605	.003

view of little long-run change, we must look at the residuals from Equation (2). If Baran and Sweezy are correct, then we might expect the residuals $(Y_i - \hat{Y}_i)$ to become negative as unemployment increased in the early 1970s.[37] Such a result would also be consistent with the traditional view of economists that the effects of a major change in the economy, such as the Civil Rights Act, may not be felt immediately, but that the adjustments will be relatively large at the beginning and then gradually taper off. On the other hand, Myrdal's view suggests no tapering off and possibly accelerating effects as changes in the economic position of blacks and white tastes for discrimination interact to improve the relative opportunities of blacks. With this background in mind, consider Table 6.4, which gives the residuals from Equation (2) for the period since 1960.

We see that there is no significant trend in the residuals since the passage of the act. (In addition, the regression line fits the more recent data for 1972 perfectly.) Therefore the experience thus far appears to provide more support for Myrdal's liberal position than for either Friedman's conservative view or Baran and Sweezy's radical one. However, it

[37] Recall that Baran and Sweezy predicted that gains for the average black would no longer occur once the economy went into a recession.

is still too early to form a definite judgment of the long-run effects of the Civil Rights Act.[38]

V. Conclusion

In this chapter we have outlined the conservative, liberal, and radical policy perspectives on the issue of racial discrimination. In evaluating these views, with regard to their success in predicting the consequences of the Civil Rights Act of 1964, we find that the liberal perspective appears to have been most successful up to this point—although the time period since 1964 is still too limited to allow a conclusive test. Moreover, it remains impossible to determine the extent to which the act is responsible for the improvement in the black–white income ratio since 1964, and even if the act does continue to have a strong continuing effect, it is not clear whether the effect comes from the symbolic value of the act or from its legal substance. Despite these qualifications, the policy prescriptions presented in the next chapter are basically both liberal and substantive. In addition to the statistical support for the liberal view, the liberal prescriptions, such as affirmative-action programs, appear somewhat more relevant in the political arena than either the radical emphasis on socialism or the conservative emphasis on increasing competition. Moreover, substantive prescriptions fall more within the author's area of competence than any symbolic analysis.

Although the statistical results do appear consistent with the liberal position, these results should not be interpreted as meaning that the liberal view is the only one with any validity. For example, the conservative view on the limitations of legislation appears to be relevant in some important cases, as we shall see in our discussion of specific policies in the concluding chapter. Moreover, future experience may yet show that the pessimism of Baran and Sweezy is more realistic than Myrdal's optimism. Finally, Sherman's radical views have not been tested. Therefore, we cannot rule out the possibility that his proposals would have led to even greater relative progress for blacks in recent years.

---

[38] For example, radicals might emphasize how large the racial income gap remains. In addition, Baran and Sweezy might question whether the increase in unemployment in the early 1970s was great enough to be classified as a recession.

7

Policy Recommendations

In Chapters 3 through 5 we have suggested that, in order to reduce the earnings gap between black and white men, the greatest potential payoffs are likely to come from policies to reduce labor-market discrimination and educational inequalities. Chapter 6 has suggested that there is empirical evidence to support the liberal policy perspective. Therefore, working mainly within the liberal framework, we shall discuss in this chapter policies to combat labor-market discrimination and to improve the relative educational opportunities of blacks. As in the preceding chapters, the analysis is primarily, but not exclusively, urban in its focus.

I. Combating Discrimination in Employment

In discussing policies to combat racial discrimination in employment, a natural starting point is Title VII of the Civil Rights Act of 1964 (as amended in 1972), which prohibits discrimination by all firms or unions with more than fifteen members. The 1972 amendments also prohibit employment discrimination by educational institutions and by

all levels of government. In analyzing the implementation of this legislation, we shall look first at the issue of enforcement procedures and then
turn to substantive issues regarding the legislation. With regard to procedures, the first question concerns the scale of federal enforcement
efforts. As of fiscal year 1972, total appropriations for "private sector
equal employment opportunities" were only forty-seven million dollars,
with administration requests up to eighty-one million for 1974.[1] Although
the projected increase is encouraging, this figure is very small in relation
to many other government activities.[2] Perhaps the most interesting comparison is with government expenditures on manpower programs, which
totaled over four billion dollars in fiscal year 1972.[3] If blacks received
the revenues of such programs in proportion to their share of the total
population, then about ten times as much was being spent on training
blacks (outside of school) as was being spent on combating discrimination.[4] This relative emphasis on manpower programs is striking in the
light of our conclusion in Chapter 5 that labor-market discrimination is
as important as skill differentials in explaining the relatively low earnings of black males, especially since benefit–cost estimates for policies
to combat labor-market discrimination, though crude, are much higher
than such estimates for most manpower and education programs.[5]

Current enforcement procedures also suffer from other limitations in
addition to meager financial resources. Until recently the Equal Employment Opportunity Commission (EEOC) set up under the Civil
Rights Act of 1964 had virtually no legal power with regard to employers,
but was limited to the role of conciliation and negotiation. Suits could
be brought only by private individuals or by the Justice Department.
Such suits can be expensive for private parties, while the activities of

---

[1] *Special Analyses of the United States Government, Fiscal Year 1974*, from *The
Budget of the United States Government, 1974* (Washington, D.C.: United States
Government Printing Office, 1974), p. 180.

[2] Note that the actual increase may be much smaller due to congressional action.

[3] *Special Analysis*, p. 120. This comparison was first suggested to the author by
James E. Jones, Jr.

[4] Since most of the manpower programs are aimed at the disadvantaged, the share
going to blacks may be greater than their share of the *total* population. On the other
hand, a significant portion of the expenditures on equal-employment opportunities is
aimed at females and other disadvantaged groups other than blacks.

[5] For rough benefit–cost estimates of antidiscrimination laws, see William Landes,
"The Economics of Fair Employment Laws," *Journal of Political Economy* 71
(July–August 1968): especially 547–549. For manpower and education programs see
Thomas I. Ribich, *Education and Poverty* (Washington, D.C.: The Brookings
Institution, 1968).

the Justice Department in this area have been limited by a small staff and lack of coordination with the EEOC.[6]

In 1972, Congress amended Title VII to enable the EEOC to sue in the courts whenever it believes a violation has occurred. While this legislation represents a significant improvement,[7] stronger procedures would have been possible and were seriously considered in the Senate. Under this alternative proposal, the EEOC would have been given the power to issue cease and desist orders. Thus, once the EEOC judged that discrimination had occurred, the firm would not have been allowed to continue that discrimination pending trial. This defeated proposal would have been more equitable since it would have given blacks (and other disadvantaged groups) the benefit of the doubt *once* the EEOC ruled that discrimination did exist.

On the other hand, the EEOC might make better use of the powers that it does have. For example, it might put more emphasis on class-action suits and less on processing individual complaints of discrimination. As Wallace puts it:

> If the EEOC could set a one-year moratorium on the processing of individual complaints and spend 90 percent of its budget on industry-wide pattern approaches and other technical assistance programs, this would be a great improvement over the present efforts.[8]

Even if enforcement procedures were greatly strengthened, however, important substantive issues would still remain.

A. Substantive Issues in Eliminating Employment Discrimination

Title VII of the Civil Rights Act of 1964 states:

> It shall be an unlawful employment practice for an employer to fail or refuse to hire or to discharge any individual or otherwise to discriminate against any

---

[6] See the discussion in *Federal Civil Rights Enforcement Effort: A Report of the United States Commission on Civil Rights* (Washington, D.C.: United States Government Printing Office, 1970), Chapter 2, Sections V and VI.

[7] For example, it appears to have contributed to the multimillion dollar settlement negotiated recently with the American Telephone and Telegraph Company and to subsequent settlements with major steel companies.

[8] Phyllis A. Wallace, "Employment Discrimination: Some Policy Considerations," in *Discrimination in Labor Markets*, eds. Orley Ashenfelter and Albert Rees (Princeton, New Jersey: Princeton Univ. Press, 1973), p. 173. This article also contains a good discussion of many other issues involving what she terms "the Equal Employment Opportunity delivery system" of the federal government.

individual with respect to his compensation, terms, conditions, or privileges of employment because of such individual's race, color, religion, sex, or national origin.[9]

While this legislation was designed to improve the economic position of minority groups, it explicitly disavows a number of actions that might be taken to improve the labor-market status of blacks and other disadvantaged groups. These restrictions are concisely summarized in a recent issue of the *Harvard Law Review*:

> The act's effectiveness in promoting minority employment was limited by the principle of color blindness. Just as the employer was not to discriminate against minority groups, he was also prescribed from showing preference to them. Employers could continue to set rigorous qualifications for their job openings and test for worker productivity, as long as they did so fairly. The act thus includes an antipreferential provision (e.g., no quotas are to be necessary), affirms the legality of professionally developed ability tests, and protects bona fide seniority systems. Help was to come to the black community, Congress reasoned, by a newfound opportunity to be judged by objective standards.[10]

While restrictions or preferential treatment might be a small price for minority groups to pay in exchange for objective standards that prohibit discrimination, it is not easy to establish such objective standards.

We start with the issue of discrimination in hiring. We define such discrimination in the following way: Assume that two identical jobs are available in a given company and that there are two equally qualified applicants; if one applicant is black and the other white, then discrimination would occur if the firm hired the white but not the black.[11]

Next, let us examine some of the problems that occur when we try to apply this definition to specific cases. The first difficulty is in determining when two applicants are equally qualified. In this area, the most controversial issue has been the role of educational requirements, either amount of schooling (e.g., a high school diploma) or scores on various kinds of tests. Recent studies have indicated that schooling is a very crude measure of worker productivity.[12] While tests might provide a

---

[9] Civil Rights Act of 1964, Section 703.

[10] "Employment Discrimination and Title VII of the Civil Rights Act of 1964," a lengthy unsigned note in the *Harvard Law Review* 84, no. 5 (March 1971): 1114.

[11] If there were only one job available and the white were hired, it would be impossible to know whether this represented discrimination or a random event—at least in the absence of any independent knowledge of the employer's intentions.

[12] For example, see Ivar Berg, *The Great Training Robbery* (New York: Praeger, 1970).

better measure, it is probably impossible to develop tests that are perfect measures of job performance. Moreover, it is expensive to develop tests that are even moderately accurate; the net costs are likely to be high even after taking account of resulting improvements in worker performance.[13] On the other hand, it may also be costly for the firm to ignore potential differences in productivity among its applicants.

The Supreme Court has ruled that requiring completion of high school or passage of a general intelligence test can be illegal if these requirements operate to disqualify blacks at a substantially higher rate than white applicants and if the requirements are not shown to be significantly related to successful job performance.[14] Although it is not yet clear what standards of proof the court will require in order for a firm to demonstrate that its requirements are job related, it appears that the courts will have to become involved in some very difficult issues involving trade-offs between efficiency and equity. As we shall argue later, there may be ways to avoid some of these difficulties by judging equity in terms of results as well as procedures.

Even if we can clearly determine when two applicants are equally qualified, there are other difficulties in determining whether or not an employer is discriminating in his hiring. Specifically, an employer's recruitment policies must be considered along with his hiring requirements. For example, many firms recruit primarily through current employees. Such recruitment procedures have significant benefits for both the employer and those considering employment with the firm.[15] However, if the present work force is virtually all white, important issues of discrimination arise.

The courts have generally ruled that such recruitment procedures are illegal if they result in a work force whose racial composition is significantly different from that of the community.[16] The natural remedy is that the employer begins advertising his job vacancies in media which

[13] For example, on many jobs a simple test and a probationary period may be a more efficient procedure than a more elaborate test.

[14] See *Willie S. Griggs* v. *Duke Power Company*, U.S. Supreme Court, no. 124 (March 9, 1971).

[15] For example, see the discussion in Albert Rees, "Information Networks in Labor Markets," *Papers and Proceedings of the 78th Annual Meetings of the American Economic Association* 16 (December 1965): 559.

[16] See "Employment Discrimination," *Harvard Law Review*, pp. 1153–1155. As that discussion indicates, however, if an employer's recruitment policies appear to be discriminatory on this basis, it seems reasonable to give the employer a chance to demonstrate that blacks have less interest or skill than whites in his line of work.

serve the black community and/or with civil rights organizations. However, the question arises: How much of this new recruitment activity must be undertaken, especially since racial quotas in employment are specifically disavowed under Title VII? Again the courts appear to have been forced into a very difficult situation.

Next, let us turn from the issue of discrimination in hiring to other issues of discrimination in employment. Perhaps the most important of these issues are promotions, layoffs, and discharges. Promotions and discharges are based partly on ability (or lack thereof) and thus qualification standards in these areas are subject to many of the same problems as hiring standards.[17] However, seniority also plays an important role in most promotions and almost all layoffs. If there is no history of discrimination in hiring, then seniority rules pose little difficulty since seniority is easier to measure objectively than most other potential criteria. However, if there has been past discrimination, then seniority rules may help to perpetuate this discrimination far into the future.

Let us assume that, prior to the Civil Rights Act of 1964, a firm employed blacks only in certain unskilled, low-paying positions,[18] and that, for whites, there was a well-defined ladder for advancement, with promotions going to the man with the most seniority among those in the next lowest job who are considered qualified. Now let us consider how blacks are to be integrated into this seniority system after passage of the Civil Rights Act. Three main possibilities have been advanced:

(1) "freedom now," requiring displacement of white incumbents by blacks who, without discrimination in the past, would have had their places;
(2) "rightful place," allowing a black to compete for a position on the basis of his total company service (without having to advance through each step of the ladder);
(3) "status quo," preserving intact the rights of white incumbents (blacks must start at the bottom of the white ladder and advance through each step on the same basis as newly entering whites).[19]

----

[17] As a result of union pressure, employers may have more carefully articulated rationales for their promotions and discharge policies than for their hiring policies. On the other hand, if a union wishes to discriminate it may not give adequate attention to grievances filed by blacks with regard to issues of promotions and discharge. Thus, policies that appear fair on the surface may be quite discriminatory in practice.

[18] If the firm (or union) is all white, a more extreme possibility is to apply the following analysis based on blacks in the community rather than on blacks in, low-paying jobs within the company. See *United States* v. *Sheetmetal Workers Local 36* 416 F.2d 123 (8th Cir. 1969).

[19] "Employment Discrimination," *Harvard Law Review*, p. 1158.

Congress clearly indicated that it was not requiring the "freedom now" approach when it protected bona fide seniority systems.[20] Of the other two alternatives, the "rightful place" test has been generally accepted by the courts.[21] Of course, there may be little practical difference between the "rightful-place" and "status-quo" approaches if skills must be learned during each job on the ladder. Consequently, even if all discrimination in hiring and recruiting should cease, it could still take a long time to eliminate all the effects of past labor-market discrimination.

B. *Affirmative-Action Requirements*

So far, we have argued that it is going to be very difficult to eliminate all discrimination in employment simply by trying to apply the "color-blind" standards of Title VII. Moreover, even if such discrimination could be eliminated, the effects of past discrimination would persist far into the future. Thus, we need to consider alternative approaches to combating discrimination.

The major alternative to the present legal concept of color blindness is the imposition of some kind of quota system. At least two variations of the quota approach are available. The first, which might be called inflexible quotas, means that firms must employ at least a certain percentage of blacks and that no exceptions will be allowed. The second, which might be called target quotas, means that the burden of proof is on the employer to show that he has not discriminated (or has fulfilled his contract commitment to take "affirmative action") if he does not employ as many blacks as stipulated by the quota. In an apparent effort to avoid confusing target and inflexible quotas, the latter are usually referred to as goals rather than quotas. While Congress clearly indicated that Title VII was not to be interpreted as requiring any quota system, the executive branch has established a system of "goals" with regard to government contractors.[22] Moreover, this system has been upheld in the courts and has been tacitly accepted by Congress.[23]

[20] However, this approach may be an appropriate remedy for a discriminatory system in effect after the Civil Rights Act of 1964 became effective. See Alfred W. Blumrosen, *Black Employment and the Law* (New Brunswick, New Jersey: Rutgers Univ. Press, 1971), pp. 202–205.

[21] "Employment Discrimination," *Harvard Law Review*, p. 1159.

[22] See James E. Jones, Jr., "The Bugaboo of Employment Quotas," *Wisconsin Law Review* 70, no. 2 (1970): 341–403, for a discussion of many of the legal aspects of the quota issue.

[23] *Contractors Association of Eastern Pennsylvania* v. *Shultz* (D.C.-E. Pa., March 13, 1970). The Supreme Court refused to review this case.

The government began its present affirmative-action program with the Philadelphia Plan, instituted in 1967. Under this plan, contractors for government construction projects in the Philadelphia area must make "good-faith" efforts to meet certain goals with regard to the hiring of minority workers. These goals are determined by the Office of Federal Contract Compliance (OFCC) on the basis of such factors as the new hiring predicted for the contractors, the number of minority-group members having the necessary skills, and, if this number is limited, the length of time necessary for training. Then these goals, indicating the number of minority employees to be hired in specified trades by specified times, are included as part of the job specifications on which the contractor bids. Although the Philadelphia Plan does set up very specific goals, these goals originally applied only to the actual government contracts and did not apply to the contractor's employment on other projects. Since firms could meet these requirements by switching black workers from their private projects rather than by hiring more black workers, the program has recently been changed to cover a contractor's total employment.

Failure to meet the specified goals does not necessarily imply that the contractor has failed to comply with the terms of the contract. In the words of the *Harvard Law Review*:

> A contractor can escape sanctions by proving that he made "every good faith effort" to meet the requirements. Signs of a good faith effort are (1) communication of employment needs to certain minority community organizations; (2) maintenance of records showing disposition of minority job applications; (3) participation in community minority training programs; and (4) notification of the OFCC area coordinator whenever the employer's efforts to meet his goal have been impeded by union referral practices. It is specifically noted that failure of a union with which the contractor has a collective bargaining agreement to send minority applicants is not a sufficient excuse for noncompliance. Though the precise procedural consequences of failure to meet goals are not outlined in the Philadelphia Plan, it has been assumed that failure to meet specific goals forces the contractor to assume the burden of producing evidence of his good faith effort to meet his goals while the government has the ultimate burden of persuasion on the issue of noncompliance with the Executive Order program.[24]

Originally the Philadelphia Plan was developed as a model to be used in other cities. However, the government's current approach is to encourage the development of "hometown plans," agreements negotiated

[24] "Employment Discrimination," *Harvard Law Review*, p. 1298.

among unions, contractors, and minority-group representatives to increase the employment of the minority group on all construction projects in the area. If no satisfactory hometown agreement is negotiated, then the government can fall back on the Philadelphia Plan approach.

After studying the operation of an imposed "Philadelphia-type" Plan in Washington and a hometown plan in Indianapolis, Rowan and Rubin conclude:

> The imposed plan provides the stick which is often needed to move contractors who would otherwise make no special effort to correct the existing practice of the past. An imposed plan, however, raises tensions and makes agencies such as the OFCC the scapegoat for unions, contractors, and minority groups.
>
> An imposed plan is not a substitute for cooperation between those who need minorities and those who know where to find qualified minority applicants . . . . On the other hand, hometown plans need some of the government pressure that accompanies imposed plans for it is the government's action or threat of action, which provides the catalyst for voluntarism . . . . If any of the various groups choose not to participate, then voluntarism is dead. Consequently, the penalties of a threatened imposed plan can be neither so light that unions and contractors would opt for them nor so hard that community leaders would prefer them.[25]

In other words, we have a clear application of the bargaining model of racial conflict discussed in Chapter 1.

So far our discussion of affirmative-action requirements has been limited to governmental activities in the construction industry. The government began its affirmation-action program in construction, possibly because

> urban renewal and government building tend to take place in areas of high minority concentration. In many kinds of work, discrimination can be concealed behind closed doors. But the presence of an all-white construction crew working outdoors in plain sight in a black community is a blatant insult.[26]

Although union jobs in the skilled construction trades pay very well, they are only a very small percentage of total jobs in this country. Consequently, it was important for the OFCC to develop an affirmative-

---

[25] Richard L. Rowan and Lester Rubin, *Opening the Skilled Construction Trade for Blacks* (Philadelphia, Pennsylvania: Univ. of Pennsylvania Press, 1972), pp. 173–174.

[26] "Employment Discrimination," *Harvard Law Review*, p. 1294. This note also suggests that allowing EEOC data on the minority employment of large firms and unions to be made public might induce such organizations to improve their employment policies.

action program for federal contractors in areas outside of construction.[27] Such a program has been developed and is currently expressed in Revised Order No. 4. This order, which was formulated in December 1971, requires nonconstruction contractors with fifty or more employees or contracts of at least $50,000 to have affirmative-action programs that include

1. a self-analysis to determine whether women and minorities are being underutilized in one or more job classifications;
2. corrective action, including goals and timetables, to remedy any deficiencies;
3. development or reaffirmation of an equal opportunity policy and dissemination of the policy both internally and externally;
4. establishment of a director or manager of Equal Opportunity Programs with many detailed responsibilities in rectifying problem areas and developing appropriate programs;
5. implementation of internal reporting systems to measure the effectiveness of the affirmative-action programs; and
6. support for community and national programs that are designed to improve the educational opportunities available to women and minorities.

Revised Order No. 4 applies to women as well as to minorities. With regard to minorities, the main differences between this program and the Philadelphia Plan are summarized by Nash:

> The primary difference between the two programs is that the OFCC or an appropriate regional organization analyzes the factors leading to appropriate goal formulation in the construction program, while under Order No. 4 each nonconstruction contractor must make his own analysis. This difference is dictated by the need for a uniform affirmative action approach by each employing entity. Most nonconstruction contractors maintain a relatively constant work force and can establish their own consistent program. But since the construction work force in any locality is in reality employed by all of the construction contractors in the area, goals and timetables for the latter, in order to have a meaningful application to employment, must be developed for the single-employer entity (all contractors) and their employees (all construction employees who move from job to job). The essential requirement of coordinated goal setting is obtained under both programs.[28]

---

[27] Affirmative-action requirements are imposed on firms that are not government contractors only as a legal remedy after a curtailing of illegal discrimination.

[28] Peter G. Nash, "Affirmative Action Under Executive Order 11, 247," *New York Law Review* 46 (April 1971): 235.

While the goals and timetables are initially set by the nonconstruction contractor, these goals and timetables can be revised by the OFCC under Revised Order No. 4. For the programs under Revised Order No. 4, as for those in construction, goals and timetables are to be based on objective factors, such as the availability of minority workers at different skill levels, the existence of training opportunities, the expected turnover of present employees, and expected changes in the size of the work force. Even though contracts can be terminated under Revised Order No. 4, this process is often too time consuming to be very effective. However, the threat of losing future government contracts as a result of inadequate affirmative-action programs still can be very effective, at least in those cases where enforcement activities are strict enough to make such a threat credible.[29]

C. The Advantages and Disadvantages of Affirmative-Action Requirements

Now that we have summarized the current status of affirmative-action requirements, let us discuss more carefully the advantages and disadvantages of this approach. The advantage of the affirmative-action requirements, compared with the color-blind standards of Title VII, is a greater emphasis on positive actions to help blacks, including the establishment of a clearer burden of proof on employers with few black employees.

Nevertheless, the present affirmative-action programs have been fairly controversial. On the one hand, the programs have been criticized for not being tough enough. Proponents of a tough approach sometimes advocate a system of inflexible quotas. However, this approach does not

[29] Ibid., p. 255. Also see Chapter 8 of Alfred W. Blumrosen, *Black Employment and the Law.* In the construction industry, specific goals and timetables are included in the contract and are subject to the same enforcement procedures as would apply to any other specifications in the contract.

Ashenfelter and Heckman find some evidence that affirmative-action requirements have been effective, by using EEOC data. More specifically they conclude: "First we find that the relative employment of black male workers increased by 3.3 percent more over the period 1966 to 1970 in firms with government contracts than in firms without government contracts, and that this difference is statistically significant. Second, we find that the relative occupational position of black male workers increased by .2 percent more in firms with government contracts than in firms without contracts, but that this difference is not statistically significant." See the paper by Orley Ashenfelter and James Heckman, "Changes in Minority Employment Patterns, 1966 and 1970," presented at a Research Workshop on Equal-Employment Opportunity held at the Massachusetts Institute of Technology, January 1974.

appear politically feasible and might reinforce racial stereotypes if black members were placed in jobs for which they were not qualified. If inflexible quotas are rejected in favor of the present emphasis on goals, timetables, and good faith efforts, then the crucial issues are (*1*) how ambitious the goals and timetables must be and (*2*) how vigorously the government pressures firms that make only a minimal effort to meet their goals.[30]

On the other hand, many feel that the whole affirmative-action approach is too stringent an antidiscrimination strategy. Advocates of this view have generally focused on three objections to the affirmative-action requirements—an efficiency argument, an equity argument, and a set of political arguments.

The efficiency argument maintains that any affirmative-action program will increase a firm's costs since the firm would be required to hire blacks when it would otherwise have been free to hire more highly skilled whites. However, the present affirmative-action programs only require an employer to make a good faith effort to meet his target for minority employment. If he has made every reasonable effort to recruit (and/or train) qualified black workers, then he would not be subject to any sanctions. While an employer might be required to undergo some extra expenses for recruiting and training black workers, it is not clear that such costs will necessarily exceed the costs that a firm might incur by ignoring the potential availability of black workers (compare Becker's view of discrimination discussed in Chapter 1). Moreover, the government and civil rights organizations can often help with recruitment and/or training, thus reducing the firm's costs.

Also recall from Chapter 6 Friedman's concern that some firms would suffer heavy costs if they were forced to hire blacks when their present employees or customers preferred the firm to remain entirely white. This argument appears to lose much of its force in the present situation, however, since all competing firms are subject to the same affirmative-action requirements; all must make a good faith effort, not only to hire qualified blacks if they apply, but also to attract such applicants.[31]

[30] For example, shortly after the 1972 election, a news article in the *New York Times* (19 December 1972) stated "The Nixon Administration has reportedly all but abandoned efforts to force Federal contractors to hire more blacks, other minority group members, and women." For another analysis of worker attitudes toward affirmative action (as well as much other valuable material on racial issues in employment) see Theodore Purcell and Gerald Cavanagh, *Blacks in the Industrial World* (New York: Free Press, 1972).

[31] Small contractors are the only ones not subject to the affirmative-action requirements. As long as they stay small, they are not likely to be too much of a threat to their larger rivals.

The equity argument maintains that, if the individual worker or employer has not discriminated against blacks, then he should not have to bear the major burden of any costs involved in improving their economic position. Instead the costs should be borne by society as a whole (e.g., through general taxation). Of course, this argument assumes affirmative-action programs do involve important costs to firms and to white workers. As we have just seen, this argument is somewhat questionable in the case of firms. On the other hand, some white workers certainly are hurt by affirmative-action programs. The greatest costs, in this regard, would occur if present white employees were laid off so that additional blacks could be hired. Such an extreme proposal has been ruled out on equity (and political) grounds. However, whites seeking new jobs will be hurt by affirmative-action programs. Two points need to be raised in this regard. First, the cost to such white workers can be minimized if the government pursues fiscal, monetary, and manpower policies to ensure full employment. Second, since the government affirmative-action requirement demands only a good faith effort by government contractors and since discrimination does still exist in the labor market, any harm suffered by whites as a result of affirmative-action programs should be viewed primarily as a cost of reducing discrimination against blacks rather than as an example of discrimination against whites. While we believe that these arguments make it difficult to attack the present affirmative-action programs on equity grounds, these equity considerations do suggest that such programs are likely to face political difficulties.

Several political arguments have been raised against affirmative-action programs. First, such programs have been criticized for dividing the working class politically and, thereby, hurting the economic position of all workers.[32] While this argument may have some validity, the lack of any significant action against discrimination may also lead to tension between black and white workers. A closely related argument maintains that blacks may be helped more (and at less political cost) if political efforts are concentrated on other policies, such as establishing and maintaining tight labor markets. But this is simply an argument for putting top priority on tight labor markets and not an argument for abandoning affirmative-action requirements.

Finally, some argue that affirmative-action programs may reinforce racial stereotypes since giving some preferential treatment to minorities suggests that they are unable to compete successfully in terms of their

---

[32] Bayard Rustin, "The Blacks and the Unions," *Harper's* (May 1971).

own ability.[33] While this argument might be valid if employers were forced to hire unqualified applicants, there is no such requirement in the present affirmative-action programs. By putting employers under more pressure to hire (and train) qualified blacks the present programs may actually help break down stereotypes by providing more examples of successful performance by black workers. Thus, none of these political arguments against affirmative action seem very persuasive.

In summary, the present affirmative-action programs are an important policy device for reducing discrimination in the labor market. While they have been attacked on several grounds for being too stringent, these attacks are not very convincing. In fact, our major concern is the relatively limited scale of enforcement efforts. Before concluding this discussion of the desirability of the present affirmative-action programs, however, we must compare these programs to some alternative possibilities.

D. Alternatives to the Present Emphasis on Affirmative Action

One alternative that has been advanced for combating labor-market discrimination is the establishment of a general system of economic incentives proposed by Duran Bell.[34] However, the present affirmative-action approach, with its legal orientation, appears preferable on the grounds of political feasibility. After all, the present program does exist and does appear to be having some impact. Consequently, it seems simpler to try to improve the present system rather than to introduce an entirely new approach that is likely to be quite foreign to the thinking of noneconomists.

A plan somewhat more closely related to the present affirmative-action requirements has been advanced by Galbraith, Kuh, and Thurow.[35] Their plan would apply to women, American Indians, and Spanish-speaking minorities as well as to blacks. Each group would have to receive a share of the highest paying jobs in proportion to their share in

---

[33] For example, see "Employment Discrimination," *Harvard Law Review*, p. 1166.
[34] See Duran Bell, Jr., "Bonuses, Quotas, and the Employment of Black Workers," *Journal of Human Resources* 6 (Summer 1971): 309–320.
[35] John Kenneth Galbraith, Edwin Kuh, and Lester C. Thurow, "The Galbraith Plan to Promote the Minorities," *New York Times Magazine* (27 August 1971).

the labor force in the area where the firm is located. Coverage would start with firms of over 5000 employees. Such firms would have ten years for complete compliance; a longer compliance period would be available for firms between 2000 and 5000 while smaller firms would be exempt. A program of educational grants to help train minority members is also included.

Three differences between this plan and the current affirmative-action requirements deserve special attention. These are *(1)* the ten-year compliance proposal, *(2)* the emphasis on large firms, and *(3)* the emphasis on top level jobs.

The ten-year compliance proposal is, perhaps, the simplest issue to discuss. Setting a specific target date for achieving an ambitious goal has the advantage of virtually ensuring equal opportunity after ten years, if the plan is fully accepted. However, the obvious danger with emphasizing such a long-range target is that the target date can easily be pushed back and even repealed.[36] Consequently, the present system which puts greater emphasis on short-run targets may be more realistic politically.

With regard to the second point, Galbraith and his co-authors argue that the plan should concentrate on the largest firms for several reasons. First, they account for most of the top level jobs in our economy. Second, such firms usually are run by professional executives who have been through a well-organized executive development program, thus facilitating the ease with which disadvantaged groups could receive the necessary training. Finally, Galbraith *et al.* expect intense political opposition from small businessmen if they are subject to any significant affirmative-action requirements. While these considerations have some validity, it appears easier to make a political (and legal) case for extra requirements on government contractors since such requirements can be viewed as a quid pro quo for the "favor" of obtaining government contracts. Given limited enforcement resources, however, it does seem efficient for the government to concentrate primarily on the largest government contractors because of economies of scale in enforcement and because of the pattern-setting influence of large firms.[37] As the largest employer in the country, it is also important for the federal

---

[36] Part of the Galbraith plan deals with intermediate goals, but these short-run targets are given much less emphasis.

[37] A reasonable analogy here may be the enforcement efforts of the Internal Revenue Service, which are aimed disproportionately at those with large incomes—partly to get more revenue per dollar of enforcement expenditure.

government to maintain successful affirmative-action programs with regard to its own employment.[38]

Finally, let us consider Galbraith's argument for limiting these plans to top level jobs:

> It will be asked why [the Galbraith Plan] is confined to the higher income jobs. Why not make it applicable to the shop floor? The answer is that no reform can accomplish everything. Existing government legislation and union rules are all but exclusively focused on the production worker and we seek to avoid conflict with these regulations, including any tangle with the unions. It is also important that our present willingness to act at the bottom be matched by a similar willingness to act at the top. As things now stand, a white construction worker can be kept out of a job by regulations that require the contractor to employ blacks. He must wonder, if he stops to think about it, why the white executive has no similar worry. Also, if women and members of the minority groups are properly represented at the top, it would seem reasonably certain that they will suffer less discrimination at the bottom.[39]

While there is merit in this argument to the extent that it seeks to reduce the present emphasis on blue-collar construction workers, it would be a mistake to limit any plan to the highest paying jobs. Discrimination applies throughout the entire earnings distribution and efforts to improve the education of minority group members will do little to help those who are already at or beyond their peak earnings period. Moreover, minority group members who do make it to the top may often be more concerned with maintaining or advancing their own position than in helping other, less fortunate, brethern.

Another approach to reducing labor-market discrimination is to assist black businessmen. For example, the government can combat discrimination in the credit market by guaranteeing loans to blacks. Such efforts to foster black capitalism would provide direct assistance to a few ambitious blacks and might also increase black employment opportunities. Since small firms are generally unprofitable, however, this approach is not likely to be successful unless it enables blacks to develop some good-sized corporations. Even then the benefits may accrue mainly to those running the corporation rather than to black workers or the broader black community. Despite the early rhetoric of the Nixon administration, the government has done little to aid black business-

---

[38] For an analysis of government efforts with regard to its own employment see *Federal Civil Rights Enforcement Effort, A Report of the U.S. Commission on Civil Rights* (Washington, D.C.: United States Government Printing Office, 1970); and Arthur J. Corazzini, "Equality of Employment Opportunity in the Federal White-Collar Civil Service," *Journal of Human Resources* 7 (Fall 1972).

[39] Galbraith *et al.*, "Galbraith Plan," p. 40.

men and the prospects for future action do not appear bright.[40] While alternatives such as community development corporations have attracted considerable attention,[41] affirmative-action programs can probably have a greater impact on the employment opportunities of the average black, at least in the short run. As a long-run strategy, community development deserves serious consideration. The issue is a complex one, however, and beyond the scope of this book.[42]

Therefore, it appears that none of the alternatives we have considered can take the place of affirmative action and that the affirmative-action programs of the federal government are generally moving in the right direction, at least conceptually. Our major concern with the present program is the need to maintain and improve enforcement efforts.

In this section, we have mainly considered policies aimed directly at combating discrimination in employment. Of course, such discrimination may also be heavily influenced by government policies that are aimed primarily at other goals. For example, employment discrimination is likely to be inversely related to the tightness of labor markets. In addition, we have argued that affirmative-action programs are likely to be much more successful when there are plenty of good jobs available for whites. Therefore, top priority in combating labor-market discrimination should go to efforts to maintain high levels of aggregate demand.[43]

Considerable emphasis should also be given to education and training programs since affirmative-action programs aimed at placing more blacks in high-level positions should have a much greater chance of success if the pool of qualified blacks is relatively plentiful. Policies to improve the educational opportunities of blacks will be discussed in the next section.

---

[40] For an interesting evaluation of the black capitalism thrust of the Nixon administration, see Arthur I. Blaustein and Geoffrey Faux, *The Star-Spangled Hustle* (New York: Doubleday, 1972).

[41] See ibid., especially Chapters 3, 4, 9, and 12. Also see the articles by Innis and by McClaughry in *Black Economic Development*, ed. William F. Haddad and G. Douglas Pugh (Englewood Cliffs, New Jersey: Prentice-Hall, 1969).

[42] Some of the issues are similar to those regarding community control of schools, a topic discussed in some detail in Section II. The complexity arises due to (*1*) the interaction of economic and political considerations and (*2*) the long-run perspective that is necessary if such an approach is to be viewed as having much chance of success on a reasonably large scale.

[43] While tight labor markets may lead to significant inflationary pressures, hopefully, such pressures can be minimized through manpower and other programs to deal with bottleneck sectors. Even if some inflationary costs must be borne, however, such costs may be a small price to pay relative to the benefits of full employment.

II. Combating Discrimination in Education

Our results in Chapter 5 suggest that earnings differentials between blacks and whites are related to skill differentials as well as to labor-market discrimination. Therefore, we need to consider what policies might be pursued to reduce racial skill differentials.

As we indicated in Chapter 2, there is considerable controversy concerning the effect of differences in school resources on educational attainment.[44] Moreover, as a result of the compensatory education programs of the 1960s, it is not clear whether black schools typically have lower expenditures per pupil than white schools. While the evidence is not conclusive, it appears that the present variation in school resources probably has relatively little impact on student test-score achievement.[45] Of course, schools can affect income in other ways, in addition to their effect on test-score performance, and there is some recent evidence showing that expenditures per pupil are positively related to the student's future income—although it is not clear whether any causal relation is involved.[46]

[44] In Chapter 2, we indicated how the Coleman report concludes that measured differences in schools' playground facilities, formal curricula, and teacher characteristics have very little effect on either black or white students' performance on standardized tests. While the methodology used by the report in deriving this conclusion has been subject to a number of fundamental criticisms, no consensus has been reached with regard to the conclusions that should be drawn from more appropriate methodology. In the recent volume edited by Mosteller and Moynihan, for example, Hanushek and Kain conclude that the Coleman report data do not enable one to determine the effect of school resources, while Jencks concludes that differences in school policies and resources have little effect on children's achievement, especially for blacks. See *On Equality of Educational Opportunity*, ed. Frederick Mosteller and Daniel P. Moynihan (New York: Random House, 1972), Chapters 2 and 3.

[45] For example, see the figures on page 293 of the Coleman report; James S. Coleman *et al.*, *Equality of Educational Opportunity* (Washington, D.C.: United States Department of Health, Education, and Welfare, 1966).

[46] See George E. Johnson and Frank P. Stafford, "Social Returns to Quantity and Quality of Schooling," *Journal of Human Resources* 8 (Spring 1973): 139–155; and Richard D. Morgenstern, "Direct and Indirect Effects on Earnings of Schooling and Socio-Economic Background," *Review of Economics and Statistics* 55, no. 2 (May 1973). With regard to the causation issue, states with higher expenditures per pupil probably also have higher per capita income. Since a person is more likely to remain in the state where he grew up than to move to any other given state, the statistical results may simply indicate that the relative position of states with regard to per capita income does not change very much over time. While this result could be attributed to educational differentials remaining relatively constant, it could also be attributed to relatively constant differentials in physical capital, natural resources, and/or interstate prices. In fact, Morgenstern finds little effect for expenditures when he includes a simple North–South dummy. Stafford and Johnson, on the other hand, make no control for current location. As this goes to press, however, more persuasive results relating school expenditures to the future earnings of students have been obtained by John S. Akin and Irwin Garfinkel. See "Economic Returns to Educational Quality: An Empirical Analysis for Whites, Blacks, Poor Whites, and Poor Blacks," Institute for Research on Poverty Discussion Paper 224-74, University of Wisconsin–Madison.

Although efforts to reduce any remaining resource inequalities should continue to receive attention, we are doubtful whether reducing such inequalities will necessarily have a major impact on either skill or earnings differentials. For example, extra money going to black schools can be spent on police instead of textbooks, teachers, and classrooms. Thus, we should consider broader educational reforms, including proposals to radically reorganize the present public school system.[47]

Proposals to reduce racial inequalities by reforming the public schools are usually based on some, or all, of the following objectives: (*1*) making the schools more responsive to the needs of black children; (*2*) reducing white tastes for racial discrimination; and (*3*) increasing the political power of the black community. Three types of reorganization proposals will be discussed: (*1*) reductions in segregation; (*2*) educational vouchers; and (*3*) increased community control of schools in black neighborhoods.

A. *Reducing Racial Segregation*

The Brown decision outlawing de jure segregation within a given school system was based on the assumption that black schools are inherently unequal. While such an argument may be valid when whites are clearly forcing the segregation, it requires strong racist assumptions to argue that all black schools are inherently inferior even if they are administered by blacks and black students attend voluntarily. Therefore, to the extent that the rationale for school desegregation is to improve the educational opportunities of blacks, it would seem reasonable to pursue the desegregation strategy if and only if it is supported by a majority of blacks.

From a practical point of view, however, the issue is not that simple. First, it is not altogether clear how to go about determining the view of the black majority. Perhaps the most basic difficulty in this regard is that the choice should be between truly integrated nondiscriminatory schools and racially separated schools supported with equal financial resources and controlled by the respective racial communities. Unfortunately, however, in this country there is little experience with schools controlled by the black community, and even desegregated schools can

---

[47] Recently Christopher Jencks has argued that schools have relatively little effect on income inequality. See Christopher Jencks *et al.*, *Inequality* (New York: Basic Books, 1972). If this conclusion is true, then it might be fruitless to seek to reduce the black–white earnings ratio by improving schools attended by blacks. While the main thrust of Jencks's argument appears reasonable, he is only talking about normal variations within the present public schools. Moreover, variations in schools could have a large effect on the relative position of blacks (our main concern) and still have very little effect on total inequality (Jencks's main concern).

still be discriminatory (e.g., if teachers, whether white or black, discriminate against black students).

Second, white opposition to "forced" integration is intense. For example, efforts to desegregate large-city schools have led to powerful antibusing lobbies and have contributed to the white migration to the suburbs. Thus, although Friedman's arguments about the futility of government efforts to combat discrimination and segregation do not appear too important in employment, they do seem quite cogent with regard to education (at least in large metropolitan areas).[48]

Despite this opposition to integration, many liberals believe that increased contact between the races is very important since it may reduce white tastes for discrimination and help dispel the myth of black inferiority—at least if the contact is on an equal basis. Moreover, they feel that whites will continue to regard black schools as inferior—and thus be reluctant to hire their graduates—no matter how good such schools may actually become. Finally, and perhaps of greatest importance, black schools may never be able to obtain adequate financial resources as long as whites are dominant economically and politically. If these arguments are correct, can the government do *anything* to reduce white resistance to integration? One interesting approach has been developed by Downs, who argues that white communities should be given a financial incentive to accept black families (e.g., by giving special subsidies to the schools in these communities).[49] As of this writing, however, there is no apparent way of judging whether a reasonable financial incentive would lead to much additional desegregation—let alone true integration, where blacks and whites are treated equally within the desegregated school.

[48] Even if the courts should rule that metropolitan-wide desegregation plans are necessary in many areas, the political opposition to busing may make such decisions very difficult to enforce and could even lead to a constitutional amendment against busing. The recent Supreme Court decision concerning the Detroit schools suggests that the courts are not likely to make such rulings, however.

With regard to employment, one hears little discussion of whites quitting or striking when blacks are hired or promoted. This difference may occur because a firm's quality is judged largely by relatively objective measures like wage rates and profits—with the lack of equivalent measures for neighborhoods and schools encouraging people to use racial composition as a proxy. Another possible explanation is that housing segregation and, thus, also de facto school segregation are valued more highly than segregation in employment since the whole family is involved in housing while only the individual is involved at work. Also there is less danger of a firm "tipping" quickly from all white to predominantly black.

[49] See Anthony Downs, "Alternative Futures for the American Ghetto," *Daedalus* 97, no. 4 (Fall 1968): 1331–1378. Also note that the federal government has deliberately helped create housing and school segregation in the relatively recent past, for example, through FHA loans to finance new homes in suburban areas for whites only.

B. Educational Vouchers

In contrast to Downs's integrationist approach, Friedman proposes to change the present public school system completely by introducing market competition into public education through a system of educational vouchers.[50] Under this approach, parents would be given a voucher that could be spent to enroll their child in any one of a number of schools. Once the child was enrolled in a particular school, that school could exchange the voucher for a cash payment from tho government. Consequently, the system would be almost like a cash subsidy to the parents, except that the subsidy would have to be spent on schooling for the child.[51] In contrast to the present public school system, the financial subsidy for education would not be restricted to a single school. Under Friedman's plan, the degree of integration would be determined entirely by parental preferences.

According to their proponents, vouchers would have three advantages. First, parents would have more direct control of and responsibility for the education of their children. This influence may be especially important for parents holding minority views within the total community. Second, vouchers should make schools more responsive to the needs of students and parents, as present schools are forced to respond to the threat (or actuality) of new schools arising and putting the older ones out of business. Third, by providing for minority views, the voucher system should encourage greater experimentation and diversity. The knowledge gained through testing various innovations should lead to improvements in other schools, as they seek to take advantage of those innovations that are judged to be successful.

Perhaps the most frequent objection to the voucher proposal is that the public schools are designed to instill a common core of values. Although we do allow parents to send their children to other schools if they are willing to pay extra costs, the case for educational vouchers rests heavily on the value judgment that "our problem today is not to enforce conformity; it is rather that we are threatened with an excess of conformity."[52] According to this view, government efforts to require integration are both an abridgement of individual freedom and an effort to enforce conformity.

Three other major arguments against the voucher system are pre-

[50] See Milton Friedman, *Capitalism and Freedom* (Chicago, Illinois: Univ. of Chicago Press, 1962), Chapter 6.

[51] In this respect, the vouchers would be analogous to the present food stamp program.

[52] Friedman, *Capitalism and Freedom*, p. 97.

sented and criticized in a document published by the Center for Public Policy.[53] These objections are based on economies of scale, the gullibility of consumers, and on inequality of educational opportunity. The economies-of-scale argument suggests that, in many areas, there are not enough students to support a variety of competing schools, especially where specialized facilities or teachers are needed, as in science and language classes. While this argument has been relevant historically and may still be relevant in many rural areas, it does not appear valid today in our large cities.

The gullible-consumer argument maintains that parents are not in a good position to judge the quality of schools, especially prior to the child's enrollment, when schools are competing for new enrollments and "putting on a good front" in a variety of ways. The main counter to this argument is that no one objects to the current system wherein wealthy parents have the option of sending their children to private schools. If wealthy parents can make a good choice, why cannot parents of modest means? While it might be necessary to maintain the current system of accreditation, it would defeat the purpose of the voucher plan if a very detailed set of curricula and other requirements were established in order for a school to be eligible for voucher payments. On the other hand, it does make sense for eligible schools to be required to make extensive, accurate information available to all parents.

Probably the most serious objection to the voucher approach is the argument that it is apt to increase inequalities in educational opportunity. For example, parents with relatively high incomes would be more likely to supplement the vouchers with additional tuition payments. As a result, there might be a high correlation between quality of schooling and the parent's income.[54] The voucher proposal of the Center for Public Policy contains a number of devices aimed at reducing this problem. First, schools would be eligible to receive vouchers only if they accept the voucher as full tuition.[55] Second, the voucher payment

[53] *Education Vouchers, A Preliminary Report on Financing Education by Payment to Parents* (Cambridge, Massachusetts: Center for the Study of Public Policy, 1970). This report was prepared under a contract from the Office of Economic Opportunity.

[54] As Friedman points out, however, freedom of choice in housing currently leads to a similar correlation, especially in large metropolitan areas.

[55] Under a revised version, schools could receive vouchers from some children and still charge higher tuition for others. In addition to the tuition issue, schools may still be sensitive to the likelihood of donations, now or in the future. Hopefully, this difficulty would be more than counterbalanced by giving larger voucher payments for children from poor families.

would be larger for children from poor families. Consequently, schools would have an economic incentive to compete for such children, thus counterbalancing the apparent preference of most teachers for "bright," middle- or upper-class children. Third, full transportation costs would be paid by the community. Finally, two restrictions would be placed on the admission policies of voucher schools:[56] (*1*) If the school has more positions than applicants,[57] it must accept all applicants; (*2*) if it has excess applicants, at least half the positions must be filled at random.[58] While up to half the positions could be filled at the discretion of the school to allow schools to develop an individual identity (e.g., emphasis on art, science, or athletics), these selection procedures could not be based on race or ethnic background. The requirement that at least half the positions be filled at random has three purposes: (*1*) to insure that schools do not discriminate to any significant extent against any category of disadvantaged applicants;[59] (*2*) to help convince parents that all children have a fair chance of obtaining admission to the school of their choice; and (*3*) to increase the chances of integration with regard to family background and academic ability as well as race.

If the various safeguards are included, then a voucher system should reduce present inequalities in educational opportunity. Since the voucher plan also appears quite efficient, at least in terms of making schools more responsive to the preferences of students and their families, the voucher system proposed by the Center for Public Policy is very attractive. Unfortunately, however, it may not be possible politically to build all these safeguards into a large-scale program.[60] Consequently we need

[56] Standards for suspension and expulsion would be determined uniformly for all schools in a given area so that the admission regulations could not be undermined by the expulsion policy of an individual school.

[57] Obviously a school would have to indicate the number of positions it had open before it knew how many applicants it would receive. If the total number of applicants for all schools exceeded the total number of positions, the publicly managed schools would have to expand so that no one would be denied a place.

[58] Present students and their siblings would be guaranteed a place.

[59] For example, the school could not discriminate against those with low IQs (at least with regard to those positions filled at random from among all the applicants).

[60] For example, the Office of Economic Opportunity had great difficulty setting up a demonstration of the voucher plan—largely because states were unwilling to pass enabling legislation. Because of this difficulty, the demonstration was ultimately limited to the present public schools of Alum Rock, a community near San Francisco.

to consider other proposals for making the schools more responsive to the needs of minority groups.[61]

C. Community Control of Schools

For those who are interested in improving educational opportunities available to blacks, but who are not optimistic about present efforts to combat de facto segregation, the most popular proposal appears to be establishing black community control of schools in black neighborhoods. There appear to be two sets of arguments in favor of black community control. The first is related directly to racial issues while the second is based on more general arguments for community control. The racial argument emphasizes the fact that present, white-controlled schools are culturally biased against blacks.[62] History is taught from a white perspective with little, if any, mention of black traditions or the achievements of prominent blacks. White styles in art and music are assumed to be superior to those of blacks. Black protest literature is usually forbidden in English classes. There are too few black teachers, especially since it is important for students to see blacks in positions of authority. Perhaps most important, teachers assume that blacks will do poorly relative to whites—an assumption that can turn into a self-fulfilling prophecy if blacks receive relatively little reward when they perform well, and thus are discouraged from working hard for future rewards in school.[63] As indicated in Chapter 2, these types of discrimination cannot be captured in the traditional measures of school inputs

[61] Another proposal to introduce more competition into the schools is performance contracting, where firms run the schools and their fee is based on improved student performance. Experiments with this approach were run and the result was not very favorable to performance contracting. See Irwin Garfinkel and Edward M. Gramlich, "A Statistical Analysis of the OEO Experiment in Educational Performance Contracting," *Journal of Human Resources* 8 (Summer 1973): 275–305.

[62] Our discussion of the racial argument draws heavily on Robert C. Maynard, "Black Nationalism and Community Schools," in *Community Control of Schools*, ed. Henry M. Levin (Washington, D.C.: The Brookings Institution, 1970); for cultural bias against blacks, see Jonathan Kozol, *Death at an Early Age* (Boston, Massachusetts: Houghton, 1967).

[63] See Robert Rosenthal and Lenore Jacobsen, *Pygmalion in the Classroom: Teacher Expectations and Pupils' Intellectual Development* (New York: Holt, 1968); and Kenneth C. Kehrer, "Education, Race, and Poverty: Vicious Cycle of Self-fulfilling Prophecy," in *Perspectives and Poverty*, ed. Dennis J. Dugan and William H. Leahy (New York: Praeger, 1973).

analyzed by economists.[64] Moreover, such discrimination is likely to occur regardless of whether blacks attend segregated or desegregated schools.

Those who favor black community control of schools in black neighborhoods argue that whites often do have such control, especially in the suburbs or other small political units.[65] On the other hand, blacks usually are a minority within large cities that are controlled by whites. Moreover, community control is an issue that can sometimes be used to unify the political energies of the black community, especially when strong opposition arises from teachers' unions or other members of the educational establishment. Therefore, community control of the schools has sometimes been a rallying cry for those who want greater black control of all institutions in black neighborhoods.

Of particular importance, black community control is likely to lead to a direct, immediate improvement in the economic position of blacks since more of the school budget would go to black employees and black firms. In other words, black community control should increase the demand for black teachers, black administrators, black publishers, and black contractors.

Next, let us consider some of the nonracial arguments for community control, arguments that are very similar to some of those made by proponents of educational vouchers. The nonracial case for community control starts with the assumption that present school systems are an inefficient bureaucratic monopoly, more responsive to the interest of professional educators than to the needs and desires of students and parents. For example, the regulations of the bureaucracy are said to stifle many creative innovations in techniques and curriculum that individual teachers would like to introduce into their classes.[66] While such charges are often leveled at all educational systems, they appear especially pronounced with regard to the school systems of large cities

---

[64] In addition, some proponents of black community control argue against the output measures used in this study (e.g., relative incomes, scores on standardized tests like the AFQT) on the grounds that these measures reflect the values of white society and do not represent black values, except to the extent that blacks have been "brainwashed" by whites. The strongest criticisms are leveled at standardized tests, which are viewed as culturally biased against blacks.

[65] Of course, this community control is subject to various constraints including state legislation and sometimes union power.

[66] This argument may help explain why there is relatively little difference in performance between students in different schools.

since such systems are larger than necessary to take advantage of most economies of scale, such as specialized programs.[67]

Splitting up large school systems into a number of smaller "community" systems is one response to this problem.[68] Hopefully, this approach would lead to better education not only by reducing bureaucratic regulations but also by getting parents more involved in the educational process. Such parental involvement could have a positive effect on both schools and students, if parents become more interested both in what is taught and in the schoolwork of their children.

The major objection to community control is based on the view that the public schools should serve to reinforce the "melting pot" tradition in this country by reducing rather than accentuating racial and ethnic differences. While the author is sympathetic with these objectives, he believes that it is highly misleading to argue that the public schools fulfill these objectives now. For example, it is difficult to see how segregated schools can act to reduce such racial differences. As we argued earlier, it appears quite unlikely that significant desegregation will occur in the public schools of large cities. Therefore, until such time as school and housing desegregation appear more likely, it is hypocritical to argue against black community control on the basis of "melting pot" arguments.

A related argument suggests that black neighborhoods are not sufficiently cohesive communities for community control of schools to be viable in black areas.[69] For example, mobility rates are very high. While this argument may be valid, community control of schools may help to build a stronger, more stable community.[70]

---

[67] In fact, such complaints are being made about many other services provided by large cities. For example, see E. S. Savas, "Municipal Monopoly," *Harper's* (December 1971). He suggests applying the voucher plan to other areas in addition to education (e.g., trash collection).

[68] Proponents of this nonracial argument would often accept the standard measures of school output, such as scores on standardized tests. Therefore, the two arguments for black community control do not lead to conclusions that are as similar as they might appear at first glance. For a further discussion of this point, see Leonard J. Fine, "Community Schools and Social Theory: The Limits of Universalism," in Levin, *Community Control*.

[69] See Harold W. Pfautz, "The Black Community, the Community School, and the Socialization Process: Some Caveats," in Levin, *Community Control*.

[70] This line of reasoning might suggest moving slowly and starting community control on a demonstration basis rather than as a large-scale program. On the other hand, teachers' unions and the educational establishment may find it easier to sabotage a demonstration than a larger program.

Other arguments against black community control focus on the problems that would occur in the transition from the present system to community control. For example, let us assume that community control takes the form of separate school districts, each with an elected board of education, covering each major black neighborhood. For this local school board to be anything more than a figurehead, it would need control over its budget and over school personnel. The school board needs the power to hire and fire teachers so that the teaching staff will be capable of working in harmony with the educational objectives of the board. On the other hand, current teachers frequently have tenure and may be represented by a union with considerable economic and political power. Therefore, the treatment of incumbent teachers involves difficult questions of equity, law, and power.[71]

Another potentially divisive issue involves the determination of the total budget for each district. We will assume that revenues are raised at the state or city level since poor communities would suffer if each neighborhood raised its own school revenue.[72] Then it would appear reasonable to allocate funds to each district on a per pupil basis, with a higher allotment for secondary school students than for those in elementary school, and, hopefully, also a higher allotment for poor students as a counterbalance to the educational handicaps presented by their home environment.[73] As long as the formula is kept reasonably simple, it should be difficult for whites to discriminate against black schools because attempts at such discrimination will be more obvious the simpler the allocation formula.

---

[71] Proponents of community control sometimes argue that such teachers simply be transferred to another district, as often happens under the present centralized structure when a teacher gets into difficulty at a particular school. However, under the decentralized system of community control, it is possible that no other district will accept the teacher. Under these circumstances, perhaps the best solution is an appeals board comprised of both teachers and community representatives. Hopefully, such a procedure would encourage compromises rather than turning the issue into one of confrontation politics. For further discussion of the relation between current teachers and black community control, see the articles by Michael H. Moscow and Kenneth McLennan, Maria D. Fantini, and Rhody A. McCoy, in Levin, *Community Control*.

[72] Following the *Serrano* v. *Priest* decision in California, many state courts have ruled that it is illegal to finance schools through a local property tax unless measures are taken to guarantee that children are not discriminated against by coming from communities with low levels of per capita wealth and income.

[73] See James and Levin, in Levin, *Community Control*, pp. 258–261, for a more extensive discussion of this issue.

With regard to the budget, it seems clear that the local board should be the major authority on spending whatever money is available. Of course, the larger community does have some stake in these decisions. Consequently, James and Levin argue that some decisions should be made by central authorities:

> Even under a decentralized plan, it is desirable that educational policies of broad social relevance be made at a highly centralized level. That is, those particular policies having implications beyond the boundaries of individual communities are rightfully determined through the consensus of a larger society than that of an individual community . . . .
>
> First, the high rate of residential mobility among American families suggests that some uniformity of curriculum is necessary in order to insure continuity of learning when students transfer from one school to another. Second, the basic skills required for participation in a modern economy should not vary according to the school that one attends. Finally, some common educational experience is required in order to have a citizenry that is informed about major areas of social policy. These factors suggest that a core of common educational needs be outlined for the community schools. This core should be designed so that considerable discretion is left to the community in fulfilling the common requirements.[74]

On the other hand, if the core is broadly defined (i.e., learning to read, write, and do arithmetic), then it seems unlikely that local districts would leave these items out of the curriculum—although they might object to the symbolic control by central administrators.

The evidence available from recent attempts to institute community control shows that little community *control* has been achieved, although there has been some increase in community influence on the schools. After examining recent experiences with "community control" and other forms of school decentralization in New York, Detroit, Washington, Los Angeles, and St. Louis, LaNoue and Smith conclude:

> It is difficult to generalize about the actual impact of decentralization on the schools. In some districts there have been curriculum changes, more bilingual programs, and some ethnic studies, but the reforms have been limited by lack of funding and by state curriculum standards. Some districts have begun to recruit staff outside the system and to experiment with accountability devices, but union contracts and other civil service requirements do not leave much flexibility. No significant evidence exists about the relationship of decentralization to student achievement. Cause and effect relationships will be so difficult to sort out that no such evidence is likely to appear in the short run.[75]

[74] Ibid., pp. 261–262.
[75] Reprinted by permission of the publisher from *The Politics of School Decentralization* by George R. LaNoue and Bruce L. R. Smith (Lexington, Massachusetts: Lexington Books, D. C. Heath and Company, 1973), p. 231.

When elections have been held to determine who would serve on neighborhood school boards (as in New York and Detroit), power has tended to shift away from "the professional big business, liberal whites who controlled the old centralized structures," [76] and toward both black and white ethnic groups.

Although blacks have increased their influence through these elections, they have not been as well represented on the community board as they are in the public schools since (*1*) the black population is more heavily weighted toward those of school age; (*2*) a higher percentage of white children attend private schools; and (*3*) voter turnout percentages have been lower for blacks than whites—as they generally are for all elections.

LaNoue and Smith anticipated frequent clashes between black and white ethnics when their power grew as a result of decentralization. However, they conclude:

> In some districts and cities the clash has occurred and the perceived gains of minority groups have accelerated the awakening of white-ethnic political consciousness. Indeed, one important result of the decentralization movement has been to mobilize white-ethnic constituencies that have felt threatened by the liberal-black Great Society programs of the 1960s. But the new activists, white or black, share some objectives, and their relationships have not been wholly antagonistic. The poor activists, generally black or Puerto Rican, are ethnics too; and in the era of ethnic pride, accomodations can be reached if there is respect for each other's turf. Furthermore, both groups have agreed on emphasizing discipline and mastery of traditional skills as educational goals. They also share a common suspicion of the professional prerogatives enjoyed by teachers and administrators. In collective bargaining, decentralization has given these new community activists access to and influence on contract negotiations . . . .[77]

Thus, the major conflicts that have appeared under community control have not been between black and white community groups, but between community groups and the educational establishment. More specifically, the authors conclude:

> The objective of many community control advocates, and a goal that has increasingly emerged as critical to school activists of many political shadings, is holding school personnel accountable. This often means, in practical terms, the right to hire, fire, and promote school personnel. The challenge to professionalism . . . has intensified in all cities where the decentralization movement was strong . . . .

[76] Ibid., p. 230.
[77] Reprinted by permission of the publisher from *The Politics of School Decentralization* by George LaNoue and Bruce L. R. Smith (Lexington, Massachusetts: Lexington Books, D.C. Heath and Company, 1973) p. 230.

The local boards, because of the distrust of the school professionals, have generally appeared to be more resistant to union pressures than city-wide officials who have been afraid to incur the wrath of the increasingly militant municipal unions. Decentralization may perhaps offer what has been conspicuously lacking in most urban political systems: an effective counterweight to the growing power of public employee unions.[78]

However, conflicts between teacher unions and community groups may divide the liberal political community, thus strengthening the hand of conservatives and working to the ultimate disadvantage of blacks. In addition, conflicts generated by community control often must be resolved in the state legislature, a political arena where blacks are generally weaker than at the city level.

To conclude the discussion of black community control, let us summarize the desirability of this alternative with regard to efficiency, equity, and political feasibility. Black community control should make many black schools more responsive to the needs and preferences of black students and their families and thus should lead to reduced skill differentials between blacks and whites. As long as the schools place a reasonable emphasis on English (as opposed to Swahili) and nonviolent political acts (as opposed to violent revolution), black community control should be efficient not only from the standpoint of the local blacks but also for the larger society. While there are likely to be administrative inefficiencies in the transition to a new system with more community control, there does not seem to be any reason why the end result need be less efficient than the present system in suburban areas.

Even if community control does little to reduce skill and earnings differentials between blacks and whites, there is still a strong equity argument for community control of schools in black neighborhoods. Since whites have the option of living in the suburbs where they can have a reasonable degree of community control, it seems only fair to give blacks a similar option. At a minimum, black self-respect should be enhanced by knowing that the important decisions affecting black schools are being made by blacks rather than whites.

Politically, there appears to be much less opposition to black community control than to meaningful housing desegregation or to school integration through busing. However, there is still considerable opposition from many school administrators and some teachers' organizations.

[78] Reprinted by permission of the publisher from *The Politics of School Decentralization* by George R. LaNoue and Bruce L. R. Smith (Lexington, Massachusetts: Lexington Books, D. C. Heath and Company, 1973), p. 233.

Since the issue generally requires action by state legislators, radical changes are unlikely to occur until either blacks obtain more political power or the issue is proposed in some form that generates considerable white support.[79] On the other hand, the threat of greater community control being instituted by state legislatures has enabled blacks and other minority groups to effect some changes in the public schools.

The discussion thus far has assumed that blacks are a political minority in the city. As blacks become a majority in more cities, their enthusiasm for community control of schools is likely to diminish. For example, blacks might then lose rather than gain jobs as a result of community control. However, the nonracial arguments for such community control remain important and many of the racial arguments will still be valid with respect to the white minority—especially when that minority is divided into different ethnic and religious groups. In addition, community control may then encourage more whites to remain in the city, thereby probably aiding both the city's tax base and its political influence at the state and possibly national levels.[80] Thus, community control of schools appears to make sense whether blacks are a political minority or majority.

III. Concluding Comments

As we have indicated in the preceding section, black community control of schools should help reduce skill (and earnings) differentials by race, as should the complementary goal of ensuring that black schools have as many resources available to them as white schools. Moreover, both policies should make school more pleasant for black children even if they have little effect on what is learned at school.[81] Thus, such policies appear to deserve support even though there is little convincing evidence that they will have any major effect on skill differentials.

---

[79] For example, there may be much more white support when blacks become a political majority in a central city. On the other hand, much of the recent pressure for decentralization appears to have come from the poverty program and other programs of the Johnson Administration. Under Nixon, those pressures have been considerably reduced.

[80] If most whites do eventually leave the city, the racial dimension of community control is automatically achieved on a de facto basis.

[81] Certainly the schools would be more pleasant for blacks if the money is spent in keeping classrooms cleaner and in better repair, or in reducing the size of classes and increasing the quality of teachers.

To reduce black–white earnings differentials, our top priority approach should be to concentrate on affirmative-action programs and other policies to reduce labor-market discrimination. In addition to having an important direct effect on earnings differentials, such policies may also have an important indirect effect by reducing skill differentials. Obviously labor-market policies should reduce differences in on-the-job training. In addition, however, they should have an effect on the educational attainment of blacks, especially if the reductions in labor-market discrimination apply mainly to jobs requiring the most education. Under such conditions, blacks will have greater incentives not only to obtain additional years of schooling, but also to take schooling more seriously.[82] Moreover, employers will have more incentive to exert their political pressure to improve the educational opportunities available to blacks. Finally, the higher incomes resulting from reduced labor-market discrimination should also affect the educational attainment of black children because of links between (*1*) the effect of family income on educational attainment[83] (e.g., through the effect of family income on food expenditures and nutrition and the effect of nutrition on education) and (*2*) the effect of neighborhood income on the quality of schools.

While reductions in labor-market discrimination are likely to reduce racial skill differentials, it should also be emphasized that improving the educational and skill levels of blacks should increase the chances of success for affirmative-action programs aimed at providing greater job opportunities for blacks, since pressures to open up job opportunities will generally be more effective when qualified applicants are readily available.

As we indicated in Section I, significant progress has been made in the enactment of legislation outlawing labor-market discrimination and in the development of affirmative-action programs. Future progress in these areas (including enforcement of present requirements), and in other

[82] For a formal argument along these lines, see Kenneth J. Arrow, "Some Mathematical Models of Race for the Labor Market," in *Racial Discrimination in Economic Life*, ed. Anthony A. Pascal (Lexington, Massachusetts: Heath, 1972). For empirical results tending to confirm this view, see Richard B. Freeman, "Decline in Labor Market Discrimination and Economic Analysis," *American Economic Review* 63 (May 1973): 280–286.

[83] See Stanley H. Masters, "The Effect of Family Income on Children's Education: Some Findings on Inequality of Opportunity," *Journal of Human Resources* 4 (Spring 1969): 158–175.

important areas such as community control of schools and maintaining tight labor markets, depends largely on the political support such policies receive. It is important, therefore, to consider how such political support might be increased.

In order to build political support for programs to assist blacks, two avenues are open. One is to increase the political power of those who are currently in favor of such programs. The other is to convince more people of their desirability. With regard to the first issue, we can apply Becker's political analysis (an analysis that is consistent with viewing discrimination in a bargaining context, which we recommended in Chapter 1). The political power of blacks and their white allies depends on (*1*) their percentage of the total electorate and (*2*) the extent to which they are organized so that they can bargain effectively with other groups. In other words, blacks need to be able to trade their support on noncrucial issues in return for more white support on issues that are crucial to blacks. Taking this analysis one step further, it appears that policies should be supported that will enable (or encourage) more blacks to register and vote—for example, the recent voting rights acts. In addition, programs that would enable blacks to control the institutions in their areas (e.g., black community control of schools or community development corporations) may increase the political cohesiveness of the black community.

While we have argued that first priority should go to the relatively noncontroversial policies such as maintaining high aggregate demand, we have also indicated that special programs to assist blacks may be very valuable. Therefore, let us now turn to the issue of convincing more people of the need for such special programs, programs like black community control of schools and affirmative-action requirements for government contractors. First, let us assume that an opponent of affirmative-action or black community control is already convinced that discrimination is a serious problem. Then, hopefully, he can be convinced by the kinds of arguments that have been presented earlier. If the opponent of special programs is not convinced that discrimination is a problem, despite the considerable empirical evidence of such discrimination, then we must refer back to the discussion of theories of prejudice presented in Chapter 6. Recall Myrdal's argument that improvements in the economic conditions of blacks will reduce racial prejudice. If that argument is correct, then it is important to inform whites of the progress that blacks are making.[84] As Allport has emphasized, indirect communication (e.g., novels, films, and television shows) is needed as well as direct communication of statistical information. As Chapter 6 indicates, the experience since the Civil Rights Act of 1964 does provide some evidence in support of Myrdal's optimistic position. However, too little time has passed since the civil rights revolution of the early sixties for one to be confident that the Myrdal dynamic will lead to continued significant improvement in the relative economic position of blacks. If future events should contradict Myrdal's optimism, and if the values and analysis presented earlier are accepted, then increased attention should be devoted to examining the radical perspective and its policy implications.

[84] In the political arena, liberals have tended to minimize these gains—probably in an attempt to maintain moral and political pressure in the Nixon administration and on public opinion. For an interesting discussion of this political strategy, see Ben J. Wattenberg and Richard M. Scammon, "Black Progress and Liberal Rhetoric," *Commentary* (April 1973): 35–44 and the exchange between these authors and Sydney E. Bernard in the August 1973 issue of that magazine.

Author Index

A

Akin, John S., 168n.
Alexis, Marcus, 11n.
Allport, Gordon W., 131, 133, 135, 141n., 183
Arrow, Kenneth J., 6–9, 22, 23, 47, 134, 140, 182n.
Ashenfelter, Orley, 20, 29, 30n., 44, 85, 120, 121, 161n.
Askin, A. Bradley, 52n.

B

Bailey, Martin, 35n.
Banfield, Edward C., 1n., 50, 51
Baran, Paul A., 15, 22n., 131, 136, 137–138, 141n., 142, 148, 149
Batchelder, Alan B., 43n., 147n.
Beale, Calvin L., 67n.
Becker, Gary S., 2, 3–10, 11, 12, 14n., 16, 19–21, 22, 28, 29, 34, 45, 46, 47, 78n., 80, 85, 132, 141n., 162, 183
Bell, Duran, 164
Berg, Ivar, 27n., 40n., 121n., 154n.
Bergmann, Barbara R., 10, 28, 29, 51n., 105n.
Bernard, Sydney S., 184n.
Blau, Peter M., 100n.
Blaustein, Arthur I., 167n.
Blinder, Alan S., 101n.
Blumrosen, Alfred W., 85n., 157n., 161n.
Bowen, William G., 76n., 114n.
Bowles, Samuel, 37, 38n.
Brackett, Jean C., 45n., 59n.

C

Cain, Glen G., 43n., 76n.
Cavanagh, Gerald, 162n.
Chiswick, Barry R., 20, 28n.
Cohen, Benjamin I., 69n.
Coleman, James S., 36, 37, 38, 40, 56n., 102, 104, 117, 120, 168n.

Coleman, Sinclair, 42
Comanor, William S., 19
Corazzini, Arthur J., 166n.

D

Daniels, Norman, 42n.
Doeringer, Peter B., 9n., 121n.
Downs, Anthony, 35n., 91n., 170, 171
Dugan, Dennis J., 174n.
Duncan, Otis Dudley, 21n., 99–104, 108

E

Engerman, Stanley L., 46n.

F

Fantini, Maria D., 177n.
Farley, Reynolds, 32n., 37
Faux, Geoffrey, 167n.
Fein, Rashi, 43n.
Fine, Leonard J., 176n.
Finegan, T. Aldrich, 76n., 114n.
Flanagan, Robert J., 20
Fogel, Robert W., 46n.
Fogel, Walter, 99n.
Franklin, Raymond S., 19, 80n., 81, 85
Freedman, Deborah, 52n.
Freedman, Donald, 52n.
Freeman, Richard B., 12n., 29n., 143n., 182n.
Friedman, Milton, 22, 131, 132, 133, 134, 140, 145, 148, 162, 170, 171, 172n.
Fromm, Eric, 139n.

G

Galbraith, John Kenneth, 164–166
Garfinkel, Irwin, 168n., 174n.
Gilman, Harry J., 31
Gintis, Herbert, 26n., 41n., 121n.
Gordon, David M., 16–17
Gramlich, Edward M., 174n.
Griliches, Z., 26–27, 29, 41, 117, 121n., 128n.
Gwartney, James, 2n., 44, 45n., 46, 102, 103 (table source), 104, 120

H

Hanoch, Giora, 29, 60n., 107n.
Hansen, W. Lee, 25–27, 29, 41, 117, 121n., 128
Hanushek, Eric A., 168n.
Harrington, Michael, 139n.
Harrison, Bennett, 29n., 69n., 86n., 90
Haugen, R. A., 36n.
Hayes, Marion, 60n., 110n.
Heckman, James, 161n.
Hein, A. J., 36n.
Heistand, Dale L., 45, 46 (table source)
Hollings, (Senator) Ernest F., 12n.

I

Innis, Roy, 167n.

J

Jacobsen, Lenore, 174n.
James, H. Thomas, 177n., 178
Jencks, Christopher S., 38n., 39n., 169n.
Jensen, Arthur R., 41
Johnson, George E., 168n.
Jones, James E., Jr., 152, 157n.

K

Kagan, Jerome S., 41
Kain, John F., 1n., 14n., 33n., 35, 36, 52n., 69n., 70n., 71–74, 75, 77, 78, 81, 86, 87, 88, 91, 92, 93, 94, 168n.
Kalachek, Edward, 43n., 69, 70n.
Karpinos, B. D., 56n., 117, 118n., 129n.
Kehrer, Kenneth C., 174n.
Kiker, B. F., 120n.
King, A. Thomas, 35
Kozol, Jonathan, 174n.
Knowles, James, 43n.
Kreuger, Anne O., 6, 7
Kuh, Edwin, 164

L

Landes, William M., 12n., 31n., 152n.
LaNoue, George R., 178, 179

Lansing, John B., 52n.
Lapham, Victoria, 35n.
Laurenti, Luigi, 35
Leahy, William H., 174n.
Levin, Henry M., 37, 38n., 39n., 40 (table source), 177n., 178
Liles, W. Pierce, 120n.
Lurie, Melvin, 52n.

M

McClaughry, John, 167n.
McCoy, Rhody A., 177n.
McLennan, Kenneth, 177n.
Marshall, Ray, 18, 21, 133
Mason, W., 26–27, 29, 41, 117, 121n., 128n.
Masters, Stanley H., 56n., 89, 111n., 182n.
Maynard, Robert C., 174n.
Meyer, John R., 69n., 70n., 71
Michelson, Stephan, 97, 98 (table source), 99, 101, 104, 108
Mieszkowski, Peter, 35
Miller, H. M., 26n.
Mooney, Joseph D., 69n., 71n., 74, 75, 76, 77, 78, 81, 86, 87, 92, 93, 94
Morgan, James M., 52n.
Morgenstern, Richard D., 168n.
Moscow, Michael H., 177n.
Moynihan, Daniel P., 66, 67
Myrdal, Gunnar, 131, 133–136, 141n., 142, 148, 149, 183, 184

N

Nash, Peter G., 160
Newman, Dorothy K., 69n., 71n., 72n.
Noll, Roger, 69n., 71, 72n., 88

O

Offner, Paul, 69n., 74n.
O'Neill, Dave M., 116, 117n.
Orshansky, Mollie, 52 (table source)

P

Pascal, Anthony H., 27n., 28, 33n., 34n.
Perlman, Richard, 43n.
Persky, Joseph J., 1n., 52, 69n., 70n., 87n., 91
Pfautz, Harold W., 176
Piore, Michael J., 9n., 121n.
Pohlman, Jerry E., 145n.
Purcell, Theodore, 162n.

Q

Quigley, John M., 35, 36

R

Rapping, Leonard A., 27n., 28
Rapkin, Chester, 36
Rasmussen, David W., 44, 45, 142
Rayack, Elton, 52n.
Reder, Melvin W., 81
Rees, Albert, 72n., 155n.
Reich, Michael, 16, 19, 20, 21
Reiner, Thomas A., 32n.
Ribich, Thomas I., 111n., 152n.
Rosenthal, Robert, 174n.
Rowan, Richard L., 159
Rubin, Lester, 159
Rustin, Bayard, 16, 21, 163n.

S

Sackrey, Charles, 50
Saks, Daniel H., 69n., 74n.
Savas, E. S., 176n.
Scammon, Richard M., 184n.
Scanlon, William J., 25–27, 29, 41, 117, 121n., 128n.
Schelling, Thomas C., 34n.
Scully, Gerald W., 27n.
Sherman, Howard, 22, 23, 131, 138–140, 141n., 149
Sjaastad, Larry A., 49n.
Silver, Morris, 15n.
Smith, Bruce L. R., 178–180

Stafford, Frank P., 168n.
Stiglitz, Joseph E., 10n.
Strauss, Robert P., 19
Sweezy, Paul M., 15n., 16, 22n., 131,
    136n, 137–138, 141n, 142, 148, 149

T

Tabb, William K., 84n.
Taeuber, Alma F., 32, 33n., 37, 51n.,
    70n., 76
Taeuber, Karl E., 32, 33n., 34n., 51n.,
    70n., 76
Taussig, Michael K., 120, 121
Taylor, David P., 29n.
Thurow, Lester C., 2n., 10–14, 15, 18, 21,
    22, 26, 164
Tobin, James, 43, 44

W

Wallace, Phyllis A., 153.
Wattenberg, Ben J., 184n.
Weisbrod, Burton A., 25–27, 29, 41, 117,
    121n., 128n.
Weiss, Leonard, 29n., 52n., 55, 111, 113n.
Welch, Finis, 6, 7–8, 29n., 47, 102n., 140
Wertheimer, Richard F., II, 49n., 52n.
Williamson, Jeffrey G., 29, 52n., 55, 111,
    113n.
Wohl, Martin, 69n., 71
Wohlstetter, Albert, 7n., 42
Wohlstetter, Roberta, 7n.
Woodward, C. Vann, 15n., 21n.

Z

Zelder, Raymond G., 34n.